Patriots for Profit

Patriots for Profit

CONTRACTORS AND THE MILITARY

IN U.S. NATIONAL SECURITY

Thomas C. Bruneau

Stanford Security Studies
An Imprint of Stanford University Press
Stanford, California

Stanford University Press
Stanford, California

Library of Congress Cataloging-in-Publication Data

Bruneau, Thomas C., author.
    Patriots for profit : contractors and the military in U.S. national security / Thomas C. Bruneau.
        pages cm
    Includes bibliographical references and index.
    ISBN 978-0-8047-7548-9 (cloth) — ISBN 978-0-8047-7549-6 (pbk.)

    1. Private military companies—United States.   2. Civil-military relations—United States.   3. National security—United States.   4. United States—Military policy. I. Title.
    UB149.B78 2011
    338.4'735500973—dc22
    2011002324

Typeset by Thompson Type in 10/14 Minion

Special discounts for bulk quantities of Stanford Security Studies are available to corporations, professional associations, and other organizations. For details and discount information, contact the special sales department of Stanford University Press. Tel: (650) 736-1782, Fax: (650) 736-1784

CONTENTS

TABLES AND FIGURES

Tables

Figures

ACKNOWLEDGMENTS

This book became possible only because the Naval Postgraduate School (NPS), awarded me six months of sabbatical leave in late 2008 and early 2009. My thanks to the Chairman of the National Security Affairs Department, Professor Harold Trinkunas, and to the leadership of NPS for their confidence and support. The Center for International Security and Cooperation at Stanford University generously granted me visiting scholar status, with the use of an office and their extensive facilities, for nine months. I am especially grateful to Professor Lynn Eden, acting codirector, for her support. CISAC was a propitious and stimulating environment in which to research and write this book.

The topic of the book, which combines an analysis of U.S. civil–military relations with the contracting out of security, required considerable study and self-education on my part. My deepest thanks for the extremely capable and responsive support of Ms. Greta Marlatt, the Dudley Knox Library's Outreach and Collection Development Manager. Greta routinely provided me with the latest research on specific themes as I developed my knowledge and dug deeper into the topic. I also was delighted, and relieved, to discover a tremendous resource at the Graduate School of Business and Public Policy at the Naval Postgraduate School (NPS) where many faculty and students are or were contracting officers. My particular thanks to Associate Professors Nicholas Dew and Rene Rendon, and Senior Lecturer Cory Yoder for their interest in my work and to the students for their generosity in allowing me to take up their class time with my questions. Their real-world experiences were invaluable to this study.

Much of the motivation and the continuing support for this project came from my colleague and frequent collaborator Major General Richard Goetze, USAF (ret.), and my longtime friend and former NPS colleague Mr. Arch Barrett, whose wealth of knowledge and experience contributed greatly to the depth of my research. They both have expended considerable time and patience over the years explaining to me how things military and governmental work in the real world. Particular thanks also go to my brother-in-law and guide to the corridors of Washington, DC, Mr. Bernard Martin. Bernie, who was a high-level OMB official for more than thirty years, introduced me to the intricacies of budgeting and the real power structure in the executive branch in Washington. He also facilitated my contacts with other experts concerning my research.

While teaching courses in the National Security Affairs Department at NPS, I have been privileged to work closely with young officer students from all the services and forty foreign countries, most of whom have now served, often several times, in peace support operations in Afghanistan and Iraq, as well as under U.N. auspices in Africa and the Middle East. From the U.S. officers I learned that civilian control of the armed forces is simply not an issue in this country; from many of the international officers I learned that civilian control is, or was, a very critical issue in theirs. Virtually all of these students have stories, some positive and many negative, about dealing with private security contractors in the contingency environments in which they served, and they have insisted that I include some discussion of PSCs in my courses. Among the many excellent students, I would like to single out two. Captain Jason Howk, USA, had worked with Lieutenant General—then Ambassador— Karl Eikenberry in Afghanistan prior to coming to NPS. After graduating, Captain Howk became aide de camp to General Stanley McChrystal, also in Afghanistan. In addition to writing a monograph on security sector reform, Captain Howk spent much valuable time describing to me his and his commanders' experiences with PSCs. LCDR Legena Malan, USN, served in Afghanistan before coming to NPS as a contracting officer. In the classroom, and while working with LCDR Malan on her thesis, I learned much about the intricacies of contracting in a contingency environment.

Several academics and policy makers read various drafts of this book to help me to avoid factual mistakes and to hone my analysis. I would like to thank in particular Lucia Dammert, Marcela Donadio, Timothy Edmunds, Jose Olmeda, and Arturo Sotomayor.

Congressman Sam Farr and his Defense Expert Permanent Staffer, Ms. Debbie Merrill, both explained to me the dynamics of congressional politics and also facilitated my access to other members of Congress and their staffers. My deepest thanks as well to Doug Brooks, president of the International Peace Operations Association (since 2010 named the International Stability Operations Association); Kara Bue, previous deputy assistant Secretary of State in the Bureau of Political-Military Affairs and a partner in Armitage International; Danny Kopp, senior writer in the office of the Special Inspector General for Iraq Reconstruction; and Jim Schweiter of Mckenna Long & Aldridge LLP. All of these busy individuals took the time to explain aspects of contracting out to me and facilitated interviews with others. In the section of this book on interviews, I have listed those forty-plus practitioners and experts I drew on most heavily in attempting to understand these topics.

I am grateful to the Director, Mr. Rich Hoffman, and Chief Operating Officer, Mr. Scott Jasper, of the Center for Civil–Military Relations, for their ongoing support of this project, both financial and moral. The National Security Affairs Department Committee on Research Grants, chaired by Professor Clay Moltz, very generously awarded me a travel grant to make three research trips to Washington, DC. In addition, both CCMR and NSA funded three more research trips, including three days of talks with Arch Barrett in Texas.

As with four of my previous publications, Ms. Elizabeth Skinner turned my half-baked ideas and awkward prose into something coherent that could be comprehended by more than the small coterie of experts on the topics covered in this book. I am most grateful for her talents and commitment in turning the rough manuscript into a book. Mrs. Cristiana Matei and I have worked very closely together in developing the analytical framework I apply in this book. She also assisted me in collecting some of the basic statistics used to illustrate a number of important issues. Geoffrey Burns, director and editor of the Security Studies imprint at Stanford University Press, has been supportive of my work ever since we discussed it at Stanford University early in the writing process. Without his encouragement, this research project might never have become a finished book. Any errors of fact or interpretation that have crept in despite all the invaluable help that I received from so many informed and competent experts are my responsibility alone.

Finally, I am as always indebted to my wife, Celia Crawford Bruneau, who tolerated her Quixote-like husband of four decades as he launched into yet one more research project. This project, more than any other since my PhD research, captured my attention and enthusiasm, which translates into time and energy. I appreciate her unflagging indulgence of my commitment to research and writing and her good humor as we try to maintain the fine balance between our conjugal life and professional enthusiasms.

I dedicate this book to our eight grandchildren: Crawford, McKenzie, Slade, Newlin, Shane, Turner, Boyd, and Nicolas. I hope that this book assists policy makers in the United States of America to strengthen its security while at the same time promoting justice at home and abroad, so that the world these children will grow up in will be a safer place than the one in which we currently live.

ABBREVIATIONS

CCMR Center for Civil–Military Relations

CBO Congressional Budget Office

CIA Central Intelligence Agency

CINC commander in chief of a U.S. regional or specified command, for eg. Southern Command or Central Command (now called a combatant commander)

CJCS chairman of the joint chiefs of staff

COR contracting officer representative

CPA Coalition Provisional Authority

CRS Congressional Research Service

CSIS Center for Strategic and International Studies

DCAA Defense Contract Audit Agency

DCI Director of Central Intelligence

DCMA Defense Contract Management Agency

DNI Director of National Intelligence

FAR Federal Acquisition Regulation

GAO Government Accountability Office

HASC House Armed Services Committee

IC intelligence community

JCS   joint chiefs of staff

JPME   joint professional military education

MEJA   Military Extraterritorial Jurisdiction Act

NPS   Naval Postgraduate School

NATO   North Atlantic Treaty Organization

NGO   nongovernmental organization

NSC   National Security Council

OMB   Office of Management and Budget

PME   professional military education

PSC   private security contractor

PNSR   Project on National Security Reform

QDR   Quadrennial Defense Review

SIGAR   Special Inspector General for Afghanistan Reconstruction

SIGIR   Special Inspector General for Iraq Reconstruction

SOFA   Status of Forces Agreement

SSR   security sector reform

UCMJ   Uniform Code of Military Justice

Patriots for Profit

INTRODUCTION

The Stockholm International Peace Research Institute reports that the 2008 U.S. defense budget, at $607 billion, is greater than the spending of the next fourteen countries combined and represents 41 percent of the world's total defense spending of $1.46 trillion.[1] There is, however, broad concern that the American people are not receiving a level of security commensurate with this huge investment of their resources. With such concerns in mind, would-be reformers have undertaken major initiatives to transform the institutions responsible for America's national security. These will be analyzed in detail in Chapter 4.

The most important of these is the Project on National Security Reform (PNSR), a congressionally funded policy think tank set up in 2006, which issued its first report in late 2008. This hefty document (702 pages) asserts that:

> the national security of the United States of America is fundamentally at risk . . . The United States therefore needs a bold, but carefully crafted plan of comprehensive reform to institute a national security system, that can manage and overcome the challenges of our time. We propose such a bold reform in this report; if implemented, it would constitute the most far-reaching governmental design innovation in national security since the passage of the National Security Act of 1947.[2]

Building on previous studies, reports, and the lessons of earlier reform efforts, the purpose of PNSR was not only to make recommendations but to bring together experts who could delineate and then implement, at the direction of the president, the necessary steps to reform the national security system. PNSR's executive director, James R. Locher III, also played an important role in the passage of the last successful defense reform legislation, the Goldwater-Nichols Defense Reorganization Act of 1986. Several PNSR members presently serve at high levels in the Obama administration's Department of Defense, Department of State, and National Security Council. Like all major reform initiatives between 1986 and today, the project's work focuses on the problem of increasing the effectiveness of the U.S. national security sector, which encompasses a daunting number of departments and agencies at all levels of government. Unfortunately, these kinds of reform efforts, culminating in the PNSR, have not received much attention beyond Washington, DC, and within a relatively small universe of policy makers and defense intellectuals.

Meanwhile, what does receive a great deal of attention in the popular media, in advocacy reporting, and in the scholarly literature is the contracting out to private firms of national security roles and missions, particularly in Iraq and Afghanistan. The importance of contracting services in wartime—the for-profit side of national security—is made evident by the fact that there were more contractors than uniformed personnel in the Iraq and Afghanistan theaters in mid-2009, at a ratio of 1.1 to 1.[3] Due to the public exposure of rampant graft, corruption, and apparently unjustifiable violence involving some private contractors, Congress stepped up its oversight, illustrated by the creation in late 2003 of the Special Inspector General for Iraq Reconstruction (SIGIR), and in 2008 of the Special Inspector General for Afghanistan Reconstruction (SIGAR), both of which produce a great variety of audits, studies, and reports.[4] The Congressional Research Service (CRS) and Government Accountability Office (GAO) also have published one study after another, while Congress itself has held many hearings on the topic of "contracting out" and at least two in-house commissions have been created that conduct studies and make recommendations for legislation. In August 2007, the secretary of the army created the Commission on Army Expeditionary Contracting (known after its chairman, Jacques Gansler, as the Gansler Commission), which made its report on October 31, 2007, and the Commission on Wartime Contracting, which submitted its interim report in June 2009 and has a final report due in July 2011.[5]

In testimony to the Subcommittee on Readiness of the House Armed Services Committee, in early March 2008, David M. Walker, comptroller general of the United States, conveyed a sense of the growth, centrality, and scope of military contracting and highlighted many of the controversial issues surrounding their employment:

> In fiscal year 2007, the federal government spent about $254 billion on *contractor services*, an amount that has more than doubled over the past decade. The Department of Defense's (DOD) obligations on *service contractors*, expressed in constant fiscal year 2006 dollars, rose from $85.1 billion in fiscal year 1996 to more than $151 billion in fiscal year 2006, a 78% increase. With this growth in spending, DOD has become increasingly reliant on contractors both overseas and in the United States. . . . The U.S. military has long used contractors to provide supplies and services to deployed forces, but the scale of contractor support DOD relies on in deployed locations today has increased considerably. DOD has recently estimated the number of contractors in Iraq and Afghanistan to be about 196,000. Further, DOD currently has the equivalent of *three brigades of contractors providing security services* in Iraq, as well as another brigade equivalent supporting these contractors—a total of about 12,000 personnel. Put another way, there are more *private security contractors* in Iraq today than the total number of contractors (about 9,200) that were deployed to support military operations in the 1991 Gulf War.[6] (Emphasis added.)

The lens of civil–military relations focuses our attention on issues of control and direction, specifically on who makes the fundamental decisions concerning the use of armed force. This volume expands and adapts that focus to include the private security contractors (PSCs) that have taken on many of the roles and missions that were traditionally the responsibility of the uniformed military. For more than thirty years now, the U.S. Department of Defense has been directed to contract out a remarkable amount of its functions rather than hire government employees. The reasons for this, and the legal bases, will be dealt with in Chapter 5 of this volume. Nowadays in many countries around the world, especially in those that receive abundant U.S. security assistance funding, the security landscape is populated by a wide variety of contractors providing technical assistance. Some are highly qualified and focused on the task at hand, but others are not. Too often these private firms seem to have no positive impact on the host nation, and even the opposite, but either way they continue to receive impressive sums of money from the U.S. government. The Quadrennial Defense Review Report of 2006 defines the U.S. "Total Force" as consisting of an "Active Component, Reserve Component, civilians and contractors."[7] The Defense Science Board refers to contractors as the "fifth force provider in addition to the four services."[8] The U.S. Army and U.S. Air Force have also included reference to contractors in their documents on doctrine.[9] Put simply, contractors are viewed as an integral part of U.S. military forces.

The academic literature on private security contractors, which has been proliferating quickly in recent years, is useful as far as it goes but has not done much more than scratch the surface of what contracting means for the nation's overall security. While Deborah D. Avant, Simon Chesterman and Chia Lehnardt, P. W. Singer, Benedict Sheehy, and Allison Stanger in particular have produced sophisticated works that contribute valuable descriptive data and analysis,[10] no book or article published so far has situated the PSC within U.S. civil–military relations, which is necessary to develop a real understanding of both. After all, these security contractors replace the military in a variety of roles and missions, including some kinds of combat; they receive the vast majority of their considerable funding from the Department of Defense; and they affect the country's ability to project force. All of this has implications not only for civil–military relations but also for decisions on the use of force.

While the problems with security contractors that are currently making news in Iraq and elsewhere arose during the administration of President George W. Bush (2001–2009), the practice goes far back, in Democratic as well as Republican administrations.[11] The solutions that have been suggested during the current Obama administration encounter very serious structural obstacles, while reforms to the national security system as a whole that have been proposed since the Goldwater-Nichols Act became law in 1986 have not been implemented. The challenge of reform is not the political orientation of those in power but rather the entire structure of U.S. national security decision making and implementation. A better understanding of the implications of contracting out military missions thus has to begin with U.S. civil–military relations and the legal and political implications of security contracting.

As Chapter 3 will argue, civilian control of the armed forces is not now, nor has it been since the earliest days of the republic, a salient concern in the United States.[12] The institutions of democracy are robust, and the armed forces are under close control in the United States, facts that are well known among civilian policy makers and at every level of the armed forces. Rather, the focus of all of the U.S. security and defense reform initiatives that come under analysis in Chapter 4 is on the effective use of the armed forces and intelligence agencies for national security and defense. This book, then, is more in line with literature on the use of force by the United States, but even those studies, unfortunately, do not deal extensively with the infrastructure and resources requirements for the armed forces and intelligence community to be able to accomplish whatever missions the democratically elected civilian leadership assigns them.[13]

The goal of this book is to propose a framework grounded in civil–military relations that can be used to analyze the main issues surrounding current U.S. force effectiveness and the contracting out of security, focusing mainly on the private security contractors. A meaningful evaluation of the national security sector requires a three-dimensional approach that encompasses reliable democratic civilian *control*, *effectiveness* in implementing roles and missions, and *efficiency* in the use of resources. These elements, taken together, capture most of what is important for the establishment of real national security reform in most countries most of the time. This three-part analytical framework also is both sufficiently flexible and reliably rigorous to be useful for decision makers. It will allow us to understand, and thereby evaluate, current efforts to reform and improve the effectiveness of those institutions involved in U.S. national security and will guide us on what is relevant to include for analysis and what is not. A critical aspect of this analysis is to develop an accurate picture of how the main components of the use of force, involving civilian decision makers and the various branches of the military, fit together.

The scope of this book relies on certain fundamental assumptions: (1) It must be amenable to comparative analysis because democracies are increasingly similar, and we must be able to compare and contrast their institutions and outcomes; (2) it must offer a contemporary viewpoint, given the changes now taking place in the security sector; (3) it must be practical, as the issues surrounding national security are vital and immediately relevant; (4) it must include a cogent discussion of government contactors because they are not only a fact of life but both a result and a catalyst of larger changes; (5) it must consider the political perspective because, at least in a democracy, reform or its absence is determined by political processes; (6) and, finally, it must include an institutional perspective. This discussion of civil–military relations and contractors is all about institutions, how they emerge, and how, as they develop support networks and resources, they become "sticky" and resistant to reform.

There is, interestingly, authoritative guidance for the addition of measurements of effectiveness and efficiency to the academic literature on U.S. civil–military relations, in Point 1 of the North Atlantic Treaty Organization's

(NATO's) "Partnership Action Plan on Defence Institution Building," which states the following:

> The Member states of the Euro-Atlantic Partnership Council reaffirm their conviction that effective and efficient state defense institutions under civilian and democratic control are fundamental to stability in the Euro-Atlantic area and essential for international security cooperation. They agree to establish a Partnership Action Plan to support and sustain further development of such institutions across the Euro-Atlantic area.[14]

The Office of Management and Budget (OMB), a key component of the executive office of the president, has found that the need to improve security effectiveness and efficiency applies as well to the United States, according to the Government Performance Results Act of 1993: "Federal managers are seriously disadvantaged in their efforts to improve program efficiency and effectiveness, because of insufficient articulation of program goals and inadequate information on program performance."[15] Studies released eight years later by the U.S. General Accounting Office (the former title of the Government Accountability Office), in June 2001, analyzed the degree to which the DOD had achieved these goals:

> DOD's progress in achieving the selected outcomes is unclear. One of the reasons for the lack of clarity is that most of the selected program outcomes DOD is striving to achieve are complex and interrelated and may require a number of years to accomplish. Another, as we reported last year, is that DOD did not provide a full assessment of its performance.[16]

Once we have a clear picture of the institutions of civil–military relations from the perspective of the three dimensions of control, effectiveness, and efficiency, it will then be possible to better analyze the implications of the private military contractors for U.S. security and defense. Using the framework to assess the performance of contractors on each of the three specified dimensions, it is both encouraging and gratifying to see how well it encompasses the main themes of ongoing auditing and research efforts aimed at contracting. Some adjustments have to be made, of course, to accommodate the comparison of public agencies, including the military, with private, for-profit, firms. The overall goal in this book is, then, to elaborate a framework for the analysis of civil–military relations, apply it to the U.S. armed forces, and then apply it as well to the private security contractors.

THE THEORETICAL FOUNDATION: NEW INSTITUTIONALISM

This book has both conceptual and practical goals. It is a work of sociological and political analysis, but it also provides an empirical basis from which to first define key issues in democratic civil–military relations and then implement institutional reform. The myopic focus on control found in most of the academic literature on U.S. civil–military relations makes this literature marginal to current national security reform initiatives, nor do these works typically appear in the reading lists prepared for the different U.S. military services.[17]

The analysis in this book will be only as good as the data in it, which are as complete and reliable as possible within a finite time period, and the conceptual framework it develops to identify what data were needed and how they should be organized and interpreted. The foremost American Weberian theorist, Reinhard Bendix, once pointed out, "You know, a little theory goes a long way."[18] This admonishes us to use just enough theory to identify key relationships that will help make sense out of political, religious, and military phenomena but not to assume that a tidy theory is enough in and of itself to end debate or obviate further study. In the course of many years' research on civil–military relations in new democracies, the Center for Civil–Military Relations (CCMR), located at the Naval Postgraduate School in Monterey, California, has developed an analytical method that emphasizes institution building and accountability. In the newer democracies, CCMR's faculty collaborate with officers and civilians to develop the institutions they need to reform their security forces and bring them under democratic civilian control. The present book will maintain the same conceptual approach as in CCMR's previous books on civil–military relations and intelligence reform, which drew heavily from Peter A. Hall's and Rosemary C. R. Taylor's seminal review article, "Political Science and the Three New Institutionalisms."[19] Those earlier works emphasized in particular the following themes. First, institutions are understood broadly as "the formal or informal procedures, routines, norms and conventions embedded in the organizational structure of the polity or political economy."[20] Second, institutions originate from the goals and motivations of the actors that create them, and we live in a world replete with these creations. Third, it must constantly be borne in mind that the process of creating and implementing institutions is all about power, and institutional power relations therefore are a primary concern of both New Institutionalism and this volume's approach to civil–military relations.

The scholars currently working in this field of New Institutionalism are engaged in comprehensive and informative debates that focus on the influence, or "functions," that institutions exercise. Claus Offe offers a useful and thought-provoking study on the functions of institutions in a chapter he wrote, titled "Political Institutions and Social Power," for an edited volume that includes some of the leading scholars in the field.[21] Five of these functions, as Offe formulates them, are directly relevant to this book's analysis and are outlined here to familiarize the reader with their terms and ideas:

a. *The Formative Impact on Actors.* "Institutions shape actors' motivational dispositions; goals and procedures are 'internalized' by actors, who adopt goals, procedures, and interpretations of the situation that are congruent with the institutional patterns. Institutions shape actors so that they (many or even most of them) take these institutions for granted and comply with their rules. Institutions have a formative, motivation-building, and preference-shaping impact upon actors."

b. *Congruent Preference Formation.* "By virtue of this formative effect, as well as the shaping of actors' expectations, institutions can provide for predictability, regularity, stability, integration, discipline, and cooperation. In the absence of institutions, actors would not be able to make strategic choices, because they would lack the information about what kind of action to expect from others, which they need to know in order to pursue their own benefit."

c. *Economizing on Transaction Costs.* "In particular, institutions increase the efficiency of transactions as they help to economize on search, negotiation, and enforcement costs of market and nonmarket interaction. To the extent that institutions are capable of cultivating their corresponding codes of conduct and the respective ethical dispositions, a by-product of their functioning is the avoidance of the costs of conflict and conflict resolutions."

d. *Frictionless Self-Coordination.* "Institutions shape actions by providing opportunities and incentives to actors so that a spontaneous order . . . results."

e. *Continuity.* "By virtue of their formative impact upon individuals, as well as their contribution to social order, institutions can be self-perpetuating. The longer they are in place, the more robust they grow, and the more immune they become to challenges. Institutions can breed conservativism. Innovation becomes more costly, both because those living in institutions have come to take them for granted, and because those who are endowed by them with power and privilege resist change. For both of these reasons, they set premises, constraints, and determinants for future developments and thus become 'path dependent' and limit change to the mode of (at best) incremental adjustment."[22]

These conceptual observations can help clarify both how U.S. civil–military relations work (or do not work) and how the PSC fit into those relations. It is the assumption of this volume that a New Institutionalist perspective best allows us to understand the centrality of institutions in the U.S. system of civil–military relations, the ways in which they support democratic civilian control but at the same time impede effectiveness, and the unequal relationship between the contractors and those who are supposed to control them.[23]

STRUCTURE OF THE BOOK

There is a wealth of books, chapters, and articles on civil–military relations as well as on contractors, located through extensive searches and the recommendations of scholars from a number of countries, that serve as the preliminary sources of information for this book. The book also draws heavily from government reports, audits, and other documents from such agencies as the Congressional Research Service, the Government Accountability Office, the Special Inspector General for Iraq Reconstruction, the Congressional Budget Office, internal reports from the Department of State and the Defense Security Cooperation Agency, congressional testimony, and think tanks such as the Center for Strategic and International Studies and several nongovernmental organizations. In addition to these are the extensive documentation and studies from the PNSR. The challenge has been to complete this book in the midst of a flurry of government publications, ongoing congressional hearings, and commission reports on several of the topics it deals with, including the PSC.

Undoubtedly the most important source for original insights and illuminating points of view were the forty-five policy makers and officials in U.S. civil–military relations, defense reform, and contracting who agreed to be interviewed for this book, some of them several times over a ten-month period.[24] The interviews proved indispensable for putting the government reports into perspective so they could be more fully understood and appreciated. Finally, the work of the instructors and students in the Graduate School of Business and Public Policy at the Naval Postgraduate School proved extremely valuable for the data and analysis presented in Chapters 5 and 6. Because much of the contracting activity is involved with various areas of jurisprudence, the research extended to articles in law review journals and interviews with lawyers in the field of contract law. The reader will discover the meaning, and significance of terms such as FAR, A-76, inherently governmental functions, CORs,[25] and much more, without which the current practice of government contracting and the expansion of the PSC cannot be comprehended.

Chapter 1 assesses the current literature on U.S. civil–military relations and discusses its limitations with regard to national security reform. As the chapter will make clear, this literature is flawed not only by its static emphasis on professions rather than the political dynamics involved in changing professions but also by its almost total focus on civilian control. Furthermore, the field is neither comparative nor amenable to a New Institutionalist analysis, a problem that will be explained in detail in the course of the chapter.

Chapter 2 elaborates on the three-part analytical framework briefly described here, comparing it to the current literature in the field of security sector reform (SSR). Several countries of Latin America provide empirical data, gathered through two recent major hemisphere-wide research initiatives, that illustrate the utility of the framework to identify and organize data for analysis. According to assessments published by the highly respected watchdog organization Freedom House, in 2009 some 119 of 193 countries were considered electoral democracies according to specific criteria.[26] If political parties and other institutions of democracy can be compared usefully, there is no reason to assume the same is not true of the armed forces because they and other security instruments have roughly similar roles and missions across different countries. In the new democracies of Latin America, the biggest challenge is indeed control of the armed forces. But the low level of resources committed to these countries' defense and security sectors is reflected in their armed forces' lack of effectiveness, a problem too often ignored by analysts and policy makers. The same points regarding challenges could be made about other new democracies in at least sub-Saharan Africa and Southeast Asia.

The issue of effectiveness as a necessary dimension of democratic civil–military relations will be taken up in Chapter 3. Drawing on a wide variety of sources, including official U.S. government reports, works by prominent journalists on current strategy and conflict, and interviews with policy makers, I will show that, although control is not an issue for U.S. national security, effectiveness most certainly is. The United States cannot afford its business-as-usual attitude or the assumption that what was good enough in the past will be adequate for the challenges of the future.

The following chapter reinforces this point as it reviews previous major reform initiatives, from the landmark Goldwater-Nichols Defense Reorganization Act of 1986 up to and including the PNSR. The issue of control never surfaces in any of these reform initiatives, although the need for greater effectiveness does again and again. Nor do these efforts at reform cover private security contractors. What becomes clear is that the success or failure of reform is determined mainly by politics in a context of institutional inertia.

Chapter 5 introduces private security contractors as a key component of U.S. national security and defense and thus of U.S. civil–military relations. The first point to understand is why the issue of contractors is so contentious. The chapter then provides data on the numbers of contractors currently employed in the broader U.S. national security sector and the many reasons for their emergence and growth in recent decades. It then focuses specifically on the PSC as opposed to the larger field of defense contractors, using Iraq for a case study due to the scope of activities and resources the PSC have there and the availability of good data on them.

Chapter 6 analyzes the PSC in terms of the threefold civil–military relations framework. Much of the documentation in Chapters 5 and 6 covers the detailed mechanisms used to keep track of funding and performance and to show that the efficiency dimension is robust. The other two dimensions, however, are not. Control can be assessed in terms of what is included, or excluded, within the definition of "inherently governmental functions." The contractors are hired to fulfill a contract, so the main focus for effectiveness must of necessity be on the contract process. That process will be analyzed in terms of our framework, and it will be demonstrated that effectiveness is problematic.

The Conclusion will update the findings on the reform initiatives, which encompass both the uniformed military and private contractors.

1 PROBLEMS WITH HOW WE THINK ABOUT CIVIL–MILITARY RELATIONS

In retrospect, the catalyst that led me to write this chapter was an epiphany I had while participating in a Center for Civil–Military Relations (CCMR) workshop in Katmandu, Nepal, in May 2007. Nepal was in the midst of yet another turbulent political upheaval, characterized by general strikes and street violence incited by Communist youth groups. The conservative, self-immolating monarchy was at its end; a tentative peace process had put the Maoist insurgent forces, which had been waging a nine-year civil war against the government, into U.N.-supervised cantonments; and the Nepalese Army were confined to barracks. The parliament was deeply divided among extremely heterogeneous and antagonistic political parties that were attempting to reach agreement on a date for general elections, with the Communist Party of Nepal-Maoist playing the spoiler. In short, Nepal's institutions and traditions were swiftly being relegated to the past, but there was no consensus on the future, and violence was pervasive.[1]

CCMR had been invited by the South Asian Centre for Policy Studies, a Nepali policy research center, to hold a series of workshops under the sponsorship of the U.S. Embassy, to assist military officers and civilian politicians find possible ways to create a stable system of civil–military relations for a future—ideally fully democratic—Nepal. In the public conferences preceding the workshops, during which I presented a framework for analysis that is the precursor to the method in the next chapter, a young Nepali anthropologist named Dr. Saubhagya Shah, who had earned his PhD from Harvard University, treated the audience to a long exposition on Samuel P. Huntington's approach to civil–military relations, which explores the difference between objective and subjective civilian control.[2] I was deeply disturbed to see this vital discussion on how to assist a country facing extremely serious political and military problems, along with high levels of violence, hijacked by abstract theoretical discursions. It became clear to me that Huntington's formulation may be useful for discussing civil–military relations in stable democracies, but it provides little help to those still in the process of reaching this state. I was thus further inspired in my attempt to formulate an approach to analysis that would be useful not only for new democracies that are struggling to engage and prepare civilians for leadership of the military but would be relevant to all democracies, new and old, including the United States.

In writing this book on U.S. civil–military relations, I had intended to mine what I assumed would be an established literature applicable at least to older democracies, even if it wasn't particularly useful for the new democracies that CCMR works with. I wanted to frame the analysis in civil–military terms, with a particular focus on the interaction between civilians, including private contractors, and the military as they confront national security challenges. Unfortunately, as I will describe in the following pages, I found that the field has not yet crystallized; there has been not only little accumulation of useful knowledge but also minimal conceptual development. So far, researchers continue to exchange disparate factual information without analyzing it according to any rigorous theoretical framework, with the result that a broader body of knowledge does not accumulate. Some ten years ago, Peter Feaver identified what he termed "an American renaissance" in the study of civil–military relations.[3] I am not so optimistic that such is actually the case. Instead of developing a conceptual base of comparative and empirical studies that could be built on by encompassing other disciplines, the field of civil–military relations remains amorphously delineated and heavily anecdotal. Those scholars who might have worked within a developing and coherent field of studies have made important contributions to areas such as military effectiveness from the perspective of historical or sociological development and strategic assessments, but in my view these contributions are not building the field of U.S. civil–military relations.[4]

One might also have hoped that current scholars are contributing to a larger analysis of the implications of the wars in Afghanistan and Iraq. Instead, the main contributions so far have been from journalists such as Thomas Ricks and Bob Woodward, from former government officials such as Richard N.

Haass and James Stephenson, and from RAND Corporation analysts led by Nora Bensahel.[5] They are writing very useful books on war and reconstruction that nevertheless lack an analytical foundation. Thus, only a minimal amount of applicable knowledge has accumulated from these extremely important events that have serious implications for civil–military relations. To explain why this is the case, I will begin with a discussion of the recognized leader in the field, Samuel Huntington; and, by drawing on the work of other scholars, I will attempt to understand where things went wrong. I will then bring this review up to date and expand it by looking at the main journal in the field, *Armed Forces & Society*.

IT BEGAN WITH HUNTINGTON

Fifteen years ago, in 1995, Paul Bracken wrote, "Theoretical treatments of civil–military relations have changed little in the past 40 years, even though the context in which these frameworks were devised has changed enormously."[6] He went on to suggest:

> One very real problem with the study of civil–military relations as it has developed in the United States is that it has petrified into a sort of dogma, so that conceptual innovation and new problem identification earn the reproach of not having applied the theory correctly. The resulting situation has tended to recycle the same problems in a way that exaggerates their significance.[7]

It is with authority that Peter Feaver, maybe the leading scholar and expert on U.S. civil–military relations, writes,

> Why bother with a model [Huntington's] that is over forty years old? The answer is that Huntington's theory, outlined in *The Soldier and the State*, remains the dominant theoretical paradigm in civil–military relations, especially the study of American civil-military relations. . . . Huntington's model is widely recognized as the most elegant, ambitious, and important statement on civil–military relations theory to date. Moreover, Huntington's prescriptions for how best to structure civil–military relations continue to find a very receptive ear within one very important audience, the American officer corps itself, and this contributes to his prominence in the field.[8]

Another recognized authority in the field, John Allen Williams, concurs: "*The Soldier and the State* remains one of the two standard reference points for discussions of military professionalism, civil–military relations and civilian control of the military."[9] Given the comments of these two widely recognized experts in the field of U.S. civil–military relations, and the remarks of the Nepali scholar I mentioned earlier, it is clear that Huntington's conception still carries enormous weight. In his magisterial *Supreme Command: Soldiers, Statesmen, and Leadership in Wartime*, Eliot A. Cohen refers to Huntington's book as the "normal" theory of civil–military relations, "the accepted standard by which the current reality is to be judged."[10] Indeed, the 2007 Senior Conference at West Point took as its theme "American Civil–Military Relations: Fifty Years after *The Soldier and the State*," and the most recent book includes extensive references to Huntington's work in all five chapters.[11]

In my view, there are three main problems with Huntington's work that have impeded development of the field. First is the tautological nature of his argument; second is his use of selective data; and third is his exclusive focus on civilian control of the armed forces. Together, these methodological weaknesses have become major obstacles to original scholarship, which, although they have been acknowledged by leading scholars, have not been overcome.[12]

First, at its core, Huntington's approach is based on a tautology—it cannot be proved or disproved. Huntington focuses on what he terms "professionalism" in the officer corps, and he bases his argument on the distinction between what he terms "objective" and "subjective" control. As Bengt Abrahamsson wrote thirty-five years ago,

> Essentially, a "professional" officer corps is one which exhibits expertise, responsibility, and corporateness. "Professionalism," however, to Huntington also involves political neutrality; as a result, "professionalism" and "objective control" are inseparable as theoretical concepts. The immediate consequence of this is to rule out the empirical possibility of establishing the relationship between the *degree* of professionalism and the *degree* of political neutrality. Huntington's thesis becomes, in Carl Hempel's words, "a covert definitional truth." In other words, professional officers never intervene, because if they do, they are not true professionals.[13]

Peter Feaver attempted to use Huntington's theory to explain how the United States prevailed in the Cold War and concluded, "The lack of fit strongly suggests that Huntington's theory does not adequately capture American civil–military relations."[14] Earlier in this same book, Feaver, more delicately than Abrahamsson, analyzed the theory of causation proposed by Huntington, which in his words has bedeviled the field from the beginning:

The causal chain for Huntington's prescriptive theory runs as follows: autonomy leads to professionalization, which leads to political neutrality and voluntary subordination, which leads to secure civilian control. The heart of his concept is the putative link between professionalism and voluntary subordination. For Huntington, *this was not so much a relationship of cause and effect as it was a definition*: "A highly professional officer corps stands ready to carry out the wishes of any civilian group which secures legitimate authority within the state." (Huntington 1957, pp. 74, 83–84). A professional military obeyed civilian authority. A military that did not obey was not professional.[15] (Emphasis added.)

Empirical research built on the foundation of a false premise forfeits its validity.

A second problem with Huntington's approach is his selective choice of data, that of the military as a profession, as the explanatory variable. "Professionalism," similarly to "culture," is not a fixed or solid concept. The qualities that make up professionalism, just like culture, are subjective, dynamic, and changing. Indeed, in Chapter 4 we will see that a fundamental goal of the Goldwater-Nichols Defense Reorganization Act of 1986 was to *promote* joint professional military education, a goal that has generally been achieved across the U.S. armed forces, but only long after Huntington wrote his book. The U.S. Congress forced the military services to educate and utilize their officers jointly and thereby changed the culture of the U.S. armed forces, something that Huntington assumed to be largely static. Other countries, including Argentina, Brazil, Chile, and Spain, are currently seeking to change their professional military education. In short, the meaning of "military professionalism" is not something static; it can be changed through intentional programs of incentivized education.

In 1962, five years after Huntington published *The Soldier and the State*, Samuel E. Finer, in his book *The Man on Horseback*, questioned Huntington's approach by arguing that "professionalism" in and of itself has little meaning, and "in fact often thrusts the military into collision with the civil authorities."[16] One has to dissect and analyze "professionalism" to determine its relevance. This is what Alfred Stepan did a decade after Finer, in his classic research on the Brazilian military and the coup of 1964. Stepan coined the term "The New Professionalism," which he described as a new paradigm based on internal security and national development, in contrast with the "old professionalism" of external defense.[17] In complete contradiction to Huntington's theory, Stepan demonstrated that, rather than keeping the military out of politics and under civilian control, the new professionalism politicizes the military and contributes to what Stepan called military–political managerialism and role expansion.[18]

More recently, in his 2007 book on the history of the U.S. Army, *The Echo of Battle: The Army's Way of War*, Brian M. Linn raises fundamental questions about the way that Huntington simplifies and glosses over major variations regarding the U.S. military profession.[19] What for Huntington was a unified officer corps becomes for Linn three main schools competing for ascendance within the Army. In contradicting Huntington, Linn states: "But as a historical explanation for the evolution of American military thought between 1865 and 1898, the thesis [of Huntington] imposes a false coherence upon an era of confusion and disagreement, of many wrong turns and mistaken assumptions."[20] The key point here is that Huntington found largely static and readily identifiable a quality that is in fact dynamic and nebulous. Professionalism is definitely not a solid basis on which to build an argument about democratic civilian control of the armed forces.

A third problem in Huntington's approach is his exclusive focus on control, to the detriment of all other aspects of civil–military relations. In the introduction to *The Soldier and the State*, he notes, "Previously the primary question was: what pattern of civil-military relations is most compatible with American liberal democratic values? Now this has been supplanted by the more important issue: what pattern of civil–military relations will best maintain the security of the American nation?"[21] Nowhere in the rest of the long text, however, does Huntington return to this issue of military effectiveness. By contrast, he devotes an entire chapter to the topic of control, where he posits his objective and subjective models of civilian control of the armed forces.

Control is the primary focus in the vast majority of literature on U.S. civil–military relations. Peter Feaver focuses on control in some of his publications, and in the second sentence of his 1999 review article, he noted that, "Although *civil–military relations* is a very broad subject, encompassing the entire range of relationships between the military and civilian society at every level, the field largely focuses on the control or direction of the military by the highest civilian authorities in nation-states."[22] More recently, Dale R. Herspring commented, "As I surveyed the literature on civil–military relations in the United States, I was struck by the constant emphasis on 'control.' A common theme was that the United States had to guard against any effort by the American military to assert its will on the rest of the country."[23] This is not to say that democratic civilian control is irrelevant, particularly in newer democracies, but the intense focus on it in the United States is misplaced and distracts from the other dimensions.[24] The issue of control itself will be dealt with in more detail in Chapter 3 and again in Chapter 4 with regard to reform initiatives.

The observations of Paul Bracken regarding a largely marginal issue in civil–military relations, the posited "civil–military gap" in the United States, still hold. Not surprisingly, the 1990s saw a plethora of conferences, op-ed pieces, and publications on the "civil–military gap" during the tumultuous presidency of Bill Clinton, but surprisingly they have continued down to the present. In 2002, one of the main authors in this line of research, historian Richard H. Kohn, published an article titled, "The Erosion of Civilian Control of the Military in the United States Today," in the *Naval War College Review*.[25] The Foreign Policy Research Institute held a conference in 2007 on the theme "Mind the Gap: Post-Iraq Civil Military Relations in America," which found that "American civil–military relations were troubled even before the Iraq war, which conflict has only exacerbated frictions."[26] A 2007 report published by the RAND Corporation, "The Civil–Military Gap in the United States: Does It Exist, Why, and Does It Matter?" refreshingly concluded that the military and civilian leadership do not differ greatly on the questions that are of most concern to the Army, despite the fact that the report used data collected during the Clinton administration, prior to the terrorist attacks of September 2001. According to the report, civilians and the military view transnational terrorism as the primary security threat; nor is there any major threat to the principle of civilian control in the United States.[27]

The question remains: Why do scholars continue to fret about a supposed "gap" at all? Any empirical support for this idea is fundamentally a matter of methodology, starting with a choice of historical case studies that support the thesis and including select questions in public opinion surveys. Bracken suggests,

> The resulting situation [a prevailing dogma in the study of U.S. civil–military relations] has tended to recycle the same problems in a way that exaggerates their significance. Is it worrisome, for example, that current civil–military relations seem strained? Is *strain* itself something to worry about at all, or can it be useful in the relationship between institutions?[28]

In my view, the U.S. system of separation of powers generates strain, not only between military and civilians, but between and among civilians themselves.

The premise of a "gap" that causes strain arises once again directly from Huntington's concept of objective and subjective civilian control, rather from an analysis of the significance this concept might have for the United States and its armed forces in light of the threat of international terrorism and the country's engagement in two wars. It also fits into the principal-agent approach, which posits certain relationships that are put into question by a "gap."[29] In short, this preoccupation with "the gap" is indicative of a larger, and in my view less-than-optimal, approach to the study of civil–military relations, one that has not been amenable to comparative testing and development and has diverted attention to less-than-fundamental issues in civil–military relations. Despite the serious shortcomings already noted, drawing on scholars from various social science disciplines, Huntington's *The Soldier and the State* still has some currency, as indicated by the Nepali PhD. I believe this has two main reasons: First, as noted by Feaver in the preceding quotation, the U.S. armed forces welcomed Huntington's notion of "objective control" as a rationalization for them to manage their own affairs; it is no accident that the 2009 publication *American Civil–Military Relations* came out of a conference at the U.S. Military Academy at West Point. Second, Huntington's book is iconic in the sense that it resonates more as normative political theory, an early effort to conceptualize the topic, than as an empirical study whose findings can be replicated. Unfortunately, the field has remained somewhat marginal to developments in the social sciences.

COMPARATIVE POLITICS AS A TEMPLATE FOR STUDY

The serious theoretical flaws in the analytical literature have impeded the accumulation of information and insights and the refining of concepts, which in turn has trapped analysts on a conceptual treadmill, with lots of activity but little gain. This applies equally to the U.S. case and to other parts of the world, where there has been very little cross-fertilization because the literature on the United States has not proven amenable to comparative analysis.[30] Yet it need not be this way. As has been demonstrated over and over again by a number of researchers and scholars, comparative studies of the spread of democracies after the beginning of the Third Wave in 1974 brought a wealth of useful insights into the creation of democratic institutions.[31] By contrast, while the field of civil–military relations is replete with case studies, there have been very few comparative ones.[32]

To illustrate this point, and thus highlight the need for the kind of comparative framework described in detail in the next chapter, this section draws

Table 1.1. The substantive scope of civil–military relations, 1989–2007.

Subject matter	Percentage of articles
Civil–military relations and/or civilian control	70.8%
Coups	12.6
Military regimes and military rule	6.8
Military participation in or abstention from politics	9.7
Total	100%

NOTE: $N = 103$.

SOURCE: The data are drawn from the Armed Forces & Society Data Set (1989–2007).

on an empirical study by José Olmeda, a senior professor at Madrid's Universidad Nacional de Education a Distancia. In an effort to delineate the field of civil–military relations based on the works of its students and practitioners, Olmeda analyzed articles in the journal *Armed Forces & Society* (*AF&S*) between 1989 and 2007 (volume 15:2 to volume 34:1).[33] Contributions to *AF&S*, which Peter Feaver has characterized as "the subfield's indispensable lead journal," offer a remarkably comprehensive universe of available material on civil–military relations.[34] Olmeda's goal was to apply an analytical framework as similar as possible to that used by Geraldo L. Munck and Richard Snyder in their methodology study, "Debating the Direction of Comparative Politics," an analysis of existing research in comparative politics.[35] Olmeda hoped to emulate their contribution to the ongoing discussion on the disciplinary direction of comparative politics by applying it to the field of civil–military relations, an objective I share in my work here. After all, civil–military relations would optimally be a subfield of comparative politics. Olmeda maps the content of civil–military relations studies as Munck and Snyder did, by considering how authors in the field handle three broad elements of the research process: the scope of research; the objectives, as demonstrated in the kinds of information produced; and the methods used, distinguishing between methods of theory generation and those of empirical analysis.

In their analysis of comparative politics, Munck and Snyder list twenty-five subject matters under five general rubrics.[36] For his study, Olmeda drew on 103 articles on the general topic of civil–military relations, out of the approximately 530 articles published over those nineteen years of *AF&S*. The sample breaks down into the divisions shown in Table 1.1.[37]

The data for those 103 show that the regions of the world tend to fall into two groups that receive very unequal scrutiny from researchers. The first set of regions receives a roughly equal level of attention: The United States and

Canada are studied in 18.9 percent of the articles; Latin America and the Caribbean (including Mexico) in 14.8 percent; sub-Saharan Africa in 11.6 percent; East Asia, Eastern Europe, and Western Europe equally in 10.5 percent; and the Soviet Union or post-Soviet republics in 9.5 percent. The second group garners strikingly fewer articles, considering that these areas are extremely important political and military conflict zones: the Middle East and North Africa are the focus of attention in 6.3 percent of the study's sample, South Asia in 3.2 percent, and Southeast Asia in 2.1 percent of the articles.[38] As opposed to *AF&S*, the field of comparative politics, which tends to concentrate on Western Europe, nevertheless studies the world's regions with a more even distribution of articles. Munck and Snyder raise a relevant point: "Comparativists thus do a good job providing broad coverage of the world's regions and have also made important strides to incorporate the study of the United States as part of comparative politics."[39] The approach to analyzing civil–military relations in the United States, by contrast, has not been amenable to comparative work.

With regard to the temporal range of research, a large number of articles in *AF&S* adopt a short-term perspective (43.1 percent) with a time span between one and five years, 31.6 percent between five and twenty years, and only 25.2 percent adopting a long-term perspective of more than twenty years.[40] In contrast, a majority of articles in comparative politics analyze a time span of more than twenty years.[41] This suggests that *AF&S* is more topical, more devoted to current affairs than to comparative politics is in general. The New Institutionalism, which is this book's analytical foundation, is attuned to long-term trends and of necessity requires a longer perspective. For example, the basic post–World War II U.S. defense reform act was signed in 1947, and Goldwater-Nichols, which I will discuss in Chapters 3 and 4, was passed more than twenty years ago, in 1986.

The field of civil–military relations is strongly oriented toward empirical analysis, as is comparative politics, though the former gives more attention to theory generation (9.7 percent for *AF&S* versus 4.4 percent for comparative politics) than the latter, as is shown in Table 1.2.[42]

The field nevertheless is much more oriented toward descriptive studies, *what* the state of the world is, than causal analysis that seeks to explain *why* the world is as it is. In comparative politics the two types of study are more balanced, with 52 percent of publications being mainly descriptive (versus 96.1 percent for civil–military relations) and 48 percent being mainly causal in orientation (versus 3.9 percent).[43]

Table 1.2. The objectives of research from *AF&S*.

Objectives	Options	Percentage of articles	Aggregate options	Percentage of articles
Theory and empirics	Theory generation	9.7%	Theory generation	49.5%
	Theory generation and empirical analysis	39.8		
	Empirical analysis	50.5	Empirical analysis	90.3
	Total	100.0%		
Description and causation	Descriptive	76.7%	Mainly descriptive	96.1%
	Descriptive and causal but primarily descriptive	19.4		
	Descriptive and causal but primarily causal	3.9		
	Causal or mainly causal	3.9		
	Total	100.0%		

NOTE: $N = 103$.

SOURCE: The data are drawn from the Armed Forces & Society Data Set (1989–2007).

Concerning methodology, or *how* the research is carried out, Olmeda also follows the minimalist approach of Munck and Snyder, in that they prefer "research that relies on words as opposed to numbers." The prevailing method of theorizing in *AF&S* is inductive and the prevailing method of empirical research is quantitative (see Table 1.3). In comparative politics, 36.9 percent of research is deductive (versus 2 percent for civil–military relations in *AF&S*), and 63.3 percent is qualitative (versus 96.9 percent in *AF&S*). Concerning the issues of method, articles in *AF&S* strongly emphasize qualitative methods for both empirical analysis and theorizing (see Table 1.4). But Munck and Snyder rightly point out "that a considerable number of studies seem not to distinguish clearly between theory generation and empirical analysis as two distinct steps in the research process; they thus offer illustrations of theory or plausibility problems rather than real tests of theory."[44] This is as true of civil–military relations as they find it is of comparative politics.

A broad variety of data collection methods are used in qualitative studies. The most frequent are secondary sources, primary-source interviews, and newspapers and news sources (see Table 1.5). There are important contrasts, however, between comparative politics and civil-military relations studies regarding the use of interviews (23.4 percent for the former versus 10.5 percent

Table 1.3. The methods of research from *AF&S*.

Aim of method	Options	Percentage of articles	Aggregate options	Percentage of articles
Methods of theorizing	Inductive, qualitative	90.2%	Inductive	98.0%
	Inductive, quantitative	7.8		
	Deductive, formal	2.0	Deductive	2.0
	Total	100.0%		
Methods of empirical research	Mixed method, dominantly qualitative	3.2%	3.2% qualitative	
	Mixed method, dominantly quantitative	3.2	5.3% quantitative	
	Quantitative	2.1		3.2
	Total	100.0%		

NOTE: *N* = 103.

SOURCE: The data are drawn from the Armed Forces & Society Data Set (1989–2007).

Table 1.4. Issues of method (percentage of articles using each method of empirical analysis) in *AF&S*.

Objective and methods	Methods of empirical analysis				
	Qualitative	Mixed method, dominantly qualitative	Mixed method, dominantly quantitative	Quantitative	Total
Theory and empirics					
Theory generation and empirical analysis	95.1%	—	—	4.9%	100%
Empirical analysis	96.2	1.9%	1.9%	—	100
Methods of theorizing					
Inductive, qualitative	94.9	50.0	—	—	—
Inductive, quantitative	2.6	50.0	—	100	—
Deductive, formal	2.6	—	—	—	—
Total	100%	100%	—	100%	—

NOTE: *N* = 103.

SOURCE: The data are drawn from the Armed Forces & Society Data Set (1989–2007).

in *AF&S*), and government sources and official documents (58 percent versus 2.1 percent). The lack of government sources and official documents in the *AF&S* studies suggest a lack of attention to ongoing institutional developments. Whether one can study the armed forces and security issues without using government sources, or understand complicated relationships involving

Table 1.5. Issues of data (percentage of articles using each method
of empirical analysis) in *AF&S*

Method of data collection	Qualitative	Mixed method, dominantly qualitative	Mixed method, dominantly quantitative	Quantitative	Total
		Methods of empirical analysis			
Analysis of secondary sources	73.0%	66.7%	—	50.0%	71.6%
Analysis of newspapers and news sources	10.1	33.3	—	—	10.5
Analysis of government sources and official documents	2.2	—	—	—	2.1
Interviews	11.2	—	—	—	10.5
Targeted surveys and questionnaires	2.2	—	100.0	50.0	4.2
Mass surveys and questionnaires	1.1	—	—	—	1.1
Totals	100.00	100.00	100.00	100.00	100.00

NOTE: $N = 103$.

SOURCE: The data are drawn from the Armed Forces & Society Data Set (1989–2007).

civilians and military officers without conducting primary-source interviews, is at best problematic. It will become obvious that I relied very heavily on both government documents and interviews in conducting the research for this book.

It is critical to address hypothesis formulation and data collection, which are central aspects of the research process, in a formalized manner so that information is transparent and open to assessment by the scholarly community, as Munck and Snyder emphasize.[45] Yet the deficiencies in the field of civil–military relations in this regard, and of comparative research in general, are obvious. Only 17.1 percent of the studies devoted to theory generation and empirical analysis formulate and use a rigorously testable hypothesis, that is, one that explicitly specifies the variables and the relationship among the variables used in a causal model. The figure for comparative politics is 28.1 percent. This percentage, however, rises to 100.0 percent in studies with mixed or quantitative methods (see Table 1.6). Regarding analytical methods, in the overwhelming majority of *AF&S* articles (95.5 percent) using qualitative methods of empirical analysis, it is either not possible to readily understand

Table 1.6. Hypothesis formulation and methods (percentage of articles with a given objective and using each method of empirical analysis) in *AF&S*

Objectives and methods	Formulation and use of a testable hypothesis			
	Yes	Partial	No	Total
Theory and empirics				
Theory generation	30.0%	20.0%	50.0%	100.0%
Theory generation and empirical analysis	17.1	39.0	43.9	100.0
Methods of empirical analysis				
Qualitative	12.8%	41.0%	46.2%	100.0%
Mixed method, dominantly qualitative	100.0	—	—	100.0
Quantitative	100.0	—	—	100.0

SOURCE: The data are drawn from the *Armed Forces & Society* data set.

Table 1.7. Data collection and methods (percentage of articles using each method of empirical analysis) in *AF&S*.

Method of empirical analysis	New data			Formal data		
	Yes	No	Total	Yes	No	Total
Qualitative	92.1%	7.9%	100.0%	4.5%	95.5%	100.0%
Mixed method, dominantly qualitative	100.0	—	100.0	100.0	—	100.0
Mixed method, dominantly quantitative	100.0	—	100.0	100.0	—	100.0
Quantitative	50.0	50.0	100.0	100.0	—	100.0

SOURCE: The data are drawn from the *Armed Forces & Society* data set.

the values assigned to the variables, or the data presented consist only of values on select units and variables (see Table 1.7). In comparative politics, the percentage of these kinds of problems is much less (74.1 percent) with 39.7 percent for the category of mixed method, dominantly qualitative (versus 0 percent in the *AF&S* data).[46]

When Morris Janowitz launched *Armed Forces & Society* in the fall of 1974, he used that first issue to advocate that the contributors engage with real-world political issues and committed the journal to devoting a section to this. There is minimal evidence, however, that contributors have aimed to produce knowledge of direct relevance to policy makers in the field of civil–military relations.[47] For their part, Munck and Snyder noted that "despite the advocacy by some scholars of an engagement with real-world political issues (Skocpol, 2003), there is little evidence that comparativists aim to produce knowledge of direct relevance to policy decisions."[48] This is even more the case in the field of civil–military relations, as demonstrated by the articles published in *AF&S*.

The results of this analysis of *AF&S* show that scholars of civil–military relations have focused mainly on matters of civilian control and general civil–military relations in different countries. Unlike comparative politics, the field is much more oriented toward descriptive studies than causal analysis, and contributors tend not to produce research that is directly relevant to policy makers. A broad variety of methods are used for data collection, but primary sources such as interviews, government resources, and official documents are largely missing. Finally, only 17.1 percent of the studies devoted to theory generation and empirical analysis formulate and use a testable hypothesis, at least in a robust manner; that is, use hypotheses that explicate the variables and the relationship among the variables used in a causal model.

In the last line of their article on comparative politics, Munck and Snyder suggest that "addressing methodological challenges such as these [they list five desiderata] will provide a far stronger foundation for producing knowledge about politics around the world."[49] The same advice would surely apply to the field of civil–military relations. Based on the preceding review of articles in the journal *AF&S*, it is evident that the field is methodologically challenged.

This review, in conjunction with my observations in the first part of this chapter on the legacy of Sam Huntington's *The Soldier and the State*, suggests that it is time for a new approach. This is what I propose in the body of this book. In line with a New Institutionalism approach to conceptualization, the analysis must be grounded in a study of institutions that includes the formal and informal procedures, routines, norms and conventions embedded in their organizational structures. Consequently, the analysis in this book strongly emphasizes the legal and institutional bases of civil–military relations, including, in Chapters 5 and 6, the private security contractors. National security reform by definition must take place in a political environment, as would be expected in a democracy; therefore the following chapters will pay close attention to the political context and implications of this study. The goal here is to provide a basis for analysis and to show the utility of a New Institutionalist conceptual approach using interview and government report data, which other researchers may find useful as a foundation to build on.

2 A COMPARATIVE APPROACH TO THE ANALYSIS OF CIVIL–MILITARY RELATIONS

In this chapter I propose an approach to the study of civil–military relations that can be used comparatively and will be equally applicable to both old and new democracies. This framework is the foundation for the following chapters, which conceptualize and then integrate the empirical material on U.S. civil–military relations and private security contractors. I started to develop the framework shortly after I began, in 1996, to conduct programs for CCMR in new democracies on four continents. While preparing these one-week seminars, which deal with virtually all aspects of what militaries and other state instruments do to achieve security around the globe, I found the available literature of very limited value. Consequently, CCMR instructors developed course materials empirically, from the ground up, and learned to adapt them to each evolving national context. This situation enabled me to use both the seminar programs abroad and the graduate resident courses in Monterey as research opportunities, where I could gather new ideas and information and test them out in different contexts on diverse audiences. This chapter thus is a further refinement of what I have learned and written over the past decade or more and an expansion of the framework so that it can be applied specifically to the United States.

In the latter part of this chapter I illustrate the utility of the framework by applying it to some recent studies from Latin America. This is not an analysis per se because I did not personally collect the data to test the framework. The two publications to which I will refer were undertaken both as scholarly projects and to provide material for civilian decision makers interested in promoting political and institutional reform. It will become clear that in all three dimensions addressed by the framework—civilian control, effectiveness, and efficiency—most Latin American governments are weak. The same points could be made with reference to other new democracies, particularly in sub-Saharan Africa and Southeast Asia, but I have chosen not to discuss them due to lack of space and the impossibility of finding material as credible as that used here for Latin America.

I will also take some time to comment on security sector reform (SSR), a model for the study of many of the same issues that is popular in Great Britain and parts of Europe. For this and the chapter in general, I draw heavily on the research my colleague Cristiana Matei and I have been doing. While we believe that SSR has much to recommend it, we do not find it a sufficiently robust alternative to our expanded approach to civil–military relations. Furthermore, the "whole of government" concept that characterizes SSR lacks the flexibility to evaluate a governmental system such as that of the United States, characterized as it is by strong federalism, the separation of powers, and extremely detailed congressional budget guidance and oversight.

It is possible to identify at least three phases in the development of analytical frameworks and literature on civil–military relations (CMR). The first, with Samuel Huntington as the main proponent, has been discussed in Chapter 1. Although some Americans and others have made reference to his ideas in their studies of democratization, the very different contexts of established versus new democracies make it clear that his approach is not of much explanatory use. Therefore, since the beginning of the Third Wave of democratization, which started on April 25, 1974, in Lisbon, with the military coup that became a revolution and gradually evolved into democracy, the focus of civil–military issues has shifted.[1] Even though neither Portugal nor Spain, whose transition began with the death of Francisco Franco in late 1975, was a military dictatorship, their militaries played key parts in the move to democracy.[2] This was even more the case as the Third Wave spread to include explicitly military regimes in Latin America, Asia, and sub-Saharan Africa. Even the transitional governments of the former Marxist-dominated Soviet bloc, while never under direct military rule, had to come to terms with their armed forces, and especially the intelligence services, once the Berlin Wall came down. Therefore, many analyses of democratic transitions and consolidation since 1974 include, of necessity, a discussion of CMR. These constitute the second phase. The major contribution by Juan J. Linz and Alfred Stepan on Southern Europe, South America, and post-Communist Europe includes different military groups, or CMR, as a central variable under the category of actors.[3] Highly regarded analysts of transitions and consolidation, such as Adam Przeworski and Philippe Schmitter, call explicit attention to the "military variable" or CMR.[4] There also are some excellent case studies of CMR in the context of transitions and democratic consolidation, or, in the case of Venezuela, deconsolidation.[5] Along with these comes a new and robust literature on intelligence reform in new democracies that captures the CMR dimension.[6]

These works evaluate the role of the military, including in some cases the police and intelligence services, in democratic consolidation. Most of these authors also take into account the institutions whereby CMR is implemented and the impediments to establishing these institutions. What these works demonstrate is that, in contrast to their authoritarian pasts, whether military or civilian dominated, the emerging democracies of South America, postcommunist Europe, South Africa, and elsewhere emphasize democratic security over national security. In other words, these new regimes focus on how to ensure civilian control over the armed forces, which in many cases were themselves previously in control of—or even constituted—the government. Those military-dominated regimes, by contrast, had tended to preoccupy themselves with national security, particularly internal security, often to the detriment of civil society. None of this literature, however, deals with what the militaries or other instruments of security are expected and able to do in terms of roles and missions.[7] This leads us to the third, and current, phase in the development of analytic frameworks for CMR.

THE THREE DIMENSIONS OF DEMOCRATIC CIVIL–MILITARY RELATIONS

I have found from my experience working with civilians and officers in consolidating democracies that the analytical focus exclusively on civilian control is not adequate either empirically or, for the purpose of developing comparisons, conceptually. In fact, militaries have long been engaged in humanitarian assistance, such as disaster relief, or to back up the police in domestic upheavals. Peacekeeping became increasingly critical in the former Yugoslavia, parts of Africa, Lebanon, and elsewhere, and more and more countries, including Argentina, Brazil, and Chile, opted to become peacekeepers; currently 117 countries furnish military, police, or gendarmerie forces for this purpose. New global threats such as pandemic terrorism require governments everywhere to reevaluate their military capabilities in terms of both control and outcomes. In short, the challenge in the contemporary world is not only to assert and maintain civilian control over the military but also to develop *effective* militaries, and other security forces, that are able to implement a broad variety of roles and missions. Therefore, while the conceptualization presented here includes civilian control as a fundamental aspect of democratic consolidation and does not assume it exists in any particular case, control is only one aspect of the overall analysis.[8] To understand what militaries and other state instruments of national security actually do, how well they do it, and at what cost in personnel and treasure, a comprehensive analysis of CMR must encompass the three dimensions of control, effectiveness, and efficiency. That is the goal of the framework presented here.

First, *democratic civilian control* comprises three aspects: civilian authority over institutional control mechanisms, normalized oversight, and the inculcation of professional norms through professional military education. Direction and guidance must be grounded in and exercised through institutions that range from organic laws that empower the civilian leadership, to civilian-led organizations with professional staffs (a ministry of defense for the military, a ministry of the interior for national police, and a civilian-led intelligence agency); one or more committees in the legislature that deal with policies and budgets; and a well-defined chain of authority for civilians to determine roles and missions. Oversight requires the executive, and probably the legislature, to have institutionalized mechanisms to ensure the security and defense organizations perform in a manner consistent with the direction and guidance they have been given. Finally, the inculcation of professional norms supports the first two elements through transparent policies for recruitment, education, training, promotion, and retirement.

The second dimension is the *effectiveness* with which security forces fulfill their assigned roles and missions. There are several basic requirements to consider in the conceptualization of this dimension. First, there is a very wide and growing spectrum of potential roles and missions for the various security forces.[9] Militaries participate in disaster relief, support the police in certain domestic situations, collect intelligence, and engage in peace support operations, counterterrorism, counterinsurgency, and warfare, to name a few. Police roles include crime investigation and prevention, law enforcement, and community relations, while intelligence personnel carry out data collection and analysis, security intelligence or counterintelligence, and covert operations. Second, the roles and missions cannot be effectively fulfilled without adequate resources, including money, personnel, equipment, and training. Third, no imaginable role or mission in the modern world can be achieved by only one service in the armed forces or one agency outside of the military, without the involvement of other services and agencies. Thus "jointness" and interagency coordination are indispensable. Fourth, to make things even more complicated, there are the paradoxes of evaluating effectiveness in the context of deterrence. When wars are avoided precisely because a country is perceived not to be vulnerable; or a program keeps at-risk youth out of a gang; or an intelligence organization supplies secret information that either prevents or induces a specific desired response, without the knowledge of anyone but those directly involved; evaluating the effectiveness in these situations means, essentially, trying to quantify a negative. Finally, most of the imaginable roles and missions for today's security services will be carried out within a web of coalitions or alliances, thus further complicating any attempts to determine a discrete service's effectiveness. In short, there are complicated methodological issues and nuances involved in evaluating effectiveness, and analysts must grapple with them to begin to understand what support the armed forces and other security forces require if they are to do what is expected of them in the contemporary world. I stipulate here, based on my experience over the past fifteen years, that effectiveness is possible only if there is a strategy that defines goals, institutions in place that coordinate the relevant agencies or ministries of government, and sufficient resources in terms of personnel and funds. I posit that these are the necessary, but not sufficient, requirements for achieving effectiveness.

The third dimension of democratic civil–military relations is *efficiency* in the use of resources to fulfill the assigned roles and missions. This dimension is of course complicated initially by the wide variety of potential roles, with their myriad missions, and the difficulty in establishing measures of effectiveness for any one, let alone a combination of them. The first requirement for an efficient allocation of resources is a statement of objectives. Most countries have not taken the important step of creating a defining document, such as a national security strategy, that lists objectives and establishes preferences for one set of goals over another. Democratically elected governments do not produce such documents for at least two reasons. Elected office holders are loath to develop and prioritize national security strategies because their opponents will quickly point out the discrepancies between the stated goals and the actual achievements. The United States only began to do so because the U.S. Congress passed the Goldwater-Nichols Defense Reorganization Act in

1986, requiring the executive to publish an annual national security strategy document. Even so, there are years when no public document is forthcoming. The second reason for not producing documents on strategy is the absence of an interagency process not only to define but also to assess priorities. This becomes even more difficult when dealing with police forces that are not organized at the national level. Very few countries have such a mechanism that is anything more than formal.

Before going further, it is important to clarify the conceptual distinctions between *effectiveness* and *efficiency*. The terms are often used interchangeably, and a review of the literature on organization theory, political transitions, and defense economics shows that the terms *effectiveness, efficiency, efficacy, cost-effectiveness*, and the like are not used in a consistent manner. The definition of effectiveness seems to garner the most agreement. Chester Barnard, in his 1938 classic *The Functions of the Executive*, states: "What we mean by 'effectiveness' of cooperation is the accomplishment of the recognized objectives of cooperative action."[10] The comparative politics scholar Juan Linz defines effectiveness in a way similar to Barnard's: "'Effectiveness' is the capacity actually to implement the policies formulated, with the desired results."[11] For the purposes of this model, then, effectiveness is the ability to achieve stated goals.

Efficiency as a concept is strongly associated with physics, economics, and organization theory. For example, in 1961 Herbert Simon stated: "The criterion of efficiency dictates that choice of alternatives which produces the largest result for the given application of resources."[12] Arthur M. Okun concurs: "To the economist, as to the engineer, efficiency means getting the most out of a given input. . . . If society finds a way, with the same inputs, to turn out more of some products (and no less of the others), it has scored an increase in efficiency."[13] A review of the literature does not offer a more useful definition. In the field of defense economics, the term used is *cost-effectiveness*, in recognition of the absence of the market and the monopoly status of a government in a given territory. While there is general recognition that the concept must be limited in the public context, agencies typically are expected to determine the most efficient use of resources.[14] I will return to this issue later in the chapter, following a more in-depth look at control and effectiveness.

It should be obvious that the three elements of CMR must be assessed as interdependent parts of a whole. Each of the three is necessary to ensure security, and individually none is sufficient. Civilian control is basic to a democracy but is irrelevant unless the instruments for achieving security can effectively fulfill

Table 2.1. Locations of authority for instruments of control over three security actors in roles and missions.

Roles and agencies	Institutional control mechanisms		Oversight		Professional norms	
	National	International	National	International	National	International
Wars—armed forces and military intelligence	High	Low	High	High	High	N/A or low
Internal wars—special forces, police, and intelligence	High	Low or N/A	High	Low or N/A	High	Low
Terrorism—intelligence, police, armed forces, and special forces	High	Low	High	High	High	Low
Crime—police, police intelligence, backup support from military	Low	N/A	Low	N/A	High	N/A
Humanitarian assistance—military and police	N/A or low	Low	N/A	Low	Low	High
Peace support operations—military, police, intelligence	High	Low	High	Low	High	High

their roles and missions. Both control and effectiveness must be implemented at an affordable cost, or they will vitiate other national priorities.

The first question to answer is, What are the major roles and missions of a nation's security forces today? What exactly is it they are expected to be effective and efficient at? These activities fall into six major categories: (1) Fight, and be prepared to fight, external wars; (2) fight, and be prepared to fight, internal wars or insurgencies; (3) fight international terrorism; (4) fight crime; (5) provide support for humanitarian assistance and disaster relief; and (6) prepare for and execute peace support operations.[15] The hypothetical location and strength of these roles and the control mechanisms are displayed in Table 2.1, along with the three main instruments for enforcing security: the armed forces, intelligence agencies, and the police. International antiterrorism and peace support operations are both activities that require international cooperation, and thus an international dimension must be included.

ENSURING DEMOCRATIC CIVILIAN CONTROL

What concerns elected leaders in most of the newer democracies is how to achieve, and then maintain, democratic civilian control over the armed forces or, in other words, to be sure they know the answer to the classic question, "Who guards the guardians?" Any armed force strong enough to defend a country is also strong enough to take over and run that country.[16] The issue is all the more important in those states where the military *was* the government and still enjoys prerogatives it negotiated during the transition to democracy.

The three main instruments governments use to achieve security are the military, police, and intelligence services, which in turn comprise a number of subdivisions. Militaries, which often have both an active and a reserve branch, typically include an army and one or more other services, such as a navy, marines, or air force. The services are divided further into activities: infantry, artillery, or surface warfare, for example. Police forces can be organized at the national (Colombia, El Salvador, Romania), state (Brazil, the United States), and municipal levels (the United States, Mexico) and may include specialized units, such as paramilitary carabinieri, gendarmerie, or so-called SWAT (special weapons and tactics) teams. Intelligence agencies typically are located within the military, national government, and police, though the gathering of intelligence can be far more widespread than that would imply. In some cases, such as Pakistan's highly autonomous Inter-Services Intelligence, a national intelligence agency may have the power to threaten the stability of the country's leadership.

The next question is how to ensure that these three instruments of state security remain under the control of democratically elected leaders. There is a wide spectrum of possible control mechanisms, but in most countries, especially newer democracies such as those in Latin America, these controls are few and weak. It is not enough to focus on democratic control of the armed forces alone because they are responsible for, at most, three of the contemporary roles security forces are expected to fulfill. Rather, a comprehensive approach has to encompass all six roles and the three instruments for enforcing security. While at the national level these may be easily understood, at a more global level things are much more complicated. Any discussion of multinational efforts to counterterrorism and crime or support peace operations, for example, must include any umbrella organizations charged with carrying out specific missions, such as NATO, the United Nations, the European Union, the African Union, or the Organization for Security and Cooperation in Europe. While each of these organizations has its own policies and bureaucracy, national governments retain control over their security forces that participate in coalition operations.[17]

Control depends less on how roles and missions are assigned to each security branch, such as the armed forces doing police work, than on how the branches themselves are institutionalized.[18] As I and others have suggested before, democratic control should be understood in terms of institutional mechanisms, oversight, and professional norms. First, institutional mechanisms are those forms of control that have been institutionalized by law, charter, or other means to ensure legal authority over the three instruments of security. These include ministries of defense, parliamentary subcommittees with authority over policy and budgets, national security councils, and officer promotion processes.[19] Next, oversight is exercised on a regular legal basis by the civilian leadership to keep track of what the armed forces or other security forces do and to ensure they are in fact following the direction and guidance they have received from the civilian chain of command. In a healthy democracy, oversight is exercised not only by formal agencies within the executive, legislative, and judicial branches but also by the independent media, NGOs (nongovernmental organizations), and think tanks.[20] The third means of control, professional norms, is institutionalized through legally approved policies for recruitment, education, training, and promotion, in accordance with the goals of the democratically elected civilian leadership.[21]

Table 2.1 indicates the level of control national and international authorities exercise over security instruments as those instruments fulfill the six major security roles. As can be seen, institutional control, oversight, and professional norms are mainly defined and exercised at the national level. Professional norms are an important facet of democratic control in all six of the roles shown in Table 2.1. Oversight and professional norms on the international level apply primarily to four roles: wars, terrorism, humanitarian assistance, and peace operations. The table also suggests that there are many potential control mechanisms that remain underused.

Measuring Effectiveness

While there are cases in which the *effectiveness* of the instruments for enforcing security in fulfilling roles and missions can be demonstrated, effectiveness generally is best determined by whether a state is prepared to fulfill any or all of the six roles outlined in the left-hand column of Table 2.1.[22] Success is very difficult to measure in many, or even most, instances. War fighting is the one role that tends to have obvious benchmarks of success and for which preparedness can be empirically evaluated through tactical and larger-scale exercises. Finding realistic measures of success for other roles gets much more complicated. For example, the United States was very good at winning the initial wars against the Taliban in Afghanistan and Saddam Hussein's regime in Iraq but not very good at the later stages of postconflict stabilization, or "nation building." This complicated issue will be dealt with in the next chapter.

When countries prepare to defend themselves or their allies against external enemies, the greatest indicator of success will be the avoidance of armed combat, whether due to the perception that the defenders possess overwhelming force, success in the use of diplomatic tools, or the integration of an aggressor into an alliance that mitigates ambitions or grievances. The best recent example is probably the Cold War, which never became hot directly between the United States and the Soviet Union thanks to the mutual deterrence imposed by the two sides' nuclear arsenals. Internal wars, including such recent cases as Colombia, Nepal, and the Philippines, have deep economic, political, and social causes that cannot be resolved by force of arms alone. Fighting tends to drag on, and it is all but impossible for either side to ever declare "victory." The fight against global terrorism, which differs from civil conflict in that terrorism is a tactic, not a cause, and has no finite locale such as a state to defend, can be considered successful when no attack occurs. It is impossible to know, however, whether there was no attack due to effective security measures or whether the lack of an attack was because the terrorists simply chose not to attack. Nor is there a clear moment when it will be safe to say, "Terrorism is defeated."

Fighting crime is ongoing, as is the provision of humanitarian assistance. Neither criminals nor natural disasters such as floods, earthquakes, or hurricanes are ever going to disappear. These are a matter of anticipation, preparation, and mitigation, with the goal of keeping the level of crime or loss of life and property within acceptable limits (leaving aside the question, acceptable to whom?). With regard to peace support operations, the issue is similar. If conflicts between parties arise due to religious, ethnic, or political differences and require intervention by foreign security forces, the troops' presence in itself will not resolve the fundamental causes behind the fighting. Rather, they may provide some stability, separate the antagonists, and allow space for negotiations. While there may be much to say about what is required for security measures to be effective, we must nevertheless be realistic about our ability to measure it, let alone explain success.

Based on studies in dozens of countries around the world of what is necessary, but not necessarily sufficient, to be effective in fulfilling any of the six roles shown in Table 2.1, there are three minimum requirements. First, as already mentioned, there must be a plan in place, which may take the form of a strategy or even a doctrine. Examples include national security strategies, national military strategies, strategies for disaster relief, doctrine on intelligence, and counterterrorism doctrine. I find that the formulation by prominent strategy analyst Hew Strachan captures the concept well:

> In the ideal model of civil–military relations, the democratic head of state sets out his or her policy, and armed forces coordinate the means to enable its achievement. The reality is that this process—a process called strategy—is iterative, a dialogue where ends also reflect means and where the result—also called strategy—is a compromise between the end of policy and the military means available to implement it.[23]

Second, there must be structures and processes both to formulate the plans and implement them. These would include ministries of defense, national security councils, or other means of interagency coordination. Third, a country must commit resources, in the form of political capital, money, and personnel, to ensure that the security sector has sufficient equipment, trained forces, and the other assets needed to fulfill the assigned roles and missions. Lacking any one of these three components, it is difficult to imagine how any state would act effectively.

The Efficient Use of Resources

The third dimension of my approach, *efficiency*, is even more complicated to conceptualize and evaluate than effectiveness. While it may generally be said that efficiency means getting "more bang for the buck," there are serious problems with both conceptualization and measurement. First, because security is a public activity where the so-called bottom line doesn't apply, there is no market mechanism to assign a value to whether an activity is being done efficiently—that is, making a profit or not. Second, competition, which logically can only be in the form of a peer provider within the same state territory vying to provide the same security, is not at play. There is, then, no objective criterion for measuring efficiency, nor, for that matter, are there incentives to achieve it. Thus the literature on private enterprises and their efficiency measures does not apply to the national security sector.

There are further considerations that must be factored in. As anyone who works in government is aware, public agencies and funds can be utilized as a "jobs program" to employ specific categories of people. This can run from simply keeping people off the dole to redressing historical inequities, from ensuring congressional or personal prerogatives are satisfied to outright nepotism. Along the same lines, government agencies are required to buy from certain suppliers, where neither cost nor quality is the major consideration. Such policies range from purchasing furniture made by prison inmates to contracting for technical support from organizations that provide money for election campaigns. No concept of efficiency alone can adequately account for these kinds of externalities.[24]

In some sectors of the public realm—education or transportation, for example—efficiency can be measured to some degree by kilometers of roads laid, numbers of bridges or schools built, or percentage of students who graduate per tax dollar spent. These rudimentary measures of efficiency do not apply, however, to the roles assigned to the security sector. How, for example, can we measure the deterrent value of the armed forces, of a nuclear capability, of submarines versus aircraft carriers versus squadrons or divisions? How should we assess the value of a "hearts and minds campaign" over "military force" in an internal war? Or how, in fighting terrorism, should we rate the efficiency of the intelligence services when success means nothing bad happens? What is the best way to determine whether engaging in peace support operations is good for the country and armed forces that are doing it or works mainly to demonstrate to the global community that the country is ready to assume its international responsibilities?

In short, the conceptualization and measurement of efficiency in the area of security is extremely problematic. What *can* be measured are the so-called hard data, such as numbers of tanks or airplanes produced, or number of troops trained or equipped, for a given cost. What these indicators tell us in terms of security and force effectiveness, however, is at the least limited and may even be misleading if we assume that, for example, lots of ships equal a strong navy. Policy makers nevertheless may rely on them to make, or more likely rationalize, decisions, when almost any imaginable issue in national security requires a broader, more strategic view than simple cost analysis. The field of defense economics, for which Charles Hitch and Roland McKean's 1960 work remains the classic text, makes some contributions, but only at the margins.[25] Those areas that can simply be quantified are not normally as important as issues of politics or strategy when it comes to deciding a defense policy or force posture.

The use of public funds in a democracy, however, requires that government agencies carry out systematic assessments of program results and their costs. Sharon Caudle, formerly of the U.S. Government Accountability Office (GAO), is a specialist in homeland security, which encompasses all three of the security instruments—the military, police, and intelligence services—discussed here. She has identified seven different approaches to what she terms "results management," or the quest for efficiency. The one Caudle most strongly recommends is "capabilities-based planning and assessment," which she describes as "planning under uncertainty to develop the means—capabilities—to perform effectively and efficiently in response to a wide range of potential challenges and circumstances."[26] This formulation is attractive because it incorporates two of the three dimensions of civil–military relations, effectiveness and efficiency. Caudle points out that institutions are necessary to oversee such planning or, for that matter, any of the seven approaches to efficiency she discusses. While this observation is obvious in the context of the United States, it might not be in countries without a history of strong civilian institutions; therefore, it is worthwhile to highlight some of the institutions that have to be in place even to begin to consider efficiency in the allocation, use, and oversight of public resources. These can include what Peter Feaver terms "police patrols," institutions whose purpose is to track and report on the allocation of resources in other agencies of the government.[27]

These institutional policing bodies would include legislative committees or subcommittees that can call hearings, legislative research agencies, inspectors general, auditing boards, executive office oversight boards, and specially created or ad hoc investigatory agencies. In the United States, these are the Office of Management and Budget and inspectors general within the executive branch. The legislative branch has the GAO, which was created by Congress to provide oversight of the executive, as well as the Congressional Budget Office and congressional oversight committees.[28] This multifaceted arrangement is not, however, unique to the United States. For example, Romania's legislature exercises control over the budget, which is ensured in various ways: Parliament approves the budget for the security institutions; annually it revises and adopts the Law on the State Budget, governing allocations to those institutions; legislative committees assess draft budgetary allocations for the intelligence agencies; parliament requires annual reports, usually during the drafting of the following year's allocations; and the Court of Audits, an independent body with budgetary responsibilities, functions in support of the parliament. Brazil has both an executive branch Secretaria de Controle Interno da Presidência da República (Presidential Secretariat for Internal Control), which oversees the executive's budget in general, and the Tribunal de Contas da União (National Audit Board), which oversees budgets and is largely autonomous. In Chile, similar to other countries in Latin America, there is the Contraloría General de la República, which has both ample authority and competence to provide oversight to public agencies and public funds.[29] This authority, however, is mainly administrative; political control is lacking because the budget process allows the legislature no, and the ministry of defense very little, opportunity to exercise control via the allocation of funds.

SECURITY SECTOR REFORM

The United States recently has officially embraced an approach, used primarily in Europe and formalized by the Organization for Economic Cooperation and Development, called security sector reform.[30] After describing what proponents of SSR mean by the concept, I will explain why I have not adopted the SSR approach, for both intellectual and practical reasons.[31]

Proponents of SSR, which is sometimes referred to as security sector transformation or security sector governance, conceptualize it on the one hand to include the more comprehensive "security community," rather than only the traditional military and police forces, in the process of democratization, civil–military relations, and conflict prevention; on the other hand, they hoped to inspire a more complex understanding of the twenty-first-century security environment.[32] Proponents point out that, because human security and development matter as much as defense against external and internal threats (of both a military and nonmilitary nature), it is obvious that armed forces alone are not sufficient to respond to these challenges. They argue that ensuring security requires a collaborative approach among a wider array of military and civilian institutions, which they term the "security sector." Despite this broad outlook, the focus of SSR is overwhelmingly on the instruments of security themselves and their democratic control and in most cases only negligibly on strategic-level roles and their attendant missions.

At a minimum, the security sector according to SSR encompasses "all those organizations that have the authority to use, or order the use of force, or the threat of force, to protect the state and its citizens, as well as those civil structures that are responsible for their management and oversight" (for example, the military, specialized peace support forces, intelligence agencies, justice and law-enforcement institutions, the civilian structures that manage them, and representatives of NGOs and the mass media).[33] At the maximum, the security sector includes all of these, plus other militarized nonstate groups that play a role, even if negative, in security issues, such as guerillas or liberation armies. More recently, some analysts working with a SSR approach have come to recognize the need to include private security contractors (PSC).[34]

SSR has made important conceptual contributions to the traditional civilian-control orientation of civil–military relations. First, the SSR agenda goes beyond considering the military to be the sole security provider of a nation and proposes a broad concept of a uniformed versus nonuniformed sector or "community," whose members must work together to achieve security. Second, it takes into account the somewhat interchangeable roles and missions assigned in recent times to the various security sector components (for example, the armed forces perform police and diplomatic tasks, as well as social development work; police and other law enforcement bodies perform military-type tasks to safeguard society against external threats, in particular after terrorist attacks), as well as the ongoing internationalization of the security agencies (multinational peace support operations and/or policing; international antiterrorism cooperation among intelligence agencies). Third, SSR tries to link directly to broader efforts toward democratization, human rights promotion, conflict prevention, and postconflict reconstruction; in this context, it encompasses the larger political, economic, social, and cultural transformations that accompany democratization; it also encourages civil society, at least theoretically, to exert more influence over policy making, violence reduction, and conflict prevention.

Despite the claim that SSR better suits the new security environment, however, it has serious problems. First is the lack of consensus among SSR proponents about what the security sector encompasses. According to Timothy Edmunds, himself an early and leading proponent of SSR, a too-broadly defined security sector that includes nonmilitary bodies (such as the health care system) jeopardizes a clear understanding of the security sector and its reform. Although such components may play a vital role in the human security and viability of a nation, the key responsibility of the security sector is the use of force.[35] Likewise, defining the security sector to include even nonstate organizations that use force, such as guerillas or liberation armies, simply on the basis of use of force, also jeopardizes the utility of SSR.[36]

Second, there is no general understanding of what SSR stands for or what its agenda, features, challenges, and effects are.[37] Research discloses at least fifteen definitions, ranging from "the provision of security within the state in an effective and efficient manner, and in the framework of democratic civilian control," to "the transformation of security institutions so that they play an effective, legitimate and democratically accountable role in providing external and internal security for their citizens," which "requires broad consultation and includes goals such as strengthening civilian control and oversight of the security sector; demilitarization and peace-building; and strengthening the rule of law."[38] In the view of one SSR proponent, Mark Sedra, the "variances in interpretation of the concept have contributed to a significant disjuncture between policy and practice."[39] In this sense, while a SSR concept has been formally adopted by various countries in their official foreign policy documents, the ways countries implement it differs greatly from case to case.[40] In addition, although several security programs were implemented as part of the broad SSR agenda, they in fact deal only with limited SSR components (for example, reform of the police or armed forces) without embracing its vaunted holistic characteristic and thus fail to comply with the SSR normative model.[41]

Third, and most importantly, SSR lacks a consistent analytical conceptualization, which is undoubtedly due to the diversity of definitions. It is put forward as either a long "checklist" that countries' security agencies need to comply with for policy reasons (such as strengthening the capabilities of the armed forces, police, and judicial bodies; improving civilian management and democratic control of the security sector; and promoting respect for human rights and transparency);[42] as a "context-depending" view (for example, developmental, postauthoritarian, or postconflict);[43] or as a "hierarchy" of programs in which the first generation of reforms focuses mainly on control, while the second generation of reforms includes effectiveness and efficiency. Of all the formulations, the approach Timothy Edmunds proposes, which acknowledges the interdependency of control, effectiveness, and efficiency, appears both most useful and most similar to the CMR framework of this book.[44]

The "whole of government" approach required by SSR is virtually impossible in the U.S. system of government with its overlapping and extremely detailed restrictions on what can be funded with foreign assistance monies.[45] Even if SSR were feasible for U.S. security assistance programs, the conceptual bases and operative elements of the approach, as it is formulated by the vast majority of its advocates, are not convincing. SSR too often serves as a checklist to rationalize, or more likely justify, programs promoted by NGOs and government agencies, rather than being the outcome of a well-researched and objectively formulated program to improve national security. Funders who use it in such a way violate the central tenet of SSR, which is supposed to be its holistic character.

ILLUSTRATIONS AND ANALYSIS FROM LATIN AMERICA

Drawing on data from new democracies in Latin America, this section will illustrate the utility of a three-dimensional approach to CMR for identifying key elements for analysis. It will show that such a framework can be used to draw comparisons among democracies across the globe, provided the necessary data is available. This initial effort at comparative analysis is made feasible by the recent publication of two comprehensive and credible reports on national security, defense, and civil–military relations in Latin America and the Caribbean. In 2008, the Red de Seguridad y Defensa de América Latina (RESDAL) published an expanded and updated version of the *Comparative Atlas of Defence in Latin America* in Spanish, English, and French (it was first published in Spanish in 2005).[46] In addition to chapters on the security apparatuses of sixteen countries in Latin America, topics include the legal bases, structures, and processes of security, defense, and civil–military relations in the region. Dozens of authors and research assistants, from Mexico to Argentina, contributed to the project. In 2007 the Facultad Latinoamericana de Ciencias Sociales (FLACSO), in Chile, published the Spanish version of *Report on the Security Sector in Latin America and the Caribbean*, a project that was coordinated by Lucia Dammert; the English translation came out in 2008.[47] This volume includes sections on the armed forces, police, and intelligence agencies, with appendices on legal foundations, structures, and processes. While there is some overlap between the two projects, they are also complementary. The FLACSO study engaged more than thirty experts as authors and researchers, from Mexico to Argentina and the English-speaking Caribbean (which the next edition of the RESDAL *Atlas* will also include).[48]

These two projects reflect growing academic interest in and collaborative research on the diverse issues surrounding national security, defense, and civil–

military relations, particularly the very serious problems of control with which many countries in the region are grappling. Both are milestones in the scholarly and policy fields of national security and civil–military relations and provide a good foundation for further research on the issues identified in their reports. The data and analysis from these two source books will help illustrate how the framework proposed here can be used for comparisons between nations.

Although neither research project was oriented by the three-dimensional approach per se, the reports provide substantial information to illustrate its utility in organizing data, and they facilitate an analysis of each of the three dimensions. The picture that emerges shows that civil–military relations are in a tremendous state of flux in these new democracies.

Democratic Civilian Control

In the new democracies of Latin America, virtually all of which were previously under military regimes, asserting democratic control has been the highest priority for civilians and for most assistance programs by foreign governments and NGOs. Consequently, it is not surprising that there is much material in the two reports on this topic. The reports provide information on two of the three posited requirements for democratic civilian control: institutions and oversight. Both reports examine the main institutions, particularly the ministries of defense and the legislatures. The RESDAL report includes a short chapter by Guillermo Pacheco on defense ministries and examines the powers of the legislatures regarding defense and the structure of the defense systems in all sixteen of the countries it covers. The FLACSO report complements the RESDAL study, first by outlining recent reforms in the defense sector and then by highlighting their weaknesses, the national variations in civilian expertise, and the scarcity of technical expertise.[49] It also goes into considerable detail on "control and monitoring" by government branches and civil society, the second critical element of control.[50] Three of the four conclusions drawn in the FLACSO report are particularly relevant for this section on democratic civilian control:

- "*Legal reforms do not necessarily strengthen institutional capabilities.* . . . Abilities to plan, civilian monitoring, permanent groups of consultants and external control mechanisms tend to be weak in the region."
- "*Lack of definition of aims and limited monitoring of their completion.* . . . reforms are implemented without adequate mechanisms

for the government to monitor, and evaluate their effectiveness. This explains why reforms are often only partially implemented in almost every country studied."

- *"Persistent levels of military autonomy.* Important levels of military autonomy in matters such as the definition of the budget, doctrine, missions and functions, modernization of the armed forces and weapons acquisitions can be seen in the countries."[51]

In short, the FLACSO study finds that although many institutional reforms have gone forward, oversight and monitoring are still weak due to lack of expertise and the continuing autonomy of the military. It highlights the importance of evaluation, monitoring, oversight, and accountability in the policy recommendation section.[52]

Neither report has much to say about the third element of democratic civilian control discussed in this volume, which is professionalization of the armed forces, mainly through professional military education (PME). This is probably because only since about 2007 have some countries (Argentina, Brazil, and Chile) begun paying any attention to the reform of PME. The RESDAL report has a chapter on military justice by Juan Rial, and there is a separate listing of the main military training and education courses in the region.[53] Interestingly enough, although the FLACSO report does not look specifically at PME, the policy recommendation section does suggest: *"Increase professionalism.* Each one of the institutions analyzed show limited levels of professionalism. Thus, it is vital to make progress to improve requirements for armed forces and police personnel, as well as the requirements for incorporation into the intelligence services."[54]

From the evidence of these reports, we can conclude that democratic civilian control remains very much in the process of being institutionalized in Latin America. Despite real interest in this dimension, and the reform and creation of institutions, there remain major gaps in civilian expertise and in the structures to promote accountability and oversight, nor has there been adequate attention to PME as a means to exercise democratic civilian control.

Effectiveness in Implementing Roles and Missions

There are a few elements in both reports pertaining to effectiveness in implementing roles and missions, but not many. This chapter earlier stipulated three requirements for effectiveness: a plan or strategy, structures including a ministry of defense and an interagency process, and adequate resources. The

RESDAL report includes sections on the definitions of defense and security and provides some information on roles of the armed forces, including peace-keeping. It also offers useful information on military budgets, which has been a major research focus for RESDAL.[55] There is nothing in the report, however, about interagency processes or more generally about what is necessary to effectively carry out roles and missions.

Several of the country studies, including Brazil and Nicaragua, make clear that defense "reforms" have not gone far. The FLACSO report highlights some trends in the kinds of roles (here referred to as missions) assigned to the armed forces:[56]

> *Missions and functions of the armed forces.* It should be pointed out that there are a wide range of definitions of the missions and functions of the armed forces. Regarding the missions, they stretch from providing defence to guaranteeing institutions and collaborating in domestic security matters. Regarding their specific tasks, the law can include roles for the military in development, control of homeland security and national emergency situations. The expansion of military functions is a highly contentious internal question.[57]

Both reports offer convincing evidence that the determination of roles and missions for the armed forces and the security sector in general is very much up in the air.[58] The process also tends to be polemical, with little attention paid to the matter of resources. Neither report goes into detail concerning the formal elements required for effectiveness, which, for understandable political reasons, has not been a priority on anyone's research agenda in the region.

Efficiency

Both reports deal only perfunctorily with matters of efficiency in the security sector, and the implementation of it is very rudimentary. The RESDAL *Atlas* includes a three-page summary by Carlos Wellington Leite de Almeida, secretary of external control, Accounting Office of Brazil, on "reserved expenses." Beyond the author's expertise, this chapter also draws on the research done by RESDAL on defense budgeting in the region:

> Reserved expenses may be defined as that spending which does not completely follow the legal rules on transparency, thus disallowing the public knowledge about one or more identification and classification elements of those allocations, such as the financial source, how resources are earmarked, the object of the expenditure, among others.[59]

Leite de Almeida calls particular attention to the reason for reserved expenses in what he terms "the culture of secrecy" that still prevails in the areas of defense. He concludes, based on experience in the region, that the persistent lack of transparency in government expenditures has a direct and negative impact on the "efficiency of the public expenditure."[60]

The FLACSO research project demonstrates that budget evaluation units are fairly common in the region, being found in eight of the eighteen Latin American countries under scrutiny: "However, the national experts who participated in this project suggested that these units generally have little authority. Less common is the existence of auditing units within the ministry to monitor spending. Such units existed in only six of the eighteen cases included in this study."[61] In only two cases (Colombia and Mexico) have ministries made the defense budget public of their own accord. In addition to the lack of institutional oversight mechanisms, the FLACSO study highlights the lack of standardized data on defense issues, let alone intelligence.[62] In short, the two reports demonstrate that Latin American countries suffer from serious gaps in the efficiency of their defense and security sectors.

Data from the FLACSO and RESDAL reports on national security, defense, and civil–military relations in Latin America show that the analytical framework proposed in this chapter can enhance our understanding of civil–military relations. Future research projects and publications are needed to fill out the three dimensions. The data on Latin America are now sufficient for the dimension of democratic civilian control; it shows that civilians are still in the process of asserting control over the defense sector and that key issues such as the lack of civilian expertise and technical capacity remain critical challenges. There has been little attention to effectiveness, however, which is not surprising as there are still confusion and debate about what the roles and missions of the security forces should be in the region. If and when this issue becomes a priority, it can be studied. The framework emphasizes institutions, and the authors of the reports agree that the institutions needed to assess efficiency are generally missing in the cases they studied. Whereas civilian control is posited in Latin America, the various institutions, from ministries of defense to congressional or parliamentary committees, to professional military education, are lacking. This lack of institutional development in turn renders the dimensions of effectiveness and efficiency practically moot. Thus, while most of the countries in the region have transitioned from military to civilian regimes, the civilians have yet to invest the political and other resources to develop institutions to ensure robust democratic civil–military relations.

CONCLUSION

This chapter seeks to describe and propose the adoption of a framework for analyzing civil–military relations. The framework is based on my work for a decade and a half in working with officers and civilians throughout the world in security and in civil–military relations. It became clear that a framework that focuses only on democratic civilian control is insufficient practically and analytically for dealing with the real issues facing contemporary military and political leaders. The framework thus includes not only control but also effectiveness and efficiency. A realistic appreciation of national security and defense, however, cautions us to be very circumspect in coming to quick conclusions on these latter two dimensions. Even if we do not go beyond national defense, by including such roles as PSO and countering terrorists, for example, it is extremely difficult to assess negative values such as the effectiveness of a nuclear deterrent or intelligence in minimizing conflict. It seems clear to me that, to be effective, security services require at a minimum a plan, institutions for implementing and coordinating policies, and adequate human and financial resources.

Going beyond effectiveness to include efficiency is even more problematic in that one cannot assess efficiency without first resolving the former issue. The biggest bang for the buck is impossible to assess without first determining what the desired bang should look like. We must be extremely cautious of phony or arbitrary measures of efficiency—those that can be drawn from economic data alone. I propose at a minimum that oversight or tracking mechanisms must be in place to determine how resources are utilized. This chapter also takes on the approach known as SSR and concludes that an approach that promises and includes everything is in fact not very useful. Rather than beginning with a conceptual core, SSR grew out of state policies for development and minimizing conflict and has yet to be distilled into a coherent conceptual basis. Thus, even though SSR includes the PSCs, it treats them no more satisfactorily than it does other actors, state or nonstate. Finally, I illustrate how my framework can be utilized by drawing on recent research from two highly regarded institutions in Latin America.

3 THE INSTITUTIONS OF U.S. CIVIL–MILITARY RELATIONS

This chapter will apply the three-dimensional framework elaborated and illustrated in the last chapter to describe how the U.S. system of civil–military relations works in practice. The academic literature in general, focused as it is on the issue of control, scarcely touches on the far more critical matters of effectiveness in its analyses of U.S. civil–military relations. The U.S. national security system is highly bureaucratized, with an enormous Department of Defense that consists of 1,421,731 active duty members within the four services, 2,646,658 civilian personnel, and 463,084 in the Army and Air Force National Guard.[1] In addition to the four armed services and eight reserve components, which compete with each other for resources, there are sixteen separate intelligence agencies, plus the Office of the Director of National Intelligence (with a staff of 1,000, not including contractors), and the Department of Homeland Security, which now encompasses twenty-one previously separate organizations with approximately 216,000 personnel.[2] This behemoth bureaucracy is controlled, funded, and regulated by the three separate branches of government, and its facilities are spread among all fifty states and the several territories. The United States has no national police force, but each of the fifty states, plus the District of Columbia, Puerto Rico, the U.S. Virgin Islands, and Guam have their own militia under the control of the governor (except for the District of Columbia, which does not have a governor), in the form of the National Guard. Federalism is a strong guiding principle. According to Amendment X of the U.S. Constitution: "The powers not delegated to the United States by the Constitution, nor prohibited by it to the States, are reserved to the States respectively, or to the people."[3]

To analyze this system, or set of systems, the concepts of New Institution-alism, which are the theoretical background to this book, offer the most com-prehensive approach. The main reform programs that will be discussed in the next chapter all focus on the institutions of security and defense, their origins, relations, and dynamics. While the profession of military service did figure in an earlier successful reform initiative, the Goldwater-Nichols Defense Reor-ganization Act of 1986, control issues, at least regarding the profession itself, were not the concern. Rather, the bill's attention focused on the relations be-tween different institutions of the overall defense bureaucracy and operational "jointness" among the services. Of the several functions highlighted by Claus Offe (see the Introduction) that figure in this discussion, two in particular are relevant. First is what Offe calls the *formative impact upon actors*:

> Institutions shape actors' motivational dispositions; goals and procedures are "internalized" by actors, who adopt goals, procedures, and interpretations of the situation that are congruent with the institutional patterns. Institutions shape actors so that they (many or even most of them) take these institu-tions for granted and comply with their rules. Institutions have a formative, motivation-building, and preference-shaping impact upon actors.[4]

These institutional norms themselves shape incentives for compliance. The second function that is indispensable to an understanding of U.S. CMR is *continuity*:

> By virtue of their formative impact upon individuals, as well as their contribu-tion to social order, institutions can be self-perpetuating. The longer they are in place, the more robust they grow, and the more immune they become to challenges. Institutions can breed conservatism. Innovation becomes more costly, both because those living in institutions have come to take them for granted and because those who are endowed by them with power and privi-lege resist change. For both of these reasons, they set premises, constraints, and determinants for future developments and thus become "path dependent" and limit change to the mode of (at best) incremental adjustment.[5]

The formative impact and continuity of institutions are central themes in this chapter. The actors take the institutions' forms and structures for granted, the institutions are self-perpetuating, and innovation is extremely difficult.

This chapter relies heavily on official documents for its information, espe-cially Congressional Research Service (CSR) reports, which tend to be thorough, bipartisan, and up to date. It further draws on reports by various investigative and advocacy groups, which in turn tend to use a variety of sources in their studies and findings. As mentioned earlier, the database of the PNSR has been extremely useful: The 702-page report, "Forging a New Shield," is a veritable encyclopedia of the U.S. national security system, and the project has also generated hundreds of pages on all components of this system. The chapter also uses accounts by reputable journalists who have investigated and written on the U.S. prosecution of the war in Iraq, an important RAND report, as well as material from the author's interviews with current and former actors directly involved in U.S. civil–military relations.

THE ANALYTICAL FRAMEWORK AND
U.S. CIVIL–MILITARY RELATIONS

U.S. civil–military relations are far too complex to be described in one chapter. Luckily, those seeking to reform the institutions of national security generally agree on the overall issues and challenges. Not surprisingly, the basis for U.S. civil–military relations, like the rest of the U.S. political system, is the Constitution of the United States. This document is the first historical example of institutional engineering. The geopolitical context in which the Constitution was framed strongly influenced how the framers dealt with national security and defense and the allocation of powers—that is, civil–military relations. The United States had just won its struggle for independence from Great Britain, a contest that pitched the colonies against the military forces of a powerful seaborne empire. U.S. naval assets were weak in comparison with those of both potential enemies and allies, including Britain, France, Spain, and Holland. The original colonies occupied a very small part of the North American continent and faced additional threats from the indigenous peoples they had displaced, as well as rebellions among the colonists themselves. In short, the new nation had clear need to defend itself. The original Articles of Confederation, which the new Constitution replaced, however, were deliberately weak, reflecting the colonists' fear of a strong central government that might repeat the perceived injustices perpetrated by Great Britain. The Constitution's framers also wanted to guarantee that the new system they were devising would not devolve into a dictatorship supported by military force. Their concern in this regard is probably best captured in Federalist No. 51: "The Structure of the Government Must Furnish the Proper Checks and Balances between the Different Departments," published in 1788:

Ambition must be made to counteract ambition. . . . If men were angels, no government would be necessary. If angels were to govern men, neither external nor internal controls on government would be necessary. In framing a government which is to be administered by men over men, the great difficulty lies in this: you must first enable the government to control the governed; and in the next place oblige it to control itself. A dependence on the people is, no doubt, the primary control on the government; but experience has taught mankind the necessity of auxiliary precautions.[6]

The author describes the importance of a separation of powers between the executive and legislative branches at the federal level and between the federal and state governments. "Hence, a double security arises to the rights of the people. The different governments will control each other, at the same time that each will be controlled by itself."[7]

The centrality of national security and defense in the U.S. Constitution has been extremely well analyzed by historians. Probably most comprehensive on this topic is the book edited by Richard H. Kohn, *The United States Military under the Constitution of the United States, 1789–1989.*[8] In the chapter "The Constitution and National Security: The Intent of the Framers," Kohn does an excellent job of describing the contemporary dynamics of national security, defense, and politics, which resulted in a federal form of government that could defend the nation and its interests but avoid the temptation of dictatorship. Of the eighteen items in the final document specifying the powers of Congress, Kohn notes that "fully eleven related explicitly to security."[9] He sums up the framers' intent:

> The framers of the Constitution thus succeeded in their first and primary task, that of empowering the new government to defend itself: to create and continue military forces in peacetime as well as in war; to control the state militias and thereby to possess a potential monopoly of military force in American society; to govern these forces, and purchase and maintain installations and stores of equipment; to make rules and laws for the operations of these forces; and, finally, to be able to use them in foreign and domestic conflict.[10]

But they also created a strong presidency. As "'Commander in Chief of the Army and Navy of the United States and of the Military of the several States, when called into actual Service of the United States,' the framers granted to the executive the power to conduct war."[11] An equally strong bicameral Congress, however, holds the power to declare war and controls the purse; "the rest," as they say, "is history." The institutional bases for contemporary U.S. civil–military relations reside in this separation of powers.[12] Notwithstanding the many extremely serious conflicts and challenges the country has faced in the intervening 220 years, there isn't any reason to believe that there is a "crisis in American civil–military relations" or a problem with the mechanisms of civilian control over those whose profession is the use of arms. Rather, as the framework presented here will demonstrate, the challenge is to make all the disparate pieces of the U.S. security system fit together so that the whole can be effective.

The next section of this chapter, on democratic civilian control of the armed forces, begins with a look at the proliferation of nongovernmental organizations (NGOs) and think tanks that exert influence over the U.S. military. Following this is a discussion of two ongoing themes or issues within the executive and the legislative branches, over control of the armed forces by civilian institutions. In the United States, the close relationship between civil society and the armed forces is hardly remarked on. It is only by contrast with other governments, especially but not only the newer democracies, that we can appreciate the powerful influence of U.S. society and politics on the control of our armed forces. Without a comparative perspective, and a framework for analysis that applies such a perspective, much of what is unique in the U.S. experience, particularly but not exclusively regarding democratic civilian control of the armed forces, is lost to view.

Civil Society

Whereas in most countries there are no more than a handful of individuals and groups in civil society concerned with issues of national security and defense, the United States has an impressive variety of them. A large and ever-growing number of think tanks, located mainly but not only in Washington, DC, focus closely on these issues, conducting studies and issuing reports on a broad range of themes within the area. For example, one quick survey of websites that posted studies and reports on national security and defense during one week, compiled by the NPS Outreach and Collection Development Manager, yielded upward of seventy such organizations.[13]

These are not sporadic or ad hoc operations but organized efforts to influence government actors, the armed services themselves, funders, or other groups. There are, in addition, NGOs such as the Federation of American Scientists, the American Civil Liberties Union (ACLU), the Washington Office on Latin America, Amnesty International, to name a very few, along with academic area experts and specialist journalists, that also seek to influence the debate on issues of national security and defense. The so-called blogosphere has become another major forum for both national media outlets and individual journalists to publish both investigative research and opinion pieces on these topics.[14] In fact, it is possible to write with confidence that larger sectors of U.S. civil society and the media follow, investigate, and seek to influence policy on issues of national security and defense than in any other country in the world. It goes without saying that these individuals and organizations are motivated by very different objectives, which are best captured by Max Weber's division of incentives into *material* and *ideal*.[15]

Military Education

By contrast, the narrow topic of military education is one that few Americans think much about unless they have contact with militaries in other countries. In most of the countries that I am familiar with, in Latin America, Africa, and Southeast Asia, the militaries themselves control the content of their forces' education. That is changing in some countries, most dramatically, to my knowledge, in Argentina, Brazil, and Chile. As will be seen later in this section, through the Goldwater-Nichols Defense Reorganization Act of 1986 and subsequent legislation, elected civilians exerted their congressional authority to force the military services to develop and offer courses in "joint professional military education," or JPME. The incentive for officers to take these courses is that they cannot be promoted to the senior ranks unless they have done so and served in joint billets. All of this process is monitored very closely by the Department of Defense and the Congress.[16]

As Arch Barrett, who served as lead House staffer on preparation and passage of the Goldwater-Nichols legislation, emphasized in a personal interview, all U.S. education, from the primary level on up, assumes a civilian-led democratic government, including civilian control of the armed forces.[17] But there are other additional elements of civilian control in the U.S. military education system. Most officers in the U.S. services have not attended the service academies (the U.S. Military Academy at West Point, the Naval Academy at Annapolis, the Coast Guard Academy at New London, Connecticut, and the Air Force Academy at Colorado Springs); rather, most of them have attended civilian universities on Reserve Officer Training Corps (ROTC) scholarships or joined the services after graduation.[18] But even the service academies operate under strong civilian control. First of all, virtually all candidates to the service academies, except those to the Coast Guard Academy, must be nominated by a member of Congress.[19] The nomination process ensures not only regional diversity but also civilian involvement in decisions regarding who becomes a military officer. All of the service academies have boards of visitors (an oversight body similar to a board of governors) in which civilians are in a clear majority. For example, at Annapolis the Board of Visitors consists of six members appointed by the president of the United States, three appointed by the vice president, four appointed by the speaker of the House of Representatives, one designated by the Senate Armed Services Committee and one designated by the House Armed Services Committee.[20] Whenever issues that are out of the ordinary administrative scope arise, such as a cheating scandal or persistent sexual harassment, a civilian-dominated ad hoc board can be convened by the academy, the service, the Department of Defense, or perhaps Congress, to investigate and report. Because the service academies are directly funded by Congress their leadership must take these reports and recommendations seriously.

Besides oversight, however, all U.S. service academies, along with DoD-funded universities such as the Air Force Institute of Technology and the Naval Postgraduate School also have to undergo the same rigorous process of periodic accreditation by regional civilian accreditation bodies as do nonmilitary colleges and universities. The accreditation process ensures not only that the quality of military education meets particular standards, as measured by the competence of the teaching staff, course content, academic requirements, and the quality of facilities, but also that each school upholds expected standards of professionalism. If a school fails to measure up, the regional body will not accredit the program. It is taken for granted in the United States that the armed forces are closely integrated into a network of relationships and institutions that ensure the exercise of civilian control.

The importance of this arrangement becomes dramatically clear when one compares the U.S. experience with that of other countries where these relationships do not exist. As noted above, this situation is changing in some countries like Argentina, Brazil, and Chile, as civilian leaders come to recognize that the way to change the culture of the armed forces, which, in the three cases already mentioned had previously imposed authoritarian juntas on their countries, is through civilian control over the institutions and content of military education.

The next section is a review of two major legislative initiatives related to civilian control of the armed forces, each of which exemplifies two main themes of U.S. civil–military relations: the unquestioned dominance of civilian leadership over the armed forces and the historic and ongoing struggle between the executive and legislative branches over the locus of control. Again, the tension is built into the system through the nature of the founding political system as defined in the Constitution and is inherent to the separation of powers.

THE GOLDWATER-NICHOLS DEFENSE REORGANIZATION ACT OF 1986

As Amy Zegart wrote in 1999, the National Security Act of 1947 was flawed in several ways. The structure that the act created for the defense establishment was completely unworkable, a product of largely successful attempts by the Navy to undermine significant reform. It established a secretary of defense, but no Department of Defense. The secretary, nominally the civilian head of the armed services, had limited powers and almost no staff. The act also created a service-dominated joint chiefs of staff without a chairman. It left the privileges and powers of the services essentially untouched and made no provision to prescribe their roles and missions. It failed to institute the unified command structures that had been a key to success in World War II. The legislation in fact proved so ineffective that it had to be amended and strengthened three times over the next eleven years. Although the changes established the incontrovertible authority of the civilian secretary over the armed forces, they failed to correct many other weakness of the act, which was still deemed seriously deficient by president and retired general Dwight Eisenhower when he left office in 1961.[21] The Goldwater-Nichols Act, passed some forty years later, was the first subsequent effort to undertake large-scale reform and modernization of the armed services. The specific flaws of the National Security Council (NSC), another creation of the 1947 act, will come under scrutiny later in this chapter.

This analysis puts forward three main points: First, the chief motivation for passing Goldwater-Nichols was not to increase democratic civilian control, which was addressed through the civilian secretary of defense's authorities, but rather to increase effectiveness.[22] In their 1998 study of the act's effects, Peter Roman and David Tarr noted: "The act clarified the chain of command by stating that operational authority ran from the president to the secretary of Defense and then directly to the CINCs [commanders in chief of the combatant commands]."[23] Goldwater-Nichols also increased the capacity of the civilian defense authorities, which logically would increase their power over the armed forces. Roman and Tarr continued:

> Goldwater-Nichols altered the advisory process between civilians and the military in two important ways. It affected the advisory process directly by establishing the chairman as the principal military adviser and making him responsible for formulating advice on a number of specific issues. It affected the process indirectly by decreasing the authority of the chiefs and their services over operational matters and increasing the power of the CINCs. By changing how the senior military leadership interacted with each other, Goldwater-Nichols changed how they would relate to civilians in the policy process.[24]

At the time the act was written in the mid-1980s, the defense system had been badly battered and demoralized by the Vietnam War and had experienced a disturbing string of operational failures in other conflict situations. The proponents of these reforms identified the key weakness in the system to be the failure of the joint chiefs, as an institution, to provide adequate, timely, and workable military advice to civilian authorities from a joint (as opposed to service-oriented) perspective.

James Locher, executive director of the PNSR, and former congressional staffer Arch Barrett both detail the resistance to reform within the service bureaucracies. It must be noted that some civilians, including Secretary of Defense Casper Weinberger and Secretary of the Navy John Lehman, along with the top-level uniformed officers in the Navy and Marine Corps, vehemently opposed the reforms, while the Army and Air Force were slightly less adamant. Even so, the official correspondence received by the House Armed Services Committee (HASC) and the Senate Armed Services Committee (SASC) opposing Goldwater-Nichols was signed time after time by all of the chiefs. Every service chief, furthermore, appeared in person at the hearings to oppose the legislation. The services, according to Locher, feared they would experience a "loss of power and influence to joint officials and organizations," a concern he describes in largely institutional terms: "The Pentagon's change-resistant culture represents its greatest organizational weakness. Because of the Pentagon's immense success in wars cold and hot, it suffers from the 'failure of success.' It is an invincible giant who has fallen asleep."[25] Therefore, this was not an issue simply of civilians versus military but also of civilians versus civilians, in which the individual services fought to maintain their autonomy even though the overall defense system suffered in terms of effectiveness.

All observers agree that the reform as it was eventually enacted was posi-tive. As Roman and Tarr observed twelve years after the act was passed: "The Goldwater-Nichols reforms have had their intended effect: a tremendous change is underway within the military." They further noted, "Civilian decision makers, virtually unanimously, have told us that the military now provides higher quality and more timely advice as a result of the Goldwater-Nichols reforms."[26] This, the most important defense reform between 1947 and the present, was not specifically about reinforcing democratic civilian control, al-though the fact that it was initiated by Congress, passed despite the opposition of the highest-level civilian in the Department of Defense, and diminished the powers of the individual services, means that it did just that.

The other major legislative reform initiative of interest here, the War Pow-ers Resolution of 1973, concerns the relative power and responsibility of the legislative and the executive branches to commit the armed forces to combat. The debate that has continued on this topic over the ensuing decades provides insights into how the U.S. system of civil–military relations operates.[27] For instance, between the administration of George Washington and the present, there have been eleven separate formal declarations of war against foreign na-tions in five different wars, the most recent being those adopted during World War II. Obviously, American forces have been deployed more than a mere eleven times over nearly 250 years.[28] The Constitution deliberately allocated different aspects of war powers between the legislative and executive branches as a way to ensure the country did not enter wars lightly, but in practice the Congress has tended to be more deferential to the executive than the legal al-location of powers would anticipate.[29]

Both the Korean War and Vietnam War were undeclared. As one analyst observed, "Many Members of Congress became concerned with the erosion of congressional authority to decide when the United States should become in-volved in a war or the use of armed forces that might lead to war. On Novem-ber 7, 1973, Congress passed the War Powers Resolution (P.L. 93-148) over the Veto of President Nixon."[30] The resolution states that the president's powers as commander in chief to commit U.S. forces into action or potential action are exercised only pursuant to: (1) a declaration of war (which responsibility lies with Congress); (2) specific statutory authorization; or (3) a national emer-gency created by an attack on the United States or its forces:

> It requires the President in every possible instance to consult with Congress be-fore introducing American armed forces into hostilities or imminent hostilities

unless there has been a declaration of war or other specific congressional authorization. It also requires the President to report to Congress any introduction
of forces into hostilities or imminent hostilities . . . into foreign territory while
equipped for combat . . . or in numbers which substantially enlarge U.S. forces
equipped for combat already in a foreign nation. . . . Once a report is submitted
"or required to be submitted," Congress must authorize the use of forces within
60 to 90 days or the forces must be withdrawn. It is important to note that since
the War Powers Resolution's enactment over President Nixon's veto in 1973,
every President has taken the position that it is an unconstitutional infringe-
ment by the Congress on the President's authority as Commander in Chief. The
courts have not directly addressed the question.[31]

The courts have not directly addressed the question because neither the
executive nor the legislative branch wants to risk having the issue decided
by an outside body, possibly to their detriment. The solution has thus been,
like so much else having to do with the separation of powers, to negotiate,
adjust, and work out ways to function. Over the past three decades, presidents
have submitted 126 reports to Congress as a requirement of the War Powers
Resolution. A report from the Congressional Research Service notes: "Debate
continues on whether using the War Powers Resolution is effective as a means
of assuring congressional participation in decisions that might get the United
States involved in significant military conflict. Proposals have been made to
modify or repeal the resolution. None have been enacted to date."[32]

Under the auspices of the Miller Center of Public Affairs, former secretaries
of state James A. Baker III and Warren Christopher cochaired a blue-ribbon
National War Powers Commission, comprising experts from all sectors of government including the military, to study the problem; it issued a report in 2008.
The report's "Letter from the Commissioners" states: "The result of our efforts
is the report that follows, which we hope will persuade the next President and
Congress to repeal the War Powers Resolution of 1973 and enact in its place the
War Powers Consultation Act of 2009."[33] In the five-page executive summary,
there is no suggestion that civilian control of the military is in any way in question. The overall sense of the report is captured well in the last paragraph of the
executive summary:

> In sum, the nation benefits when the President and Congress consult fre-
> quently and meaningfully regarding war and matters of national security.
> While no statute can guarantee the President and Congress work together

productively, the Act we propose provides a needed legal framework that encourages such consultation and affords the political branches a way to operate in this area that is practical, constructive, fair, and conducive to the most judicious and effective government policy and action.[34]

This recent report, by a very high-profile group of civilian and military experts, conveys very well the reality of U.S. civil–military relations. There is no crisis; rather, the tensions among the different branches of government in all areas of policy, including in the areas of national security, defense, and use of the armed forces, are deliberate in the Constitution and inherent to liberal democracy. The issues of control are not controversial in the United States. Therefore, we need touch only briefly on the three instruments of civilian control here.

Institutional Control Mechanisms

The mechanisms of control include the specific structure of the Department of Defense, which is headed by a civilian secretary nominated by the president and confirmed by the Senate. The same is true in the various lower echelons, to the assistant secretary level, and in each of the military services, which also are led by civilians. While there is a mix of military and nonmilitary personnel throughout DoD, political appointees are clearly and unquestionably in charge. While the joint chiefs of staff (JCS) are active-duty military and the joint staff itself is overwhelmingly military, the chairman of the JCS (CJCS), in line with Goldwater-Nichols, is not in the chain of command. Rather, the National Command Authority is constituted by the president and the secretary of defense. Directives pass from the president and/or the secretary to the combatant commanders (formerly called CINCs), who are directly responsible for fighting the wars. These directives are transmitted through the CJCS, who also serves as top military advisor to the president.[35] Through the executive office of the president, and especially the Office of Management and Budget (OMB), the White House influences funding for the entire defense establishment. Congress has extensive control over the nuts and bolts of defense through its responsibilities for the budget process, force levels, promotions, and major legislation like Goldwater-Nichols.[36]

Oversight

All of these institutional control mechanisms are monitored through ongoing reports and investigations. The executive closely monitors all areas of military activity, primarily through OMB, the CJCS, and the civilian side of DoD. Specific committees within both houses of Congress exercise oversight by holding hearings and requiring rigorous reports on virtually all aspects of defense and security, in addition to what comes to them from the Government Accountability Office (GAO), the Congressional Research Service (CRS), and the Congressional Budget Office (CBO).[37] The budget, the approval and oversight of which also lie entirely with Congress, itself entails a rigorous and extremely detailed process. In our conversations, Arch Barrett called my attention to a particularly important oversight mechanism that I was not familiar with: Congress has the power, which it exercises from time to time, to establish and disestablish the offices and officials in the department of defense who serve under the secretary of defense and the secretaries of the military departments. Moreover, Congress specifies the positions that require presidential appointment and those that require both presidential appointment and confirmation by the Senate. The latter positions include the levels of deputy secretary, undersecretary, and assistant secretary. At their confirmation hearings, nominees have to agree to uphold the legal obligations of their office, which now include the provisions of Goldwater-Nichols. Later, in their oaths of office, the appointees swear to uphold the Constitution of the United States. Barrett noted that, by expanding the numbers of such political appointees, the Senate "puts the tentacles of civilian control into the military."[38]

Professional Norms

Professional norms are inculcated throughout the whole professional military education system, from commissioning right up through the Capstone course for new generals and admirals. They are buttressed by the civilian educational system, from which a majority of the officers come, and by virtually all aspects of society.[39] Major efforts are made in the war colleges to mix civilians, from other agencies or departments in the executive branch and elsewhere, with the student officers. On commissioning, the officers swear an oath to uphold the U.S. Constitution. In addition, the officer promotion process mixes military and civilian expertise in selecting those who will be recommended for promotion. Boards of military officers make the initial selection, with guidance—called precepts—from the service and/or defense secretary. These precepts, among other guidance, charge the promotion board to select a given number of the best-qualified eligible candidates in certain career paths where DoD sees a need; for instance, lawyers or medical officers. The service promotion board recommendations are forwarded through the service secretary to the secretary of defense for review and approval and then to the White House for the president's review and approval. The White House then nominates them, and they go to the Senate for final confirmation. Thus, in the U.S. system, civilians in both the executive and legislative branches have the final say on all officer promotions.[40]

While democratic civilian control over the armed forces in the United States clearly is not an issue for concern, this does not mean that there are not different professions and perspectives at play. The greatest potential tension lies between professional politicians and professional military officers, who tend to have very different time horizons and incentives, but that is not the main fault line of politics, or even of bureaucratic politics. The fault line in terms of control concerns the division of power and responsibilities between the different branches of the government. The military sector fits into this process with its own political calculus but not as an independent protagonist.

EFFECTIVENESS IN IMPLEMENTING ROLES AND MISSIONS

As described in the preceding pages, the roles of the armed forces, most of which are shared with other security instruments including the police and intelligence agencies, fall into six broad categories: external wars, internal conflicts, terrorism, crime, humanitarian assistance, and peace-support operations. In most cases, it is extremely difficult to say definitively whether the armed forces have successfully fulfilled these assigned roles and their associated missions. What did not work, as in the case of intelligence failures or lost wars, is relatively easy to analyze.[41] By contrast, to prove that something that did not happen, such as a full-scale war between the Soviet Union and the United States, or another successful terrorist attack along the lines of September 11, 2001, was prevented by effective deterrence or intelligence work, is very difficult indeed.

What we can do, and what is the central theme of this piece of the analytical framework, is to identify and examine three requirements without which effectiveness is impossible. First, at a minimum, there must be a workable plan or strategy for achieving a given goal; second, there must be a proven process in place to coordinate policy (in the huge U.S. bureaucratic system this of necessity is an interagency process); and finally, sufficient resources in the form of money, facilities, and personnel must be available to carry out the plan. In the case of the United States, it will become clear that two of these three requirements are problematic.

Strategy

In the children's fantasy *Alice in Wonderland* by Lewis Carroll, the heroine, Alice, converses with the rather Zen-like Cheshire Cat about her journey:

> "Cheshire-Puss," she began, rather timidly, as she did not at all know whether it would like the name: however, it only grinned a little wider. "Come, it's pleased so far," thought Alice, and she went on: "Would you tell me, please, which way I ought to go from here?"
> "That depends a good deal on where you want to get to," said the Cat.
> "I don't much care where," said Alice.
> "Then it doesn't matter which way you go," said the Cat.[42]

These lines pretty well capture the whole idea of strategy, that is, to know where you want to go and have a plan to get there. Those who work in this area identify four requirements, or phases of planning: First, determine where you are; second, determine where you want to go; third, plan how to get there; and fourth, evaluate how well you are progressing along the way until you reach your goal.

The U.S. government offers to help other countries develop national planning processes and strategy documents, through security assistance programs that include education, training, and technical assistance. In most other countries, it is up to the executive, whether this is a president or prime minister, and typically the minister of defense to formulate national security strategies, and these officials generally have little interest in developing such documents. This is because, if the administration develops and makes public a national security strategy that includes clear goals and means of evaluation, it will open itself up to criticism by its opponents for the very likely gap between aspirations and achievement. Therefore, politicians behave rationally if they do not develop a strategy and leave no paper trail with which to compare what they intended to achieve and their actual achievements. As a consequence, few national security strategies are formulated anywhere in the world.

Colombia presents a rare exception to this rule. Former President Álvaro Uribe's administration (2002–2010) published, adhered to, and regularly assessed Colombia's Democratic Security and Defense Policy of 2003.[43] There are two main reasons for the publication and implementation of this strategy. First, Colombia had, for over a decade, faced a serious existential threat from a spiral of political violence mainly linked to the Revolutionary Armed Forces of Colombia (FARC) and exacerbated by counterinsurgent militias. Uribe was elected president in May 2002 on a tough security platform intended to reverse the mistakes and inertia of his predecessor, who attempted to negotiate in good faith with the FARC between 1998 and 2002. That trust had proved utterly misguided, and the FARC used the hiatus in fighting to strengthen their organization, better arm themselves, and expand their reach throughout the country. Thus, the election of Uribe by an absolute majority in the first round of voting gave him a mandate to fight the FARC and other illegal armed actors (the Army of National Liberation and the Union of Autodefense Organizations of Colombia). It was, then, in the interests of the president to develop a practical strategy to determine, and then communicate to the country, how his government would prevail in the internal conflict.

Second, Uribe and his government were told by U.S. government representatives in very clear terms at least once, and probably many times, that the United States needed to know that Uribe had a plan to combat the FARC. Washington had been giving the Colombian government a high level of logistical and funding support to combat the insurgents under what was known as Plan Colombia; if this support was to continue, it had to bring clear results. I was present at one of these meetings, in July 2002, when this message was forcefully communicated to the president's representatives. A CCMR team, along with other government experts, provided their Colombian counterparts with a few concepts and insights into what is involved in developing a national security strategy, during a one-day seminar for the president-elect and his government. The U.S. team then left the Colombians to develop their own strategy. Within a year they had produced one, which was extremely well thought-out and logical, and they continued to implement it until the end of Uribe's term in mid-2010.[44] His successor, former defense minister Juan Manuel Santos, has engaged one of the authors of the national security strategy, Mr. Sergio Jaramillo, to be his national security advisor. Whether Mr. Jaramillo develops the legislation for a formal national security council, and a new national security strategy, remains to be seen in early 2011. But creating a formal structure would be a step in the right direction.

Given the impressive number of documents dealing with national security policy and strategy that the federal government publishes, it would be logical to assume that the United States itself is well prepared in terms of strategy to meet security challenges. In the epilogue to his book, Locher details requirements in Goldwater-Nichols to encourage the executive branch to formulate strategy and contingency planning; furthermore, as will be discussed in the following pages, Goldwater-Nichols requires that a national security strategy be developed and published on a periodic basis.[45] The DoD alone addresses four major policy categories: the national security strategy and national defense strategy, along with the Quadrennial Defense Review (QDR) report and the national military strategy. A CRS report describes how these plans should function: "The military strategy written by the Chairman of the Joint Chiefs of Staff describes how the military will operationalize the defense strategy written by the Secretary of Defense, which in turn covers those aspects of the security strategy for which the Department of Defense is responsible."[46] The Quadrennial Defense Review informs the president, Congress, and the public on how well these plans are working and what has changed. Most civilians and officers in DoD are probably aware of these strategy documents, but it is likely that many think they are produced at the initiative of the executive, DoD, or the JCS. This is not the case. Rather, "all of the strategies are mandated by law, and their contents are prescribed in some detail. To date, execution has not always precisely matched the letter of the law."[47]

The National Security Strategy is issued by the office of the president and pertains to the U.S. government as a whole: "The current mandate for the President to deliver to Congress a comprehensive, annual 'national security strategy report' derives from Section 603 of the Goldwater-Nichols Act of 1986." The legislation provides extensive detail on the requirements for the report, including the categories for its content. Whereas the George H. W. Bush administration (1989–1992) submitted three and the William J. Clinton administration (1993–2000) seven, the administration of George W. Bush submitted only two between 2002 and 2008. Furthermore, in neither of these did that administration follow the guidelines of the law.[48] It is up to Congress to enforce adherence to the law, but in the case of requirements for the executive branch to formulate strategy, it rarely does so.

Specifically, the requirement for the National Security Strategy comes from section 104 of the Goldwater-Nichols Act, which both stipulates that the report will "take into consideration the content of the annual national security strategy report of the President under section 104 of the National Security Act of 1947 for the fiscal year concerned," and defines what should be included.[49] What is supposed to be included is very extensive. Arch Barrett, who was one of the authors of this stipulation, reported that this was an initiative of Senator John Warner (R-Virginia) and that while the executive branch initially complied, by the time of the George W. Bush administration compliance had lapsed. Barrett also noted that whereas the joint education section of the Goldwater-Nichols Act was finally implemented through the efforts of a panel on joint education chaired by Congressman Ike Skelton, Congress mounted no corresponding effort with respect to the requirement for the National Security Strategy.[50]

The National Defense Strategy and the QDR are mandated from the 2000 National Defense Authorization Act (NDAA).[51] The legislation describes in detail fifteen items that the QDR report to Congress must include. The George W. Bush administration generally adhered to the guidelines from Congress regarding these two requirements.[52]

Promulgation of a biennial National Military Strategy (NMS) and its content also are mandated in the U.S. Code:[53]

> The legislation permanently mandates a biennial review of national military strategy, by the Chairman of the Joint Chiefs of Staff in coordination with the other members of the Joint Chiefs of Staff and unified commanders. A written report based on that review is to be submitted to the Committees on Armed Services of the Senate and House of Representatives by February 15 of even-numbered years. The report is required to be consistent with national security strategy and the most recent QDR.[54]

Although a NMS was issued in 2004, the subsequent reports due to the Armed Services Committees in February 2006 and February 2008 were never issued.[55]

From CRS reports and discussions with officials in the legislative and executive branches, there appears to be a general consensus that these mandates for codifying a national security strategy are not working out as intended. Consequent proposals to remedy the situation focus on such issues as frequency, synchronization of timelines, relationships among strategic documents, prioritization, roles and responsibilities, and fiscal constraints. Two representative criticisms note, "As a rule, current strategic documents do not prioritize the objectives or missions they prescribe, nor are they required to do so by law," and, "The national security strategy, the national defense strategy and QDR, and the national military strategy are not required by legislation to be fiscally constrained."[56]

While the CRS reports typically are not very candid or blunt, a quote from another source captures the sense that the strategic documents fail to serve their intended purpose: "None [of the strategies] can purport to involve the detailed articulation of achievable, minimum essential ends, the balanced adjudication of ways and means, and a thorough analysis of the risks associated with action and/or inaction."[57] Michèle A. Flournoy, a well-respected defense expert and policy maker now serving as undersecretary of defense for policy in the Barack H. Obama administration, put it forcefully: "For a country that continues to enjoy an unrivaled global position, it is both remarkable and disturbing that the United States has no truly effective strategic planning process for national security." She goes on to detail the absence of a planning process, the reasons for it, negative implications, and possible solutions.[58]

In sum, the DoD, probably even more than the rest of the U.S. government, churns out reports, studies, position papers, and other policy documents. All of those concerning national security are mandated by Congress. As Barrett wryly observed, however, "Laws are not self-executing." There has been limited congressional follow-through on the National Security Strategy requirement of Goldwater-Nichols, often for political reasons similar to the reasons the documents are not written in the first place. Unlike the JPME provisions that, according to Barrett, were subjected to at least eight years of intense congressional oversight, few of the strategic reporting mandates are followed. Therefore, while the U.S. government does produce an enormous number of national security strategy documents, they ironically do not provide an accurate picture of what U.S. national security strategy actually is.

THE IMPERATIVE FOR STRATEGY IN WARTIME

The absence of a national security strategy, or other strategies to implement the grander designs of a NSS, might not be important but for the fact that the United States is at war.[59] As one military analyst put it, "The Iraq War proceeded in the absence of a governing grand strategy and persistently fails to live up to expectations as a result."[60] This harsh assessment has become widely accepted as accurate.

Investigative reporting by several credible journalists on the U.S. involvement in Iraq provides useful documentation and insights on many of the key themes of civil–military relations. Of the several well-researched and informative books that have come out on this subject, the most complete, and arguably most credible, are by journalists Thomas E. Ricks and Bob Woodward, and U.S. Agency for International Development (USAID) Mission Director James Stephenson.[61] There is consensus regarding the U.S. war in Iraq, among virtually all of the authors consulted for this study—journalists, RAND Corporation researchers, and Department of Defense policy makers—that the absence of strategic planning has been a major factor in the war's missteps and failures.[62] A few illustrative quotes from *Fiasco: The American Military Adventure in Iraq* by Thomas E. Ricks highlight the key points here. At the start of Chapter 7, "Winning a Battle," Ricks writes,

> It now seems more likely that history's judgment will be that the U.S. invasion of Iraq in the spring of 2003 was based on perhaps the worst war plan in American history. It was a campaign plan for a few battles, not a plan to prevail and secure victory. Its incompleteness helped create the conditions for the difficult occupation that followed. The invasion is of interest now mainly for its role in creating those problems.[63]

The title of a section in Chapter 7, "Franks Flunks Strategy," is telling but possibly too arbitrary, as will become clear in the following discussion. Nevertheless, it was indeed up to General Tommy Franks, then-CENTCOM combatant commander in charge of U.S. operations in the Middle East region, and thus of the war, to formulate and implement a viable strategy. Ricks goes on: "The inside word in the U.S. military long had been that Franks didn't think strategically. . . . Franks' plan for making war in Iraq was built around U.S. technological and mechanical advantages. . . . So where Frank's plan should have been grounded in a wide-ranging strategy, it instead was built on a series of operational assumptions, many of which proved incorrect."[64] Ricks, however, makes the most important point relating to the control dimension of U.S. civil–military relations:

> There is no doubt that Franks executed the mission given him. As a military professional, he should have done more to question that mission and point out its incomplete nature. Ultimately, however, the fault for the lapse in the planning must lie with [Donald Rumsfeld, Bush's first secretary of defense], the man in charge. In either case, it is difficult to overstate what a key misstep this lack of strategic direction was—probably the single most significant miscalculation of the entire effort. In war, strategy is the searchlight that illuminates the way ahead. In its absence, the U.S. military would fight hard and well but blindly, and the noble sacrifices of soldiers would be undercut by the lack of thoughtful leadership at the top that soberly assessed the realities of the situation and constructed a response.[65]

Finally, Ricks states, "By failing to adequately consider strategic questions, Rumsfeld, Franks, and other top leaders arguably crippled the beginning of the U.S. mission to transform Iraq."[66] The responsibility for strategy in the U.S. system lies with the civilians, not the generals.

In his more recent and even more comprehensive book on the war in Iraq, Bob Woodward focused on another U.S. Army general, General George Casey, who served as first commanding general of the multinational force in Iraq from July 1, 2004, to February 10, 2007, and then as chief of staff of the Army from April 10, 2007, a position he holds as of this writing. In his former position, Woodward writes of him: "Casey didn't feel at all patient. Neither Rice [Condoleezza Rice, the president's national security advisor] nor Hadley [Stephen Hadley, deputy advisor] had come up with a national strategy for the Iraq War or found a way to make sure it was properly resourced."[67] Later in the book, Woodward notes: "No one ever articulated a grand strategy about what the heck the United States was doing. Nearly everything fell to the military."[68] In short, while the government produces a great many documents on strategy, when a strategy became actually necessary for going to war in Iraq, none was forthcoming. Or, rather, there were several, but their sum total was incoherent, and there was no plan available to be implemented at all when the initial fight was finished.[69]

Finally, in the lead-up to the troop "surge" of 2007, which eventually enabled U.S. forces to start moving out of Iraq's cities in July 2009, a strategy began to cohere, but from the sidelines. The most accurate description of this shift is captured in the following quote from a more recent book by Tom Ricks:

> It would take nearly 12 more months, until late in 2006, for senior officials in the Bush administration and the U.S. military to recognize that the U.S. effort was heading for defeat. Then, almost at the last minute, and over the objections of nearly all relevant leaders of the U.S. military establishment, a few insiders, led by Keane [General Jack Keane, ex-vice chief of staff of the Army and member of the Defense Policy Board], managed to persuade President Bush to adopt a new, more effective strategy built around protecting the Iraq people.[70]

How this new strategy was adopted, bypassing the statutory role of the CJCS as stipulated in Goldwater-Nichols, provides insights into the ad hoc decision-making process of the country's leadership at the time.

Interagency Process

The lack of a coherent strategy for the war in Iraq, and indeed in most areas of U.S. national security and defense, was directly linked to the weak interagency process, at least during the George W. Bush administration and possibly before. If any organization should be developing the inputs and the consensus on a national security strategy, it seems likely this would be the NSC.[71] This crucial point comes through in virtually all the written sources and interviews gathered for this book: The common refrain in Washington, DC, through late 2008 was "the interagency is broken." In *Fiasco*, Ricks assigns blame broadly for the fiasco of the war:

> It takes more than one person to make a mess as big as Iraq. That is, Bush could only take such a careless action [going to war in Iraq] because of a series of systemic failures in the American system. Major lapses occurred within the national security bureaucracy, from a weak National Security Council (NSC) to an overweening Pentagon and a confused intelligence apparatus.[72]

In his book, Bob Woodward also comments frequently on the lack of a viable interagency process. He quotes Leon Panetta (former congressman, director of OMB, chief of staff of the Clinton White House, and later director of the CIA), during a meeting of the Iraq Study Group, demanding:

> "Where is the central authority for dealing with politics in Iraq?" Panetta asked. He knew from his experience as President Clinton's chief of staff that someone in the White House had to take charge of such issues. But the Bush administration seemed to have no such authority. "Who controls policy there? Is it Hadley? Is it Rice? Is it Rumsfeld? Is it the National Security Council?" The others agreed it was an important question. Panetta tried to get an answer but never did.[73]

Earlier in the book, Woodward points out:

> But from the start, no one in the administration had control over Iraq policy. In the early days of the war, the president's national security adviser, Condoleezza Rice, and Hadley, her deputy at the time, had worked on Iraq nonstop and yet they never got control over the policy making. They were no match for Rumsfeld. The president had signed a directive before the invasion, giving the authority for an occupation to the Defense Department. Bush and Rumsfeld's selection of L. Paul Bremer, a career diplomat, to act as the viceroy of Iraq further diminished the role of Rice and Hadley, as well as Powell at the State Department. Bremer all but ignored the National Security Council.[74]

On the issue of deciding to disband the Iraqi military and the ruling Ba'ath Party, it became clear from interviews with those involved in the formal interagency process of the time that the decision was made by Bremer, without coordination, and was counter to previous guidance from the president on this issue. This view is confirmed by Woodward:

> As secretary of state at the time of the invasion in 2003, Powell said he wasn't told about the decision to dissolve the Iraqi army until it happened. It was a monumental decision that disbanded the entire Iraqi army with the stroke of a pen, and its enactment was contrary to previous briefings that had been given to the president and to Powell. Nor was Powell told in advance about the sweeping de-Ba'athification order banning members of Saddam's Ba'ath Party from many levels of government.[75]

Another authoritative source on this same crucial issue is Nora Bensahel of the RAND Corporation, who led the major RAND study of the Iraq war. She writes: "During both the planning and implementation phases of post-conflict reconstruction in Iraq, the U.S. government lacked effective interagency coordination. A formal coordination structure did exist, but it provided only general policy guidance and failed to mediate key tensions among its members, particularly between the Departments of State and Defense."[76] In somewhat broader terms, in her previously cited article, Michèle Flournoy states:

> The Government currently lacks both the incentives and the capacity to support strategic thinking and long-range planning in the national security arena. While the National Security Council (NSC) staff may develop planning documents for their respective issues, they do not have the ability to conduct integrated, long-range planning for the President. While some capacity for strategic planning exists in the Department of Defense (DOD), no other department devotes substantial resources to planning for the long term.[77]

The result is clearly negative: "In sum, the absence of an institutionalized process for long-range planning puts Washington at a strategic disadvantage."[78] The PNSR pays particular attention to the interagency process and its many and fundamental problems. One of its members, Cody M. Brown, wrote a separate report for the project specifically on the NSC.[79] Former Deputy Assistant Secretary of Defense for Stability Operations Dr. Joseph J. Collins writes with considerable credibility about many of the errors in decision making and execution regarding the invasion of Iraq and the aftermath. On interagency decision making, he observed: "U.S. decisionmaking problems in Iraq have much in common with problems present in other complex contingencies, such as Somalia, Bosnia, Kosovo and Afghanistan. All of these cases have demonstrated the limitations of our interagency decision making and policy execution processes."[80]

The wide recognition that the national security decision-making processes are not effective has resulted in several initiatives to reform them, which are summarized in two CRS Reports for Congress, one on the effects of interagency dysfunction on national security and the other specifically on the NSC.[81] In the former report, the authors state:

> Doubts about the adequacy of the system to meet 21st century security chal-
> lenges have been catalyzed by recent operational experiences, including Opera-
> tion Iraqi Freedom, Operation Enduring Freedom, and responses to hurricane
> Katrina. In the view of many defense and foreign affairs analysts, these opera-
> tions revealed deep flaws in the ability of the U.S. government to make timely
> decisions, to develop prioritized strategies and integrated plans, to resource
> those efforts, and to effectively coordinate and execute complex missions.[82]

They continue, "The 'outdated bureaucratic superstructure' of the 20th century is an inadequate basis for protecting the nation from 21st century security challenges, critics contend, and the system itself, or alternatively, some of its key components, requires revision."[83]

RESOURCES IN TERMS OF FUNDS AND PERSONNEL

The U.S. commitment to national security and defense is tremendous. As noted in the Introduction to this book, in 2008 the Department of Defense budget alone stood at $607 billion, greater than the spending of the next four-teen countries combined. At 4.3 percent of GDP, how could such an amount for a total active force of approximately 1.6 million[84] troops not be enough? In comparison with the rest of the world, where resources are minimal, the U.S. defense budget is robust and extremely impressive. Furthermore, as will be described in the following pages, these resources are held to strict oversight, with the intention to minimize loss due to inefficiency. Defense contractors, which are the subject of the latter part of the book, however, also use this DoD funding, not to mention funds from the Department of State, USAID, and other U.S. government agencies. In short, resources in terms of both money and personnel are not the reason for lack of effectiveness; rather, it is the absence of strategy and a functional interagency process.

Efficiency in the Use of Resources

The United States has multiple diverse and extremely competent institutions in place to monitor the use of resources. In this system, which includes national security and defense, all branches of the federal government are involved in monitoring or oversight, and so are civil society and the media. As will be clear in the last chapter of the book on the contractors, these oversight mechanisms do have some impact on policy. Arch Barrett was able to give me a personal sense of what is involved in oversight, thanks to his many years of government service, first as a military officer, then as a House staffer, and then as principal deputy assistant secretary of the Army for manpower and reserve affairs. The following discussion comes from his observations.[85]

Congress has several nonpartisan instruments reporting to it with information about the functioning of government, including the Government Accountability Office (with more than 3,000 full time employees), on which Barrett often relied; the Congressional Budget Office; and the Congressional Research Service. The CRS, which has a staff of 300 researchers, provides written and oral analyses to members of Congress and their staffs with the goal of providing context and options for future activities. Members and staff can request a memo, report, or briefings; depending on in-house expertise and other workload considerations, CRS analysts provide very timely assistance.[86]

Instruments of the executive branch include the Office of Management and Budget, which serves as a very powerful check on DoD. There has been a high level of interaction between OMB and DoD, including at the political level. The DoD inspector general's office, whose staff of lawyers is part of DoD, is a hybrid: Created by Congress, the IG reports to both Congress and the executive and is regularly tasked by Congress.[87] Both the IG and GAO must testify to Congress about their reports when called on to do so. Staff can be cross-examined and are able to interact with the committee members.

As noted in the previous chapter, efficiency in the use of resources in the government sector is extremely difficult to fully conceptualize. This is even more the case in national security and defense, for several reasons: There are at least six distinct major roles for the armed and intelligence services; measuring the effects of deterrence is logically complicated; secrecy further impedes evaluation; and policy choices, such as using public funds to address social priorities, introduce unquantifiable "externalities." To keep track of where resources go and how they are used, the U.S. government has developed a very robust set of institutions.

In addition to the official mechanisms, civil society and the media play a very large role in democratic oversight. Some proportion of the electorate is interested in the powerful combination of questions concerning the ways in which huge sums of the people's money are used, how the United States defends itself, and the ways in which the government decides whether to put their sons and daughters in harm's way. NGOs that deal with national security from every point of the political spectrum are an extremely active community, and so are the media. It should be noted that most of the best books on the conflicts in Iraq and Afghanistan have been written by journalists who write regularly for leading newspapers such as the *New York Times*, *Washington Post*, and *Wall Street Journal*, among others.

CONCLUSION

The Government Performance Results Act of 1993 begins with a section on findings and purposes. Under "(a) Findings—The Congress finds that— (1) waste and inefficiency in Federal programs undermine the confidence of the American people in the Government and reduce the Federal Government's ability to address adequately vital public needs; (2) Federal managers are seriously disadvantaged in their efforts to improve program efficiency and effectiveness because of insufficient articulation of program goals and inadequate information on program performance." One GAO report reads:

> DOD's progress in achieving the selected outcomes is unclear. One of the reasons for the lack of clarity is that most of the selected program outcomes DOD is striving to achieve are complex and interrelated and may require a number of years to accomplish. Another, as we reported last year, is that DOD did not provide a full assessment of its performance. We also identified weaknesses in DOD's strategies for achieving unmet performance goals in the future.[88]

The rest of the report documents these negative findings by the GAO regarding efficiency and effectiveness. This report, written in June 2001, before 9/11, the wars in Afghanistan and Iraq, and the devastation of Hurricane Katrina, would surely be even more negative in terms of effectiveness if it were done today. What this chapter has attempted to demonstrate, following the three-dimensional framework for analyzing civil–military relations, is that democratic civilian control of the armed forces in the United States is not an issue. Civilian control in and of itself, however, does not necessarily lead to effectiveness in achieving roles and missions, which remains problematic. An analysis of the institutions that make up the security and defense sector, with a strong focus on incentives and continuity, can explain a great deal of the problems, but even well-established institutions are not enough to ensure effectiveness. Very few senior military leaders attempted to push back against what turned out to be flawed policies in Iraq, despite any misgivings they may have had. The difficulty with evaluating effectiveness is not a theoretical or hypothetical exercise but has proven to be critical in many situations, with the most dramatic recent examples being the wars in Afghanistan and Iraq. Vietnam was another. The next chapter will explore the many efforts that have been made or are being undertaken to remedy the situation.

4 DEFENSE REFORM

Institutional and Political Impediments
to Effectiveness

Chapter 3 analyzed U.S. civil–military relations in terms of the three-dimensional framework that is at the heart of this book. While democratic civilian control is not the issue in the United States that it is in most of the world, and although the executive and legislature wield an impressive number of instruments to oversee the efficient use of resources, the *effectiveness* of the security sector is recognized to be problematic by virtually all policy experts. As the only remaining superpower, with commitments across the globe, the challenges concerning U.S. national security and defense are real in terms of blood and gold and have to be dealt with seriously. Not surprisingly, there have been many diverse efforts to improve the effectiveness of the U.S. defense and security sector.

This chapter will review the most important reform efforts in recent years, beginning with the Goldwater-Nichols Defense Reorganization Act of 1986. The other reform initiatives reviewed here all began after the events of September 11, 2001, which signaled the dramatic end of false tranquility in the United States and saw a renewed emphasis on the emerging threat environment. This in turn led to the so-called Global War on Terror and the invasions of Afghanistan in 2001 and Iraq in 2003. Besides the Goldwater-Nichols Act, the chapter will review the findings and recommendations (released in July and August 2004) of the National Commission on Terrorist Attacks upon the United States, commonly known as the 9/11 Commission; the 2005 Center for Strategic and International Studies (CSIS) report, "Department of Defense Reform: Beyond Goldwater-Nichols"; the CSIS "Smart Power Initiative" of 2007;

and the Project on National Security Reform (PNSR), which was initiated in 2007 and continues to the present. No reform initiative can be successful unless it is enacted into law, necessitating action by both the legislative and executive branches in the American political system. Furthermore, unless they are funded by Congress and implemented by the relevant agencies, the reform initiatives have no impact. This was the case, as seen in the previous chapter, regarding the production and publication of a national security strategy and other security documents over the past decade.[1]

The reform initiatives reviewed in this chapter validate the three conditions for effectiveness described in Chapter 3 as necessary, though not necessarily sufficient in and of themselves: a comprehensive plan or strategy; an institutional means to coordinate policy, such as an interagency process; and sufficient resources to see the plan through. All of the reform initiatives focus on institutional relationships rather than professions, for example, and include exactly what is posited here as indispensable to success. The high degree of relevance that emerged from this review of the reform initiatives was somewhat unexpected and also highly gratifying.

The CRS report, "Organizing the U.S. Government for National Security: Overview of the Interagency Reform Debates," offers a useful compilation of the relevant problems to be solved, the proposed reforms, and the key proponents of the most recent reform initiatives.[2] It lists seven topics in the current debates, all of which focus on effectiveness, and notes that every initiative calls for "a reexamination of how well the U.S. government, including both the executive branch and Congress, is organized to apply all instruments of national power to national security activities."[3] As the reform efforts highlight, there are serious problems in U.S. national security and defense, but civilian control of the armed forces isn't one of them, and there is not a single mention of the issue in this detailed CRS report. Nor is there anything in these reform initiatives but for a very brief reference in the current PNSR concerning the use of contractors. This last omission, by contrast, is a real problem.

BUILDING ON SUCCESS: THE MODEL OF GOLDWATER-NICHOLS

The CRS report notes that "in the current debates, calls for a 'Goldwater-Nichols for the Interagency' typically refer not to the content of the 1986 Act, but to aspects of the process that produced it: a comprehensive review of current legislation and approaches; bipartisan leadership of the reform effort; relatively sweeping solutions; the use of legislation to prompt closer integration."[4] Virtually all informed observers agree that Goldwater-Nichols substantially improved military effectiveness, a fact that has been proven in all of the military campaigns between its implementation and the present day. Therefore, an evaluation of my framework for analysis of defense reform must begin with this law and the process that resulted in it. This point is further reinforced by the CRS report:

> The [current] debates could follow the model of the Goldwater-Nichols process of the 1980s, which led to the Goldwater-Nichols Department of Defense Reorganization Act of 1986, October 1, 1986 (P. L. 99-433). That landmark legislation ushered in fundamental defense reorganization aimed at diminishing inter-Service rivalries and promoting greater jointness, through streamlining the chain of command, enhancing the military advisory role of the Chairman of the Joint Chiefs of Staff, and adjusting personnel policies and the budgeting process.[5]

The successes of Goldwater-Nichols are reflected elsewhere in recent government policy and recommendations. The 9/11 Commission Report refers to a Goldwater-Nichols approach to jointness.[6] In a policy directive issued in May 2006 and amended in September 2009, the director of national intelligence established policy and procedures for the permanent appointment or temporary detail of intelligence community (IC) employees to joint IC duty positions. This is intended to develop a joint culture, similar to that achieved through the Goldwater-Nichols legislation.[7] The Project on National Security Reform is under the overall guidance of one of the two key former Congressional staffers who formulated the Goldwater-Nichols legislation, James R. Locher III.[8]

    To keep the analysis consistent, I will use six criteria to describe each of the five reform initiatives as they relate to the problem of effectiveness: (1) the specific problem the reform is intended to address; (2) the proposed solution to the problem; (3) the agency that takes the lead in the reform process; (4) the strategy, which frequently involves both U.S. government and nongovernment elements; (5) immediate legislative results, if any; and (6) the long-term impact, if any. The three requirements for success—a plan, structures and processes to implement the plans, and resources—are included within these categories and, as will become apparent, are central to all five reform initiatives in question.

THE GOLDWATER-NICHOLS DEPARTMENT OF DEFENSE REORGANIZATION ACT OF 1986

As the Introduction to "Beyond Goldwater-Nichols: Defense Reform for a New Strategic Era" states:

> In the mid-1980s, a series of operational military failures in the field—the botched attempt to rescue the American hostages in Iran, the Beirut embassy bombing and the interoperability problems during the invasion of Grenada— convinced Congress that the Department of Defense was broken and that something had to be done. Despite intense resistance from DoD, over four years of Congressional hearings, investigation, and analysis finally culminated in the Goldwater-Nichols Department of Defense Reorganization Act of 1986 (Goldwater-Nichols)—a landmark of U.S. defense reform.[9]

I was fortunate to be able to discuss the Goldwater-Nichols Act with Arch Barrett, who, along with Locher, was a lead player in the formulation of the Act for the House Armed Services Committee (HASC).[10] The Goldwater-Nichols legislation, according to Barrett, was unique, a view that is supported by the evidence. None of the initiatives that followed is similar in terms of the combination of factors supporting reform. The problems Goldwater-Nichols dealt with had been widely recognized by defense experts for a very long time, said Barrett, but it took a unique combination of factors to make passage of the law possible. First, the military had experienced a series of failures, the fundamental causes of which were known to be structural, stemming from the relationships between different organizations within the defense sector or the delineation of authority and responsibilities of each one in relationship to the others. Second, because Barrett had been tasked to summarize a series of studies on defense reform initiated by Secretary of Defense Harold Brown during the Jimmy Carter administration (1977–1981), he was in a unique position to grasp the underlying structural problems in the DoD and bring them to the attention of important members in Congress. With the outbreak of the Iranian Revolution in early 1979, the secretary's initiative ended, but Barrett, then a USAF colonel, was detailed to National Defense University for two years, where he wrote a book highlighting the organizational issues that inhibited defense reform.[11] From there he retired and went directly to join the permanent staff of the House of Representatives, working with Congressman Richard C. White, chairman of the investigation subcommittee of the HASC. The orga-

nization of DoD (the Office of the Secretary of Defense, the military departments and their constituent services, the joint chiefs of staff and joint staff, the
unified and specified field commands throughout the world, and the defense
agencies) was within the purview of Congressman White's subcommittee.

Third, when Chairman of the Joint Chiefs of Staff (CJCS) General David
C. Jones testified before the HASC on February 3, 1982, regarding fundamental problems in defense organization that impeded operational effectiveness,
Barrett told me that his work the previous three years on defense organization
allowed him to grasp the significance of the general's testimony.[12] No incum-
bent member of the joint chiefs, much less a chairman, had ever acknowledged
the organizational flaws described by the department's multitudes of outside
critics. Barrett was concerned, however, that the historic moment might not
have registered with the members of Congress, whose experience with defense
organization had been limited for decades to mundane issues such as adding
or eliminating an under- or assistant secretary position, often to accommodate the request of the current secretary of defense. Congressman White soon
initiated investigations subcommittee hearings to examine the issues Jones
raised in his testimony. Barrett structured the hearings with key military and
civilian defense officials, as well as private sector national security experts,
to ensure a thorough, evenhanded examination of the issues brought to light
by Jones.

Fourth, Congressman William F. Nichols, who had succeeded White as
investigations subcommittee chairman, personally knew some of the families of the 241 men who died in the terrorist attack on the U.S. Marine barracks in Beirut, Lebanon, on October 23, 1983. Nichols's intellectual interest
in reorganization was now reinforced by heartfelt conviction. The success of
the Beirut attack crystallized for many, including Representative Nichols, the
endemic weaknesses in the command structure and training of the current
armed forces and further spurred the drive to bring fundamental change to
the DoD. Fifth, and very importantly, this potentially divisive issue of reforming U.S. defense organizations was handled in a bipartisan manner. Whereas
Congressman Nichols, who took the lead in the House of Representatives, was
a Democrat, Senator Barry Goldwater was a Republican, and a conservative
Republican at that.

Following the lead from the House, the Senate did become involved, and
Locher has summarized that series of events thoroughly in his 2002 book.[13]
It should be kept in mind that this was the era when the Ronald Reagan

administration pushed through massive budget increases for the Pentagon, and the legislative oversight process raised serious questions about whether there was a corresponding increase in effectiveness resulting from these increases in funding. Those supporting reorganization were opposed by all of the armed services, most emphatically the Navy, Secretary of Defense Caspar Weinberger, and the Reagan White House. Barrett noted that while the legislators who backed reorganization did benefit from supporting studies done by the Center for Strategic and International Studies, the Heritage Foundation, and the President's Blue Ribbon Commission on Defense (known as the Packard Commission, convened by President Ronald Reagan to study issues of defense management), these were complementary but not central to the overall political process that resulted in the success of the reorganization initiative.

While Jones, along with White and Barrett, focused on organizational issues, the opponents in the military claimed that organization didn't matter and that what they really needed were "better personnel." (While Goldwater-Nichols includes an entire title on Joint Officer Personnel Management, the 1982 hearings did not pay any attention to personnel matters. So many witnesses referred to the need for joint personnel to bridge the gaps between the services, however, that the committee decided to look at the issue. Aspin eventually adopted it as something that should be included in the legislation).

The Goldwater-Nichols legislation is particularly advantageous for the purposes of this analysis. It was passed and has been implemented over the last quarter-century, and the results can be seen and analyzed in the real world of combat and JPME. There is one very good book available on the political process that led up to the law's passage, written by a key actor in that process, and a ten-year retrospective that includes chapters by some of the main figures who helped get the act passed.[14] Others have taught on the topic and have collected substantial documentation for its analysis, including this author.[15]

The Problems Identified

The National Security Act of 1947 created the post–World War II national military establishment. As noted in Chapter 3, it prescribed a weak secretary of defense, established the joint chiefs of staff (with no chairman), and retained the powerful military departments, now joined by the U.S. Air Force; the service secretaries served both in the Cabinet and as National Security Council (NSC) members. It also created the National Security Council. In 1949 the Department of Defense was created, and the office of the secretary was strengthened in subsequent legislation in 1953 and 1958. The position of chairman of the JCS was created in 1949 as well, but initially it was without a vote in JCS deliberations. The military departments were downgraded with the creation of DoD and the service secretaries removed from the Cabinet and NSC; they were taken out of the operational chain of command in 1958. A goal of the 1958 legislation was to strengthen the unified and specified commanders, such as Pacific Command (PACOM), European Command (EUCOM), or Strategic Air Command (SAC). Between 1958 and 1982 there were several frustrated, aborted, or failed reform initiatives, all of which foundered, in the words of Locher, on "the unyielding alliance between the services and Congress."[16] In short, despite the National Security Act of 1947, and the improvements made between 1949 and 1958, the institutional framework did not fundamentally change.[17]

These organizational problems, which centered mainly on how the services link up through the chain of command, might not have been considered serious enough to warrant action but for several dramatic operational failures that included the Bay of Pigs debacle; the disastrous war in Vietnam; North Korea's seizure of the USS *Pueblo* on January 23, 1968; Cambodia's seizure of the USS *Mayaguez* in May 1975; the aborted Iranian hostage rescue mission on April 25, 1980; the aforementioned bombing of the U.S. Marine barracks in Beirut in 1983; and the U.S. invasion of Grenada in October 1983, when the inability of the Army and Marines to communicate jeopardized the invasion by the superpower United States of a small island defended by a few hundred Cubans.

Locher identifies four basic weaknesses arising from the U.S. military's dysfunctional structural arrangements, which led to these operational failures: inadequate military advice, a lack of unified operations in the field, the inability of the services to operate jointly, and dysfunctional chains of command. He also considers the legitimating of the process that would lead to the Goldwater-Nichols Act in 1986 to have begun with the testimony of JCS chairman General Jones, concerning the organization of the DoD.[18] Locher then lists the ten "Fundamental Problems" that Goldwater-Nichols sought to remedy: an imbalance between service and joint interests; inadequate military advice to the secretary of defense; the inadequate qualifications of joint-duty military personnel; an imbalance between the unified and specified command chiefs' (CINCs) authority and responsibility; confused and cumbersome operational chains of command; ineffective strategic planning; inadequate supervision and control of defense agencies and DoD field activities; confusion over the service secretaries' roles; an unnecessary duplication of functions among the military department headquarters; and finally, congressional micromanagement.[19]

Proposed Solutions to the Problem

Locher lists nine proposed solutions to those ten problems, all of which ultimately were included in the Goldwater-Nichols Act: Strengthen civilian authority (not in terms of control so much as by influencing the uniformed military to act in line with civilian goals); improve the quality and timeliness of military advice going to the executive; place clear responsibility on the CINCs for mission accomplishment; ensure that a CINC's authority is commensurate with the responsibilities; increase attention to strategy formulation and contingency planning; plan for the more efficient use of resources; improve training for joint officers and boost their management skills; enhance the effectiveness of military operations; and improve DoD management and administration.[20]

Leadership Toward a Solution

The lead for this basic reorganization came from Congress, specifically Senator Barry Goldwater and Congressmen Les Aspin and Bill Nichols, assisted by their professional staffs with Locher and Barrett in the lead.[21] Over time, those pushing for reorganization came to include, apart from members of Congress, the JCS chairman, Admiral William Crowe (privately, but not in public), the NSC staff, and the Packard Commission. As already mentioned, the chief opponents were Secretary of Defense Weinberger and the White House, the U.S. Navy led by Secretary of the Navy John Lehman, the Marine Corps, and, to a lesser but significant extent, the Army and Air Force.[22]

Strategy to Develop Political Momentum for a Solution

As Locher reports, the strategy to gain support for defense reform involved helping members of Congress become knowledgeable enough of the issues to reject Pentagon opposition and to be willing to alter the historic Congress–service alliance.[23] Influential congressional leaders holding key committee leadership positions, particularly Goldwater and Sam Nunn, also enabled Congress to push back against resistance from the Pentagon. Senator Goldwater, at that point a very senior member of the Senate and scheduled to retire, pushed the bill as his "swan song"; it was in the end a large part of his legacy. The creation of the Packard Commission in July 1985 further legitimized the reform movement. Locher's book and other sources highlight the many angles of the proponents' comprehensive strategy, which involved developing an action plan to inform and activate the news media concerning the problems with the current system and the need for reform. The CSIS study "Beyond Goldwater-Nichols" takes ample credit for their role:

> External studies and expert groups were central to creating the momentum and consensus for tackling necessary reforms. The Center for Strategic and International Studies (CSIS) played a critical role in building the analytic and political foundation for Congressional action—in particular, through its path-breaking report, *Toward a More effective Defense*. CSIS also convened a Blue Ribbon commission to help promote the importance of military reform.[24]

More accurately, the reformers in Congress used think tanks such as CSIS as forums for discussion of the issues and to influence the legislative process and also involved such noted academics as Sam Huntington on the side of reform. This was part of a very broad-based strategy to mobilize support and overcome resistance in the services, especially the U.S. Navy and the Department of Defense, to the reorganization.

The Resulting Legislation

The key provisions of the act, as mentioned earlier, are ten in number. The report's language stipulates: "The secretary has sole and ultimate power within the Department of Defense on any matter on which the secretary chooses to act."[25] The Goldwater-Nichols Act:

- designates the JCS chairman as principal military adviser to the secretary of defense and the president;
- creates the JCS vice chairman position;
- directs the JCS chairman to manage the joint staff;
- specifies that the military chain of command extends from the president to the secretary of defense to the combatant commanders (bypassing the JCS);
- prescribes and greatly expands the authority of the combatant commanders;
- requires the CJCS to prepare fiscally constrained strategy;
- requires the secretary of defense to provide contingency planning guidance;
- assigns ten new duties to CJCS on resource advice;

- establishes a joint officer personnel system; and
- consolidates military department acquisition and financial management offices under the civilian secretaries.[26]

In addition, and as indicated in the previous chapter, "The current mandate for the President to deliver to Congress a comprehensive, annual 'national security strategy report' derives from the *National Security Act of 1947*, as amended by the *Goldwater-Nichols Department of Defense Reorganization Act of 1986*."[27] The legislation also assigns to the CJCS the responsibility for developing joint doctrine, which has, in the words of "Beyond Goldwater-Nichols," "led to the creation and regular updating of a comprehensive body of joint publications."[28] All three of the requirements for effectiveness described at the beginning of the chapter are included in the resulting law: It requires a plan in the form of an annual national security strategy; it details the structures and processes for achieving effectiveness; and it stipulates, in at least two sections, the resource requirements for meeting its goals. The Goldwater-Nichols Act is the very model of how to achieve effectiveness according to my proposed framework. It was considered revolutionary at the time, and it is no wonder that there has been no successful reform initiative in the intervening twenty-five years.

Long-Term Results

All observers, including civilian policy makers and senior military officers, agree on the positive results of Goldwater-Nichols.[29] Improvements were demonstrated in virtually all of the combat operations the United States has been involved in since that time, including Panama in 1989, the first Gulf War of 1991, and the combat operations of the last decade in Iraq and Afghanistan. In the epilogue to his book, Locher summarizes the accomplishments of Goldwater-Nichols and indicates the areas still requiring work. One of the reports that has been mentioned here and will be reviewed later in the chapter, "Beyond Goldwater-Nichols: Defense Reform for a New Strategic Era," takes up some of the remaining business of reform, nearly twenty years after the law's enactment.[30] The initial section of this report, titled the "Phase 1 Report," reviews the legislation's goals and assesses how well they have been met. The main focus of the assessment is not what the author terms the "unintended consequences" of the 1986 reform but rather the post–Cold War threat environment characterized by "pervasive uncertainty." The report also highlights the continuing weakness of the interagency process, which becomes the main focus of this and later reports.[31] An important point not in the report is the following: To be promoted to flag rank, military officers must serve in a joint position, and the CJCS has the authority and obligation to review promotion lists to ensure that is happening. This was Les Aspin's idea, was included in the Goldwater-Nichols legislation, and has worked out extremely well.

THE IMPACT OF SEPTEMBER 11, 2001, ON DEFENSE REFORM: THE 9/11 COMMISSION REPORT

It is not hard to list a number of events that have taken place worldwide over the past two decades that have had a profound impact on all elements of U.S. national security and defense, including the size and composition of the armed forces themselves. Such a list starts, of course, with the collapse of the Soviet Union and the end of the Cold War. It continues with the spread of democracies to most regions in the world; the reignition of historic hostilities in the Balkans, southern Caucuses, and sub-Saharan Africa with the end of Soviet and U.S. involvement and the concomitant rise in importance of peacemaking and peacekeeping as new military roles; and the quick and successful U.S. combat operations in the Persian Gulf War, Afghanistan in late 2001, and the 2003 Iraq War. Most observers agree, however, that the Department of Defense, in response to these global shifts, did not so much reorient or restructure itself, or modify the bureaucracies responsible for its various operations, as simply cut down the size of the forces and call that reform.[32] It was only with the horrific terrorist attacks on U.S. soil on September 11, 2001, (hereinafter, 9/11) that a critical mass of experts and officials within the defense and security sector came to the mutual conclusion that America's national security and defense structures had to change, and dramatically, to deal with stateless international terrorism. The first major effort to reorganize the U.S. national security and defense structures after 9/11 emerged from the findings of the National Commission on Terrorist Attacks upon the United States, the so-called 9/11 Commission, which was created by Congress and the White House (Public Law 107-306, November 27, 2002) to find out what went wrong, and who, if anyone, was to blame for the failure to predict and prevent the attacks. The commission and its report focused on three main areas of reform, one of which, titled "Reforming the Institutions of Government," takes on the intelligence community. Because the IC is a central element in the effectiveness of national security, and a key concern for democratic civilian control of the security sector as well, it is appropriate to pay particular attention to it here.[33]

The Problem Identified

The Central Intelligence Agency was created by the National Security Act of 1947. By 2001, the U.S. intelligence community consisted of fifteen separate agencies, or major organizations within agencies, engaged in some part of the intelligence cycle. Professor Amy Zegart identified a critical weakness of the resulting bureaucracy, as she wrote in 1999:

> The Central Intelligence Agency never succeeded in centralizing intelligence. Instead of exerting discipline over the far-flung intelligence community, the CIA only added to the crowd, producing its own reports and developing its own independent collection capabilities. In addition, the agency pursued a series of illegal and quasi-legal activities that eventually triggered citizen outcries and congressional intervention.[34]

The intelligence function is admittedly difficult, particularly for a democracy. By its very nature, the gathering, processing, and dissemination of intelligence must be to some degree secret, yet democracy as a system of governance is based on public accountability that requires transparency. There is, then, a tension, or even paradox, inherent to intelligence operations under democratic scrutiny, that is experienced in even—perhaps especially—the oldest, most well-established democracies, where citizens are accustomed to asserting their constitutional rights. While there was one significant period in the 1970s when democratic civilian control over the intelligence sector was a salient issue in the United States, following alleged assassination attempts, allegations of domestic spying by the CIA, and the constitutional crisis of the Watergate scandal, during most of the post–World War II era any concern there might have been was over effectiveness rather than control. This is not the case in the vast majority of new democracies, where civilian officials struggle to assert control over the intelligence agencies and only secondarily worry about their effectiveness.[35]

In 1949, only two years after the National Security Act was passed that created the CIA, the first proposal to reorganize the IC was formulated but never successfully implemented. Over the half-century between 1949 and the 9/11 Commission Report, none of the subsequent proposals was successful, either. As a CRS Report states:

> Proposals for the reorganization of the United States Intelligence Community have repeatedly emerged from commissions and committees created by either

the executive or legislative branches. The heretofore limited authority of Directors of Central Intelligence, and the great influence of the Departments of State and Defense have inhibited the emergence of major reorganization plans from within the Intelligence Community itself.[36]

A review of this detailed CRS report makes clear that while democratic civilian control over the intelligence sector has been increased, mainly through oversight, effectiveness has not improved as long as operations continue to require coordination from the top by the director of Central Intelligence (DCI), who until 2005 simultaneously served as director of the Central Intelligence Agency.

In an internal, unclassified, study, "The U.S. Intelligence Community: Reform Studies since 1947," Michael Warner, chief historian to the office of the director of national intelligence, "examines the origins, context, and results of 14 significant studies that have surveyed and sought to improve the American intelligence system since 1947."[37] The study demonstrates that there have been some successful reforms during the intervening fifty-seven years. Warner concludes his report, however, by highlighting the main structural obstacles to reform:

> Intelligence reform is difficult because it involves two branches of government—Congress which diffuses its two houses' authority among their committees, and the Executive Branch, whose departments and agencies each respond to both political and institutional pressures. Within the Executive Branch, the Intelligence Community itself is fragmented, with the principal fault line between the DCI and his CIA on the one hand and the Secretary of Defense and his Department on the other. The studies we've examined nonetheless reveal that, despite these systemic difficulties, reform is possible when most of the key political and bureaucratic actors agree that something must change—even if they do not all agree on exactly what that change should be.[38]

The terrorist attacks of September 11, 2001, and the 9/11 Commission created by the legislative and executive branches on November 27, 2002, provided the impetus for major change.

The 567-page Commission Report does an excellent job of outlining the emergence of terrorist threats to the United States and describes the fecklessness of the government's response to the emerging threats. It points out, for example, "The road to 9/11 again illustrates how the large, unwieldy U.S. government tended to underestimate a threat that grew ever greater," putting heavy blame on the bureaucratic or organizational features of the security system.[39]

Proposed Solutions to the Problem

In view of the commission's analysis of the problems with U.S. intelligence, it is not surprising that the report's final chapter is entitled: "How to Do It? A Different Way of Organizing the Government." Four of the five subsections in that chapter are on "unity of effort," two of which deal specifically with intelligence and information sharing. The report makes seven specific recommendations for intelligence reform: (1) Create the position of director of national intelligence; (2) set up a National Counterterrorism Center; (3) create an FBI national security workforce; (4) define new missions for the CIA director; (5) create incentives for information sharing among departments, agencies, and subagencies in the IC; (6) stimulate government-wide information sharing; and (7) promote homeland airspace defense.

Who Takes the Lead in the Reform Process

In the aftermath of the horrific attack on the U.S. homeland, it was clear to everyone that something serious had to be done to prevent another. It was not surprising then, that the legislative and executive branches eventually agreed that a bipartisan commission be created to investigate events leading up to the attacks and formulate recommendations for change, despite strong opposition from President George W. Bush and the Republican leaders in Congress. As Kenneth Kitts notes in his study of the process, there were many early proposals for a commission. He documents the active resistance of the Bush administration and how this resistance was overcome, chiefly, according to Kitts, through the pressure of the victims' families, an increasing body of information on the failures of the administration's security policies, and outside criticism.[40] Whether it was the most serious attack ever on U.S. soil, or on a par with the bombing of Pearl Harbor in 1941, it was clear that someone had to document as thoroughly as possible why the attack was successful and, based on that information, map out a strategy for the future that would minimize the likelihood of another such attack.

A Strategy Involving the U.S. Government and "Outside" Elements

In view of the layers of politics involved, including but not limited to bureaucratic politics, which both exacerbated the lack of cooperation among the agencies and promoted general inertia, the fact that the recommendations were passed into law, and to some degree implemented, is an important political story in itself. Kitts states that this was the "most important commission in U.S. history."[41] There is at least one book, Philip Shenon's *The Commission: The Uncensored History of the 9/11 Investigation*, that goes into great detail on the strategy involved in developing sufficient consensus for the commission to complete its report and arrive at recommendations.[42] The political momentum carried the recommendations into law, in the Intelligence Reform and Terrorism Prevention Act of 2004, hailed by some as the most important intelligence legislation since the National Security Act of 1947.[43]

Immediate Results in Law

Several government reports assess the degree to which the recommendations have been implemented.[44] Because of the close involvement of Congress in these issues, CRS publishes quarterly reports on "Intelligence Issues for Congress," which analyze the status of reform initiatives in the intelligence community. The three dimensions of effectiveness posited above are clearly included in the legislation. With regard to a plan or strategy, a CRS report on legislative mandates notes:

> The Intelligence Reform and Terrorism Prevention Act of 2004 (December 17, 2004, P.L. 108–458) alone includes the following requirements for strategies: from the Secretary of Homeland Security, a National Strategy for Transportation Security (#4001); from the Director of the Central Intelligence Agency, a strategy for improving the conduct of analysis by the CIA, and a strategy for improving human intelligence and other capabilities (#1011); from the Director of the National Counter-Terrorism Center, a "strategy for combining terrorist travel intelligence, operations and law enforcement into a cohesive effort to intercept terrorists."[45]

The requirement to reform structures and processes is addressed with several important institutional innovations, such as the creation of the office of the director of national intelligence; the setting up of the National Counterterrorism Center; and new missions for the CIA director. To address the issue of resources, the legislation created incentives, including funds and personnel benefits, for a national security workforce, to promote information sharing among government agencies and government-wide.[46] Of particular importance is the CRS quarterly publication, "Intelligence Issues for Congress," which keeps a spotlight on key issues and possible weaknesses. The impressive output of CRS reports on a wide variety of intelligence topics and their increasing availability through such organizations as the Federation of American Scientists have helped promote a broad debate and discussion and thus further education and research, about intelligence issues.[47] Funding has increased substantially; the public release of overall figures indicates that, whereas the total appropriation authorized by Congress for intelligence in fiscal year 2006 was $43.5 billion, in fiscal year 2009 the total was $49.8 billion.[48]

Long-Term Impact, If Any

As already noted, evaluating the effectiveness and efficiency of the intelligence sector is very tricky. The Intelligence Reform and Terrorism Prevention Act of 2004 clearly meets the three criteria necessary to improve the effectiveness of the intelligence sector; if there are weaknesses, they lie in increasing the powers of the DNI.[49] A comparison of this legislation with the Goldwater-Nichols Act highlights a few key elements. Both require periodic strategies or plans to be produced by the executive branch, although the National Security Strategy was largely neglected by the George W. Bush administration. Both have resulted in extensive changes within the target organizations and in their relations to one another. They have both put in place new incentives for achieving their desired goals. One telling lapse so far with the intelligence reform legislation, however, is a lack of progress in regard to jointness, at least in intelligence education.[50] This lapse may furnish some insight into the causes of the intelligence failure regarding the attempted terrorist attack on December 25, 2009, aboard Northwest Airlines Flight 253 coming into Detroit. News reporting demonstrates that the IC failed to piece together bits of evidence, despite the creation of the office of the DNI, with its National Counterterrorism Center.[51] As averred by Dennis C. Blair, director of national intelligence, in his testimony to the Senate Homeland Security and Governmental Affairs Committee on January 20, 2010, "The counterterrorism system failed and I told the President we are determined to do better."[52] While the causes of the intelligence failure will be debated indefinitely into the future, as other plots are uncovered, there appears to be general agreement that the different components of the IC continue to "stovepipe" information. President Barack Obama therefore issued a directive to most of the executive branch on January 7, 2010, observing that "immediate actions are necessary given inherent systemic weaknesses and human errors revealed by the review of events leading up to December 25th."[53]

BEYOND GOLDWATER-NICHOLS: DEFENSE REFORM
FOR A NEW STRATEGIC ERA

In this report, which was presented in two parts, Phase 1 (March 2004) and Phase 2 (July 2005), the study team "concluded that the U.S. national security apparatus requires significant reforms to meet the challenges of a new strategic era."[54] "It also looked beyond the scope of the original Goldwater-Nichols Act to address the problems that significantly affect how DoD operates today, including the conduct of interagency and coalition operations as well as its relationship with Congress."[55] After reviewing a number of problems with DoD operations after Goldwater-Nichols and the terrorist attacks on 9/11, the report notes: "These problems all impede the full potential of the U.S. government to fulfill its national security responsibilities."[56] It stresses that, although the Goldwater-Nichols Act improved military effectiveness, DoD interagency operations still functioned poorly. This project under the auspices of CSIS was, in the authors' terms, "an enormous effort." Begun in November 2002, the study involved over 120 former civilian and military officials in five working groups that met several times during 2003 and presented their draft results for review in January 2004. The second phase began in May 2004 and was supported by seven working groups consisting of over 220 current and former civilian and military officials. The sessions to review the draft results for Phase 2 were held in February and March 2005. If one scans the list of participants, it is hard to imagine a civilian or retired military defense expert within a reasonable commute of the Washington, DC, area who was not involved at some point in this nearly three-year project. A number of the defense experts who participated in this project, including Michèle Flournoy, also have contributed to the PNSR.

The Problem Identified

The title of this project, "Beyond Goldwater-Nichols," is apt. It begins with a review of the act's original goals and actual accomplishments and concludes that the defense reforms originating from the legislation were successful for the challenges and environment of the time. What was not anticipated by its creators in 1986 was the current security environment, in which the United States must cope with "pervasive uncertainty." In addition, as the U.S. military has become more involved in what the authors term "complex contingency operations," also called "peace support operations," it has become increasingly clear that the interagency process is not robust enough: "The NSC needs to play a greater role in coordinating policy planning and overseeing policy execution during America's involvement in regional crises. The weaknesses of other U.S. federal government agencies have forced DoD to bear the main burden of nation-building."[57] The authors identify weaknesses that include, among others, outdated organizational structures, inefficiencies in resource allocations, and lack of civilian expertise in government: "These problems all impede the full potential of the U.S. government to fulfill its national security responsibilities."[58] If the problems are relatively obvious, readily identified, and generally agreed on, what stands out in these two reports are the huge scope and complexity of the proposed solutions.

Proposed Solutions to the Problem

The Phase 1 report focuses on six main areas for reform: (1) Rationalize organizational structures in DoD; (2) improve the efficiency of the resource allocation process; (3) promote joint capabilities; (4) strengthen civilian professionals in defense and national security; (5) improve interagency and coalition operations; and (6) strengthen congressional oversight.[59] The authors list twenty-three recommendations to remedy problems of ineffectiveness in these six areas.[60]

The Phase 2 report identifies eleven general areas for reform: (1) Create a more integrated and effective national security apparatus; (2) coordinate and unify efforts in interagency operations; (3) build operational capacity outside the department of defense; (4) elevate and strengthen homeland security policy; (5) determine joint capability requirements; (6) reform defense acquisition; (7) organize logistics support; (8) improve governance of defense agencies; (9) update the officer management system; (10) modernize professional military education; and (11) organize DoD for planning and operations in space and cyberspace.[61] Taken together, the two phases of the project result in sixty-one recommendations. Not surprisingly for such a comprehensive set of recommendations, all three requirements for effectiveness are included, often in several areas. One recommendation that is included in both the Phase One and Phase Two reports would lead to a new NSS and a classified National Security Planning guidance.[62] At least twenty-five recommendations concern structures and processes, and at least another twenty-three address the management of financial and human resources.

While the authors do an excellent job of evaluating the impact of the Goldwater-Nichols legislation, there is a problem with the way they describe its goals, which needs clarification because it can be misleading. Following the sixty-one recommendations is a review of various efforts at reform. The chapter begins: "One of the unique qualities of the American approach to governance is the persistent pursuit of reform. This spirit is vividly demonstrated in the quest for greater defense effectiveness."[63] It then reviews five major defense reform initiatives, including Goldwater-Nichols and the 9/11 Commission Report. While the former is, in the report's words, "a clear success of ambitious military reform,"[64] it goes on to discuss a number of areas that either have not been implemented or were unanticipated, such the emergence and virulence of global terrorism. The report claims, "The legislation's twin goals were straightforward: to strengthen civilian authority and improve military advice."[65] For those unfamiliar with the situation of civil–military relations in much of the rest of the world, this statement could be misinterpreted to mean the act needed to reassert civilian control over an autonomous military in the United States. As this book has repeatedly demonstrated, such is clearly not the case. For example, in a 1989 report to Congress on military education, Goldwater-Nichols author Arch Barrett wrote: "The primary objective of the Goldwater-Nichols Act is to strengthen the joint elements of the military, especially the Chairman of the Joint Chiefs of Staff (JCS) and the commanders in chief (CINC) of the combatant commands. The act's primary method is to change organizations and their responsibilities."[66] Nor is this observation on civilian control in the Phase 2 Report supported in the documents, interviews, or implementation.[67]

"Beyond Goldwater-Nichols" points out that the success of the Goldwater-Nichols legislation dwarfs the results of the three subsequent reform initiatives (which are not being reviewed here to avoid redundancy): the 1995 Commission on Roles and Missions, the 1997 National Defense Panel, and the Phase III Report of the U.S. Commission on National Security of the 21st Century.[68] Its analysis of the 9/11 Commission Report and the resulting legislation in 2004, however, was too close to the fact to provide many insights into those efforts' successes or failures. The authors of "Beyond Goldwater-Nichols" review the conditions that they think would allow reform, contrasting their current recommendations to those that came between the successful Goldwater-Nichols Act and this one, and assess the prospects for reform. The final sentence of the Phase 2 Report is remarkably candid, and ultimately accurate: "The BG-N study team believes this report will add to a growing body of literature and national level commentary that shows defense reform is not only necessary, but immediately possible."[69] Of course, literature and national-level commentary are one thing, and reform is another.

It has to be noted that "Beyond Goldwater-Nichols" makes no reference to private security contractors, the outsourcing of DoD functions, or anything related to contracting in any of the recommendations. This is so despite the fact that it includes eleven recommendations regarding DoD personnel reform. Ironically, personnel issues, specifically a lack of qualified personnel within DoD, constitute one of the reasons used to justify turning to PSCs.[70]

THE CSIS COMMISSION ON SMART POWER

The CSIS commission, chaired by Richard L. Armitage and Joseph S. Nye Jr., published its report in 2007.[71] The commission's report concerns, as the title of John J. Hamre's foreword reads, "Restoring America's Inspirational Leadership." It studies and recommends institutional reforms in five large areas of international relations: alliances, partnerships, and institutions; global developments; public diplomacy; economic integration; and technology and innovation. The executive summary notes, "Implementing a smart power strategy will require a strategic reassessment of how the U.S. government is organized, coordinated, and budgeted."[72] This section looks at the institutional reforms recommended by the report.

The Problem Identified

In 2006, the CSIS invited Armitage and Nye to chair a bipartisan Commission on Smart Power to formulate a guiding vision for the future of U.S. foreign policy.[73] The final report was oriented toward whomever became the next president following the national elections of 2008; that, of course, is one reason why this commission, like all the rest, was bipartisan. The first part of the report uses global public opinion surveys to document the waning influence of the United States in the world. It identifies five main causes for "America's declining influence": the country's sole superpower status; a general reaction against the effects of globalization; U.S. isolation from agreements and institutions with widespread international support; the U.S. government's response to 9/11, particularly the so-called Global War on Terror; and perceptions of U.S. incompetence. As the report states, "Taken together, these factors have produced a startling erosion of standing in the world."[74]

A Proposed Solution to the Problem

The CSIS Commission determined that the United States must mitigate its current heavy reliance on "hard power," or armed military might, with what has come to be called "soft power." The report explains,

> Soft power is the ability to attract people to our side without coercion. Legitimacy is central to soft power. If a people or nation believes American objectives to be legitimate, we are more likely to persuade them to follow our lead without using threats and bribes. Legitimacy can also reduce opposition to— and the costs of—using hard power when the situation demands.[75]

It argues that a combination of these two broad capabilities will result in "smart power":

> Smart power is neither hard nor soft—it is the skillful combination of both. Smart power means developing an integrated strategy, resource base, and tool kit to achieve American objectives drawing on both hard and soft power. It is an approach that underscores the necessity of a strong military, but also invests heavily in alliances, partnerships, and institutions at all levels to expand American influence and establish the legitimacy of American action.[76]

There are three main obstacles to implementing a true smart power strategy. First, as the result of a long trend that has accelerated in recent years, U.S. foreign policy overrelies on hard power at the expense of diplomacy and other means of influence: "The Pentagon is the best trained and best resourced arm of the federal government. As a result, it tends to fill every void, even those that civilian instruments should fill."[77] U.S. foreign policy experts are still struggling to develop soft-power instruments. Those that exist are often not quite appropriate and are not sufficiently funded, while U.S. foreign policy institutions such as the Department of State and the U.S. Agency for International Development are underfunded and underused. The report further notes: "Coordination where there is any, happens either at a relatively low level or else at the very highest levels of government—both typically in crisis settings that drive out long-range planning. Stovepiped institutional cultures inhibit joint action."[78]

Who Takes the Lead in the Reform Process

A smart power strategy can only be implemented by the highest levels of the U.S. federal government. At the beginning of the third section, "Restoring

Confidence in Government," Anthony C. Zinni, a retired Marine four-star general and CINC CENTCOM, points out, "Having a winning strategy is meaningless without the means to implement it."[79] In this key chapter, the authors examine the ten main historical impediments to better integration of hard and soft power:[80]

1. Negotiators have little room for making trade-offs at the strategic level because there is no office below the president's where programs and resources come together.
2. Programs promoting soft power lack integration and coordination.
3. The U.S. government has not invested sufficiently in civilian tools, and by default the military fills the void.
4. Civilian agencies have not been staffed or resourced for extraordinary missions, whereas the Pentagon can mobilize resources in emergencies. The military services have a "float" that other agencies lack. This means the DoD has 10 percent more officers than it has jobs at any one time and uses the extra 10 percent for training, education, and assignment to other agencies. The recruitment and training of civil service personnel for roles in crisis mitigation and disaster relief are completely inadequate.[81]
5. Diplomacy today requires new methods compared to traditional diplomacy. Again, training in the civil services has not kept up.
6. Insufficient authority resides in field organizations, due at least in part to communications technology that allows Washington to micromanage events in the field.
7. Civilian agencies lack regional operational capabilities, which the DoD has through its regional combatant commanders.
8. Short-term exigencies tend to drive out long-term planning, including at the level of the NSC.
9. Congress and the executive branch need to overcome their current adversarial gridlock and reach a new understanding on how to make progress in areas of national security.
10. Finally, many of the tools that promote change are not in the hands of government: "Vast deposits of soft power reside in the private sector, yet the U.S. government is largely oblivious to these resources and does not know how to tap them for coordinated affect."[82]

The primary focus of the CSIS Commission on Smart Power was to convince the next president (in this case the Democratic candidate, Barack H. Obama, elected in November 2008) to use his political resources to implement a strategy that combines hard and soft power to achieve "smart power." Again, its seven recommendations encompass the three requirements for effective reform postulated in this book. It must be stressed that the commission's goal, which is to reverse the decline in U.S. influence in the world through institutional reform, is broader than those of the previous reports. Its recommendations thus combine the hard power reforms of the previous three initiatives with the mechanisms of soft power they identify as crucial to the future of U.S. global leadership. Two recommendations deal with the need for a plan or strategy. The first, which is to establish a quadrennial smart power review, would complement the current Quadrennial Defense Review and National Defense Strategy with a parallel process for the civilian tools of national power. The second recommendation, to establish a new institution as a nonprofit, nongovernmental entity for international knowledge and communication, would create the means to communicate more credibly with populations abroad.

Four of the seven recommendations deal with structures and processes. These include the creation of a "smart power deputy" at the level of the National Security Advisor and the director of OMB, adding greater coordinating capacity to the executive secretariat at the level of the National Security Council, the creation of a Cabinet-level voice for global development, and strengthening civilian agency coordination on a regional basis. Finally, the report recommends that the government resource a "float" for civilian agencies, by adding 1,000 foreign service personnel so that they can take advantage of the float, currently limited only to DoD personnel, for advanced education, training, and exposure to other agencies.

Immediate Results in Law, and Long-Term Effects

The strategy, as with most of the think tank-based initiatives, is to engage opinion leaders and decision makers in the challenge of reorganizing the U.S. government. There were several hearing on Capitol Hill to discuss the findings of the commission, and some members of Congress were enthused by what they heard. But, as one interviewee put it, implementation will require a budget, and it will require a "forcing mechanism" to make the changes the commission identified as necessary.[83] Smart power is predicated on a reordering of current priorities and a readjustment of the government apparatus to position the United States to more effectively address current and likely future global challenges. The commission member emphasized that all of the reform initiatives lead in the same direction: to create a government that can address new global challenges. There are many proposals, and a great deal of rhetoric, floating around Washington on how to make U.S. power more "smart."[84] Although Secretary of State Hillary Clinton uses the term *smart power*, as do others in DoD and the Department of State, it remains to be seen whether the necessary reforms can actually be implemented.

THE PROJECT ON NATIONAL SECURITY REFORM

The Project on National Security Reform,[85] which builds on reform efforts going back to Goldwater-Nichols, is both the most recent initiative for national security reform and by far the largest in scope. It is led by James R. Locher III, the former Senate staffer who played a key role in Goldwater-Nichols; later served as assistant secretary of defense for special operations and low intensity conflict; is author of *Victory on the Potomac*, about the fight for reform; and, more recently, was chairman of the Defense Reform Commission of the Organization for Security and Cooperation in Europe in Bosnia and Herzegovina, 2002–2003.[86] The list of 300 high-level participants, research and analysis staff, and political and legal affairs staff includes retired generals and admirals, civilian defense policy makers, retired members of Congress, and academics. Funding and other support comes from a long list of organizations, as well as from Congress through the 2008 National Defense Authorization and Defense Appropriations Acts, and again in the 2009 budget.

The PNSR's ten analytic working groups conducted thirty-seven major case studies and sixty-three smaller studies, resulting in, by a rough calculation, some 1,500 pages of reports.[87] The project began in September 2006, and by late 2008 the teams had reviewed all aspects of the U.S. institutions of national security and defense decision making and implementation. While originally based in a Washington, DC, think tank, the Center for the Study of the Presidency, and later at facilities provided free of charge by a defense contractor in Arlington, Virginia, the project is clearly politically linked through the two major U.S. political parties to both the executive and legislative branches, with implementation geared for the new administration that came into office on January 20, 2009. The initial PNSR report, "Forging a New Shield," was delivered to President Bush in November 2008, and the follow-up, "Turning Ideas into Action: A Progress Report," was given to President Obama on September 30, 2009.[88] Given the sheer magnitude of PNSR, it will be possible here only to touch on some of the key themes, all of which focus on changing those institutions that impair U.S. national security.

The Problem Identified

The problem PNSR was created to find solutions for is summarized succinctly in the executive summary of the full 702-page report, "Forging a New Shield":

> We, twenty-two members of the Guiding Coalition of the Project on National Security Reform, affirm unanimously that the national security of the United States of America is fundamentally at risk. The U.S. position of world leadership, our country's prosperity and priceless freedoms, and the safety of our people are challenged not only by a profusion of new and unpredictable threats, but by the now undeniable fact that the national security system of the United States is increasingly misaligned with a rapidly changing global security environment.[89]

The PNSR begins its review with the National Security Act of 1947, highlighting the dramatic changes and major global trends in the world and the United States in the intervening sixty-plus years. It then describes five major defects of the U.S. national security system and concludes, "Taken together, the basic deficiency of the current national security system is that parochial departmental and agency interests, reinforced by Congress, paralyze interagency cooperation even as the variety, speed, and complexity of emerging security issues prevent the White House from effectively controlling the system."[90]

Proposed Solution to the Problem

"Forging a New Shield" goes into detail on seven key recommendations, presented as a single integrated proposal.[91] These, in summary, are as follows: Adopt new approaches to the national security system design that focus on national missions and outcomes, emphasizing integrated effort, collaboration, and agility; focus the executive office of the president on strategy and strategic management; while centralizing strategy *formulation*, decentralize policy *implementation* by creating Interagency Teams and Interagency Crisis Task Forces; link resources to goals through national security mission analysis and mission budgeting; align personnel incentives, personnel preparation, and organizational culture with strategic objectives; greatly improve the flow of knowledge and information; and build a better executive–legislative branch partnership. Together these ideas includes a rigorous assessment of the national security system's performance based on the three criteria of "outcomes, efficiency, and behaviors," the first two of which correspond exactly with the standards of effectiveness and efficiency proposed in this volume. They also include my three posited requirements of a plan, an interagency process, and resources. Regarding outcomes, the report warns: "As the analysis of the case studies also shows, the security system failures have become more common in recent years. The security system has failed more frequently of late because it has confronted an increasing number of problems and issues it was not designed to deal with."[92] The report's evaluation of efficiency focuses on the use of resources and raises concerns about sustainability. Notably absent from the report is the issue of civilian control.

The PNSR study results in what its authors term six "Twenty-First Century Imperatives," involving organizational design, innovation, effectiveness, and cohesion.[93] It must be noted that the PNSR report, unlike any of the earlier studies and reports reviewed for this volume, at least briefly touches on the problems arising from an increasing reliance on contractors. Under the rubric of "Human Capital. Problem 1," titled "The system is unable to generate the required human capital," the report states: "When government departments lack the right staff, they are forced to look to contractors to fill roles that government employees previously held."[94]

Who Takes the Lead in the Reform Process

In my meetings with James Locher to discuss the strategy to bring the proposals to implementation, he stressed that there are many different approaches, which he divided into "intellectual" activities, such as the production of studies and documents, and the "political." This latter approach includes having those members of the PNSR Guiding Coalition who occupy key positions in the Obama administration brief members of the legislative and executive branches, with the goal of engaging virtually all interested actors in the reform effort. Summarizing the status of those efforts when we met on February 23, 2009, Locher noted that "the stars are aligned" in some respects, especially as several PNSR alumni (General Jim Jones, Admiral Denny Blair, Jim Steinberg, and Michèle Flournoy) had been appointed to key positions in the Obama administration. The project's proponents are seeking to create a sense of urgency within the government to make progress on the implementation of its proposals, and the focus of their efforts is on the president.[95]

Immediate Results in Law

According to a CRS Report quoted at the beginning of this chapter, there are four summary characteristics of a "Goldwater-Nichols for the Interagency": a comprehensive review of current legislation and approaches; bipartisan lead-

ership of the reform effort; relatively sweeping solutions; and the use of legislation to prompt closer integration.[96] So far, the PNSR has achieved the first two
and is working to achieve the second two.

At our meeting in February 2009, Locher noted that he thought Congress
would have new authorities passed into law in relatively short order, given the
administration's stated intentions on implementing reforms. When I met with
him on June 15, he said that this would not in fact be possible. Instead, the
PNSR team was working on six priority projects to demonstrate how change
could be implemented.[97] The next time we talked, on September 16, Locher
observed, in response to my question on timing, that he knew going into the
project that it would take ten years to see real results. Some nine months into
President Obama's term, Locher was very expansive on the impediments to
reform that the project was encountering. Coming from the horse's mouth,
as it were, his assessment highlights the inertia of established institutions and
the need for some real political clout behind the effort to promote national
security reform: First of all is the monumental difficulty of getting bureau-
crats to think intellectually about change in a system that is now sixty-two
years old; second is the even higher political hurdle of promoting change in
institutions people are invested in, where their "rice bowls are filled"; third is
the sheer complexity of how to change gigantic bureaucracies with countless
moving parts; fourth, no single entity owns all of the institutions that require
change; and finally, all of the players who would have to be working together
on this project are already totally consumed with the work of today and, in
many cases, tomorrow.[98] The interim report, "Turning Ideas into Action: A
Progress Report," lists eight building blocks of reform. While seven of these
require the initiative of the executive branch and finally will necessitate congressional action, one requires specific congressional action from the start.
It is termed "Congressional Responsibilities" and reads, in part: "Instead of
structuring itself to catalyze interagency approaches, Congress reinforces outdated, department-centric practices. . . . It will take aligning congressional
structures to 21st Century challenges to change this."[99]

Long-Term Impact, If Any

At this stage, given the realities previously outlined and the very short time
since the PNSR reports were presented to the White House, there is little concrete results from PNSR initiatives, aside from lobbying from key positions
within the government and developing a larger and larger web of informed

Table 4.1. Selected national defense and security reform initiatives since 1986.

National defense or security reform initiative	Problem identified dimensions	Proposed solution dimensions for effectiveness	Takes lead	Strategy for success	Results in law	Long-term impact	Contractors included
Goldwater-Nichols, 1986	Effectiveness Efficiency	Strategy Institutions Resources	Congress	Congress and wide-ranging momentum	Yes	Yes	No
9/11 Commission	Effectiveness	Strategy Institutions Resources	9/11 Commission	Commission engaging public widely	Yes	Dubious	No
Beyond G-N	Effectiveness Efficiency	Strategy Institutions Resources	CSIS	Cajoling	No	No	No
Smart Power	Effectiveness	Strategy Institutions Resources	CSIS	Cajoling	No	No	No
Project on National Security Reform	Effectiveness Efficiency	Strategy Institutions Resources	PNSR	Executive and wide-ranging momentum	Not yet	Not yet	Minimally

and supportive actors on which to evaluate how the PNSR strategy for national security reform is progressing. As Locher put it in June 2009, "The PNSR is doing the heavy lifting in demonstrating how reform can be implemented." Progress on the PNSR agenda will be reviewed in the Conclusion.

CONCLUSION

This chapter reviewed the main efforts at reforming the national security and defense institutions, from the successful Goldwater-Nichols Act of 1986 up to the present Project for National Security Reform. They are illustrated in Table 4.1. Several points in particular stand out. First, reform is extremely difficult. The only clearly successful wide-scale reform was Goldwater-Nichols, which dealt with the institutions of security and defense and used incentives as a means to change the culture of the military. The fate of the Intelligence Reform and Terrorism Prevention Act of 2004, aside from reorganizing the IC components, was not one of success, as was demonstrated on December 25, 2009. "Beyond Goldwater-Nichols" and "Smart Power" have been generally subsumed within the PNSR. Second, the problem is not with people in general or the resistance of individuals to change but is caused by inertia, in both the executive (civilian and military) and, to a lesser degree, referring to the members of Congress in the legislative branches. All of the studies, analyses, and proposals focus on how to change the institutions and the relations between and within them. Obviously, there have to be incentives for individuals to accept and implement reform, but they are individuals operating within institutions and interacting with other institutions. This is why a New Institutionalism approach to analysis can at least sensitize us to the ways in which institutions can themselves become obstacles to change.

Third, democratic civilian control of the armed forces is not an issue in any of the reform initiatives I examined here, nor in any of the other reform initiatives I am aware of in the United States. Instead, the focus is on effectiveness, which is impeded by the institutions, and their relationships with one another. In fact, the overlap in institutions and the extremely strong separation-of-powers principle in the United States strengthen democratic civilian control by multiplying the loci for access and influence in the executive branches. Fourth, the necessary requirements that I posit for effectiveness—a plan or strategy, coordinating institutions, and resources—all figure as integral aspects of each reform initiative. Fifth, even though national security and defense are typically matters of state, in reality the direction they take is determined by the goals, strategies, and resources of different political actors. This is not to say that the American armed forces are politicized but that precisely because civilians are in such absolute control of strategy and policy, virtually all issues of government, including the reform of institutions and personnel, are worked out, or more commonly kicked down the road, in a highly politicized environment. Sixth, except for the PNSR, there is no mention of contracting out national security and defense in any of the reform initiatives. This, as will become apparent in subsequent chapters, has serious ramifications for the future of U.S. national security and all attempts at reform.

5 THE SCALE AND POLITICS OF CONTRACTING OUT PRIVATE SECURITY

This chapter's discussion moves from the military's implementation of the roles and missions assigned to it by elected officials to the private firms that make a profit by doing work in the security sector. This will expand the analytical framework that has been presented and illustrated in earlier chapters to include the private security contractors (PSCs). Table 4.1, near the end of the last chapter, shows that, among the reform initiatives discussed in that chapter, only the Project on National Security Reform (PNSR) made a very brief mention of private contractors. None of the others went even that far (though to be fair, security contracting was not nearly as widespread in 1986, at the time of the Goldwater-Nichols legislation, as it was even ten years later). When I asked James R. Locher III, the director of PNSR, about this in our interview on February 23, 2009, he responded frankly that, while his staff had "flirted" with the issue of the contractors, the project had more than enough areas of interest to tackle in the official government sector without getting into contracting.[1]

I had met earlier with Professor Christopher Lamb, director of research for PNSR, at which time he told me that, in addition to the already daunting scope of the project, he believed that such an important and complicated topic would exceed the capacity of the Human Capital working group.[2] That comment confirmed my own observation that the extant scholarly work on the PSCs lacks a readily adaptable and convincing framework for analysis. PSCs already make up a significant proportion of the total defense and security force, are involved in operations alongside active and reserve forces, and, most importantly, have assumed a number of the missions that previously were the exclusive responsibility of uniformed military personnel.[3]

MUDDYING THE WATERS: POLEMICS, DATA, AND METHODOLOGY

Two issues need clarification before this chapter turns to the scale and politics of contracting out. First is the polemic that has tended to surround this issue, and second are the difficulties of gathering reliable data and finding a way to analyze what is available. Contracting out national security and defense is becoming an increasingly tendentious issue, one that is rapidly spawning a great quantity of books and articles, both academic and popular, from radically different perspectives. Some of the more lurid titles include *Licensed to Kill: Hired Guns in the War on Terror*; *Big Boy Rules: America's Mercenaries Fighting in Iraq*; *Blackwater: The Rise of the World's Most Powerful Mercenary Army*; and *From Mercenaries to Market: The Rise and Regulation of Private Military Companies*.[4] This tendency to sensationalist points of view derives, I believe, largely from the perception that the state rightfully has a monopoly on the use of force. It is worth reviewing the most relevant concepts that underlie that perception, to better understand the very extreme positions we can find in writings and discussions on the use of PSCs.

The other, larger obstacle to studying and making sense of the phenomenon of contracting out security is the difficulty of getting good data and then organizing it in a way that facilitates meaningful analysis. Reliable information is hard to come by, for several reasons, mostly having to do with the fact that private security firms are, well, private. Government transparency rules do not apply to them, and their extraordinarily rapid expansion in the past decade has outstripped normal mechanisms of oversight. Furthermore, because these firms are free to take on whatever missions promise the most profit, it can be hard to find a solid basis from which to make comparisons or draw general conclusions about them. The three-part framework of control, efficiency, and effectiveness, however, offers a way to do just that, by focusing on outcomes rather than actions. This will be the topic of the following chapter.

The Problem with Polemics

The first basic concept to grasp for this discussion is that of the sovereign state, which in Western history originates with the Peace of Westphalia of 1648. Max Weber probably best posited that a state requires a monopoly on the use of force: "The claim of the modern state to monopolize the use of force is as essential to it as its character of compulsory jurisdiction and of continuous operation."[5] This notion of the centrality of coercive power, a monopoly on the use of force that is normally exercised by the military in the modern state, is a central theme of leading contemporary political sociologists such as Theda Skocpol.[6] Integral to this since the first professionalization of armed forces in Prussia in the nineteenth century, a trend that spread globally during the twentieth century, was the general assumption that a state's monopoly of force is exercised through professional militaries; later, this came to include professional, state-controlled intelligence and police organizations.[7] In this conceptualization, in which the state is assumed to hold a monopoly on the use of violence, exercised through a professional military, the privatization of armed force is an anomaly, something that should not happen and, if it does, must be explained.[8]

The great political theorist Niccolo Machiavelli, writing in 1513, had this to say about mercenaries: "Mercenaries and auxiliaries are useless and dangerous. Any man who founds his state on mercenaries can never be safe or secure, because they are disunited, ambitious, undisciplined, and untrustworthy—bold fellows among their friends but cowardly in the face of the enemy; they have no fear of God, nor loyalty to men."[9] The perception that there is something abnormal, illegal, shady, and just not right about the privatization of security and defense continues to influence many authors 500 years later.[10]

Reinforcing these concepts about the dangers of privatizing security are two perceptions that came directly from the occupation of Iraq following the 2003 U.S. invasion. The first is that private guards engage in torture and murder, which arose from the torture of prisoners at Abu Ghraib prison, in which contractors from CACI International Inc. and Titan Corporation were involved, and the infamous 2007 case in which Blackwater USA personnel are accused of killing seventeen innocent Iraqi civilians in Nisoor Square, Baghdad. For many authors—and probably many Americans—these have become the defining characteristics of PSCs.[11] The second assumption is more tempered, but it assumes that even if the contracting firms are effective in fulfilling the terms of their specific contracts, such as Blackwater personnel protecting their Department of State "principals" in Nisoor Square, they may set back the overall war effort and America's prestige in the world by employing mercenaries who appear to be out of control.[12] With these violent images coloring our perceptions of who private security contractors are, contracting out must appear anomalous or worse. It just should not happen.

In complete contrast to this popular image, the contractors themselves and those in government who employ the contractors and their lobbyists and strategic communicators point out that contracting out is legal, based on U.S. law and government policy. The contractors are acting in accordance with what they have been contracted to do. Given these competing perspectives, the rhetoric on both sides is bound to become polemical. The legal basis for contracting, the Federal Acquisition Regulation (FAR), has no prohibition against a firm making a profit.[13] In fact, the whole premise for replacing government employees with private contractors rests on the assumption that competition for profit in an open marketplace guarantees the best-quality product or service for the least cost. An increasing number of federal policy documents, such as the Quadrennial Defense Review, include contractors as an integral element in U.S. national security and defense policy.[14] This is such an important topic, one that I developed an awareness of and appreciation for in meetings with contractors, lawyers, lobbyists, and Pentagon officials in the course of my research, that it deserves serious discussion before going any further.[15]

Contracting out national security and defense functions became especially relevant in the United States with the unrelenting drive to "privatize" government services during the William J. Clinton administration, and even more so during the George W. Bush administration.[16] Contracting out had been a major theme during the Ronald Reagan administration as well, but not under President George H. W. Bush, as his Office of Management and Budget (OMB) director, Dick Darman, was not a big fan of the practice. During the Clinton administration it was used mainly in the Department of Defense and was pushed by Undersecretary for Acquisitions Jacques Gansler. This trend in the United States is in contrast to other countries, particularly in Europe, where the public and private sectors remain far more distinct. Several important studies and books by talented scholars do a good job of analyzing the trend; especially noteworthy are those by Paul C. Light and John D. Donahue.[17] A 2008 Congressional Research Service (CRS) report gives a sense of what is involved, and the extensive legal basis, for government privatization:

> Sometimes called contracting out, "outsourcing" refers to an agency engaging a private firm to perform an agency function or provide a service. . . . Federal outsourcing policy is governed by the FAR and the Federal Activities Inventory Reform (FAIR) Act of 1998 (P.L. 105-270). FAIR requires agencies to produce inventories of "commercial activities"—those that are not "inherently

governmental" and able to be acquired from the private sector—that may be put up for competitive sourcing. OMB's Circular A-76 provides agencies with specific directions for undertaking competitive sourcing.[18]

OMB Circular A-76, which provides the legal basis for outsourcing, has also been reviewed in other CRS reports.[19] There is an extensive literature on this topic, which conveys a sense of the extremely proprivatization environment of the U.S. government. I will never forget the direction I received from then superintendent of the Naval Postgraduate School in 2003, RADM David Ellison, when I wanted to hire government employees for an expanding CCMR; he said I could not and had to contract the positions out. In a certain sense, there is a "dialogue of the deaf" on this issue. Social scientists, some journalists, and sectors of the general public see contracting out functions in national security and defense as anomalous, even somehow shady, whereas those within government have come to view it as standard operating procedure.

The Obstacles Posed by Data and Methodology

There are several challenges regarding the gathering of data about and methodologies for studying PSCs, but a wealth of government documents has become available since the Special Inspector General for Iraq Reconstruction (SIGIR) was founded in late 2003 and the Democratic Party took control of Congress after the November 2006 elections. Legislators have mandated the conduct and release of a considerable stream of audits and studies by SIGIR, the Government Accountability Office (GAO), the Congressional Budget Office (CBO), and CRS. This study will take Iraq as its focus and draw most of its data from official sources and interviews because these changes in the availability of data have made analysis of the invasion and occupation of Iraq uniquely worthwhile. Some of the basic difficulties regarding data on contracting out in national security and defense, which I will describe in detail in the following pages, are highlighted by Peter Singer and Christopher Kinsey.[20] The issues they raise can help explain the limitations in earlier publications.

First, as *private* providers, security contractors are exempt from the transparency required of government agencies, even if the vast majority of the contractors' money comes from these agencies. Their information and documents are considered proprietary and, unlike government agencies and the U.S. military, the Freedom of Information Act does not apply to them.[21]

Second, they are profit-making businesses that, to succeed, must be entrepreneurial. This means that the contractors expand and contract in response to supply and demand, move in and out of different areas of activity where and when they see opportunity, and are sold and acquired depending on market forces.[22] There are hundreds, maybe thousands, of PSCs based both in the United States and abroad, and there is no responsible agency or centralized database for keeping track of them.

Third, each contractor offers different product lines or services, which are diverse and extremely dynamic. A single contractor may well have programs in the United States, Kosovo, Liberia, and Colombia, for example, making it impossible to be sure that any sample of programs is representative of a larger set or to come to general conclusions about the whole.

Fourth, as I will document in the following discussion, the wars in Afghanistan and Iraq have triggered an explosion of contracting, measured both in amounts of money and numbers of personnel. Any phenomenon that is so dynamic is extremely difficult to track, even if there were adequate legal bases and qualified personnel to track them. For all of these reasons, even though the PSCs are engaged in many of the same missions as the U.S. military, there is little visibility into their operations, whether for oversight or monitoring purposes, and even less for scholarly analysis. As the next chapter will show, this deficit is a frequent theme in SIGIR reports and audits.

Fifth, private security contractors tend to be highly secretive, for a number of reasons. These firms deal with security in frequently violent situations in expeditionary or contingency environments, which demands a certain level of operational secrecy. Most personnel are former police or military, for whom secrecy is part of their standard mode of operation. These firms operate in a wide-open marketplace, with ever-increasing numbers of competitors and virtually no regulation, so secrecy is seen as a necessary aspect of protecting their market share. Finally, it is very difficult to get access to PSC staff for interviews if management doesn't want them to talk. They of course are under no obligation to talk with researchers or anyone else, and their employers frequently put real disincentives in place to prevent them from doing so.

Despite these obvious difficulties with reliable data and analysis, there are an increasing number of credible sources to draw on in the case of Iraq. Congress mandated the creation of SIGIR in 2003 to study and issue quarterly reports on the war and occupation, which are readily available online.[23] The GAO has been tasked to conduct a number of efficiency studies, as well, and is investigating the shortcomings in DoD's management and training of contractor support to deployed forces since 1997. The CRS and CBO have also been doing related studies.[24]

It became clear in the course of my interviews in Washington, DC, in early January 2009, that the contract itself—the nexus between the contracting firm and the funding agency, such as DoD, DoS, or USAID—is key to understanding their relationships. With this insight, my research benefited tremendously from my access to the students and faculty of the Contract Management curriculum at the Naval Postgraduate School. The instructors are all former procurement specialists with long experience in contracting, who regularly publish the results of their own research. All of the students have done contracting work for the government, many for operations in Afghanistan and Iraq. Not only do several of their theses contribute to this study, but the students themselves proved to be invaluable sources of information over the course of three meetings I had with them. A group of students and faculty also conducted surveys of the PSCs and developed databases from which it became possible to make some generalizations, thereby countering to some degree the obstacles already noted. This book thus benefits from better and more reliable data than previous studies have had. Personal interviews with contractors, their lawyers, lobbyists, the regulators, investigators, and other primary actors helped both guide the research and fill in gaps in the empirical data. The three-part framework has proven very useful in conceptualizing and organizing this data.

The nature of the contract, as already noted, is central to the contracting process.[25] The Gansler Commission (named for its chairman, former undersecretary Jacques Gansler), which studied U.S. Army arms acquisition and program management practices in Kuwait, Iraq, and Afghanistan, for example, has forcefully made this point:

> Contracting is the nexus between our warfighters' requirements and the contractors that fulfill those requirements—whether for food service, interpreters, communications operations, equipment repair, new or modified equipment, or other supplies and services indispensable to warfighting operations. In support of critical military operations contractor personnel must provide timely services and equipment to the warfighter.[26]

Although most government documents and expert testimony typically are neither conceptual nor analytical and can be very tedious to wade through, for the committed researcher they contain a wealth of data for the most part yet to be tapped.

THE SCALE OF CONTRACTING IN NATIONAL SECURITY AND DEFENSE

The growth of PSCs has come a very long way since Robert Mandel wrote, less than a decade ago, "In the United States alone, there are at least twenty legitimate private military companies, with the largest grossing $25 million a year in overseas business."[27] While there are many different sources for the data on the scope of contracting in Iraq, one of the most useful is an August 2008 CBO report, "Contractors' Support of U.S. Operations in Iraq," which "examines the use of contractors in the Iraq theater from 2003 through 2007."[28] Table 5.1 provides comparative data on the use of contractors in different U.S. military operations. Following are some key points:

- "From 2003 through 2007, U.S. agencies awarded $85 billion in contracts for work to be principally performed in the Iraq theater, accounting for almost 20 percent of funding for operations in Iraq."
- "The Department of Defense (DoD) awarded contracts totaling $76 billion, of which the Army (including the Joint Contracting Command—Iraq/Afghanistan) obligated 75 percent. The U.S. Agency for International Development and the Department of State obligated roughly $5 billion and $4 billion, respectively, over the same period."
- "Although personnel counts are rough approximations, CBO estimates that as of early 2008 at least 190,000 contractor personnel, including subcontractors, were working on U.S.-funded contracts in the Iraq theater."
- "The United States has used contractors during previous military operations, although not to the current extent. According to rough historical data, the ratio of about one contactor employee for every member of the U.S. armed forces in the Iraq theater is at least 2.5 times higher than that ratio during any other major U.S. conflict, although it is roughly comparable with the ratio during operations in the Balkans in the 1990s."[29]

The CBO report discusses the different product lines or services contractors are providing, in a table that is vague and unclear because of incomplete data, which is a common problem in attempting to analyze contractors. As

Table 5.1. Presence of contractor personnel during U.S. military operations.

Conflict	Estimated personnel (thousands)		Estimated ratio of contractor to military personnel[a]
	Contractor[a]	Military	
Revolutionary War	2	9	1 to 6
War of 1812	n.a.	38	n.a.
Mexican-American War	6	33	1 to 6
Civil War	200	1,000	1 to 5
Spanish-American War	n.a.	35	n.a.
World War I	85	2,000	1 to 24
World War II	734	5,400	1 to 7
Korea	156	393	1 to 2.5
Vietnam	70	359	1 to 5
Gulf War	9[b]	500	1 to 55[b]
Balkans	20	20	1 to 1
Iraq Theater as of Early 2008[c]	190	200	1 to 1

SOURCE: Congressional Budget Office based on data from William W. Epley, "Civilian Support of Field Armies," *Army Logistician,* vol. 22 (November/December 1990), pp. 30–35; Steven J. Zamparelli, "Contractors on the Battlefield: What Have We Signed Up For?" *Air Force Journal of Logistics,* vol. 23, no. 3 (Fall 1999), pp. 10–19; Department of Defense, *Report on DoD Program for Planning, Managing, and Accounting for Contractor Services and Contractor Personnel During Contingency Operations* (October 2007), p. 12. Data in the public domain.

NOTE: n.a. = not available.

a. For some conflicts, the estimated number of contractor personnel includes civilians employed by the U.S. government. However, because most civilians present during military operations are contractor personnel, the inclusion of government civilians should not significantly affect the calculated ratio of contractor personnel to military personnel.

b. The government of Saudi Arabia provided significant amounts of products and services during Operations Desert Shield and Desert Storm. Personnel associated with those provisions are not included in the data or the ratio.

c. For this study, the Congressional Budget Office considers the following countries to be part of the Iraq theater: Iraq, Bahrain, Jordan, Kuwait, Oman, Qatar, Saudi Arabia, Turkey, and the United Arab Emirates.

one SIGIR report explains: "DoD, DoS, and USAID have not been required to systematically identify financial data for private security contractors (PSCs) providing physical security services such as guarding sites, escorting individuals and equipment convoys, and providing security advice and planning."[30] The CBO report makes clear that, in the current conflict, "Contractors also perform some functions, such as security, that traditionally have been reserved for the military."[31] This is a key finding: Contractors are now filling missions that were traditionally the purview of the state. The report continues, "Total spending by the U.S. government and other contractors for security provided by contractors in Iraq from 2003 through 2007 was between $6 billion and $10 billion. As of early 2008, approximately 25,000 to 30,000 employees of private security contractors were operating in Iraq."[32] To be clear, this sum is for *security* alone, whereas the $85 billion total mentioned in the report is for contracting in general.

The most complete and updated data regarding the PSCs comes from SIGIR, which is working at the direction of Congress to compile and analyze them specifically. The mandate regarding SIGIR's comprehensive and focused study of the PSCs is as follows:

> In accordance with Section 842 of the National Defense Authorization Act (NDAA) for Fiscal Year 2008 (P.L. 110-181) and through discussions with key congressional staff, the Special Inspector General for Iraq Reconstruction (SIGIR) in consultation with other agencies developed and is implementing a "comprehensive plan for a series of audits of contracts, subcontracts, and task and delivery orders . . ." relating to the performance of security and reconstruction functions in Iraq. Specifically, this plan identifies and describes a series of contracts and activities relating to companies that provide physical security services to protect the personnel, facilities, and property of the U.S. government and contractors, subcontractors, and other parties supporting the U.S. mission and military in Iraq since April 2003. These companies are commonly known as *private security contractors* (PSCs).[33]

As of October 16, 2008, SIGIR had identified seventy-seven individual PSC companies that have provided security services to U.S. agencies working in Iraq since 2003. In the May 2009 update of the report, SIGIR identified another sixteen, bringing the total to ninety-three companies that have provided physical security services in Iraq. The report estimates that since the war's inception in 2003, DoD, DoS, and USAID have spent $5.9 billion on contracts and subcontracts for PSCs. In interviews at SIGIR in February and June, 2009, officials emphasized that the PSCs are extremely important in the overall reconstruction effort and could become even more important as U.S. forces withdraw, first from the major cities and finally from the country by the end of 2011.[34] Drawing from the previously cited CBO report, they noted that actual expenditures are probably double the $5.9 billion that they have so far traced in their ongoing audits; in some service contracts, security is up to half of the total costs.

The October 2009 SIGIR report to Congress estimated that, as of mid-2009, there were 25,500 private security personnel under contact in Iraq.[35]

SIGIR, however, does not claim to have developed a precise definition of just what a PSC is. Several federal agencies including SIGIR define a PSC in terms of the following four functions:

- *Static security:* protect fixed or static sites, such as housing areas, reconstruction work sites, or government buildings;
- *Convoy security:* protect convoys traveling in Iraq;
- *Security escorts:* protect individuals traveling in unsecured areas in Iraq; and
- *Personal security details:* provide protective security to high-ranking individuals.[36]

It must be noted that these four functions, which fit within the roles and missions related to fighting wars, internal wars, and peace support operations, require that the contractors be armed. This means they can either respond to hostilities, or, if they perceive an imminent threat, they can preempt it by initiating the use of force. Based on their empirical research, Nicholas Dew and Bryan Hudgens note the tension between the concept of guns for hire and the free market:

> Overall, we think this data will alarm some observers and satisfy others. Some people will be alarmed to find out that there are around 200 firms offering military competencies of various kinds for sale in the marketplace. From this perspective, it is rather worrisome that there is an industry that specializes in fielding various kinds of (private) mini-armies to the highest bidder. Others will find this fact reassuring rather than worrisome—for them, a significant number of firms means competition which means efficiency.[37]

The missions taken on by PSCs are largely those that military service members themselves previously provided. And, while these particular missions may not be associated with what are generally referred to as "trigger pullers," they were previously carried out by personnel who were part of the regulated, civilian-controlled military structure described in Chapter 3. It is therefore not surprising that the U.S. Congress and those who are responsible for implementing congressional guidance in terms of research and policy are now paying a great deal of attention to the PSCs. This focus is captured in the title of SEC. 862 of the National Defense Authorization Act (NDAA) for Fiscal Year 2008, Public Law 110-181 (December 5, 2007): Contractors Performing Private Security Functions in Areas of Combat Operations.[38] SIGIR published a "Comprehensive Plan for Audits of Private Security Contractors to Meet the Requirements of Section 842 of Public Law 110-181," updated on May 8, 2009, which provides detailed information on the PSCs and the audits and other studies being conducted on them.[39] In addition, the main focus in the office of the secretary of defense, assistant deputy undersecretary (logistics & material readiness/program support) is on implementing the guidance of Section 862. In short, the greatest amount of attention regarding contractors is on the PSCs, and in my view this is precisely because their missions most closely approximate those traditionally conducted by the uniformed military.

MOTIVATIONS FOR CONTRACTING OUT SECURITY AND DEFENSE MISSIONS TO PSCS

A major weakness of earlier studies of the PSCs arises from the difficulty of identifying the universe of contractors and understanding how it is configured. For this reason, before elaborating on the four specific reasons that contracting out security has become the standard way of doing business in Iraq, it will be useful to look at some analyses of the hard data on the rise of private defense and security providers for a clear picture of the industry's development since 1970.

The Naval Postgraduate School Studies

The conceptualization of private security contractors presented in the following paragraphs draws from research by faculty and students in the Graduate School of Business and Public Policy at the Naval Postgraduate School, who gathered extensive industry information for a database that would permit them to define and draw conclusions about the key characteristics of the PSCs. Led by Associate Professor Nicholas Dew, several teams of graduate students contributed to the development of a list of 550 firms that have been named by one source or another as active in this sector at some time since 1970.[40] Given the dynamism of the sector and the fact that these firms all engage in more than one activity, the NPS teams focused on the specific capabilities offered by the firms to classify them.[41] They eventually compiled approximately 2,500 individual capabilities in their data set. This form of analysis, based on empirical data collected from the 550 firms in the study, demonstrates a great deal more heterogeneity than other studies or the basic four security functions for facilities and people considered by federal agencies. As the NPS study notes, "This data points clearly to the intermingling of service provisions up and down the

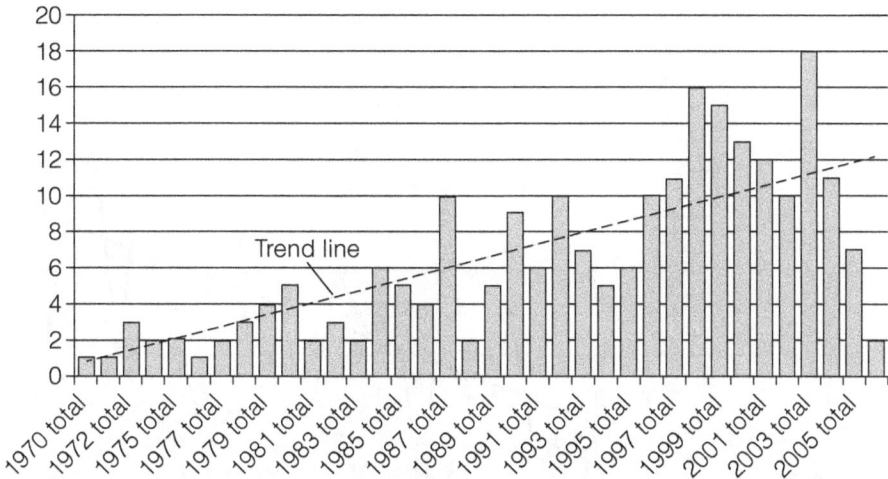

Figure 5.1. Founding of PSCs by year, 1970–2006.

spear that Avant and Singer (and others) have remarked on as a characteristic of the sector."[42] Based on this data set, they determined that the following percentages of PSC firms provide the following services: 25 percent protective services, 35 percent as training and advisory support, and 40 percent as support services of various kinds; all of these are functions that militaries have traditionally been engaged in.[43] Figures 5.1 through 5.4 come from this study.

As Figure 5.1 shows, private security contracting is a young, post–Cold War industry.[44] The NPS study traced data on 550 firms that appear to have been active in the PSC sector from 1970 through 2006. Of these, they were able to establish the founding dates of approximately 230 firms, which yielded data on industry growth. The *x*-axis is years. The *y*-axis is the total number of firms founded in each year of the sample of 230 for which data were available.

Figure 5.2 shows that the U.S. market has grown far more quickly than have markets in other parts of the world, while Figure 5.3, for a shorter period, makes clear that the privatization of national security is a post–Cold War phenomenon.[45] Nicholas Dew and Bryan Hudgens observe that the surge in PSCs is a consistent feature of the post–Cold War era, driven mainly by new U.S. firms entering the industry, rather than a post-9/11 phenomenon as is commonly assumed. Figure 5.1 shows, however, that there was indeed a tremendous spike in the numbers of PSCs at the start of the Iraq war, and Figure 5.3

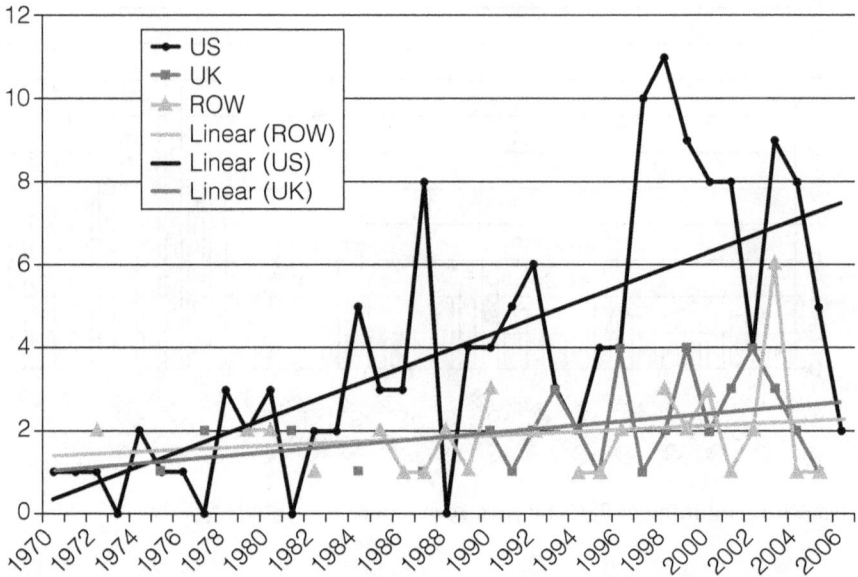

Figure 5.2. Founding of PSCs by region.

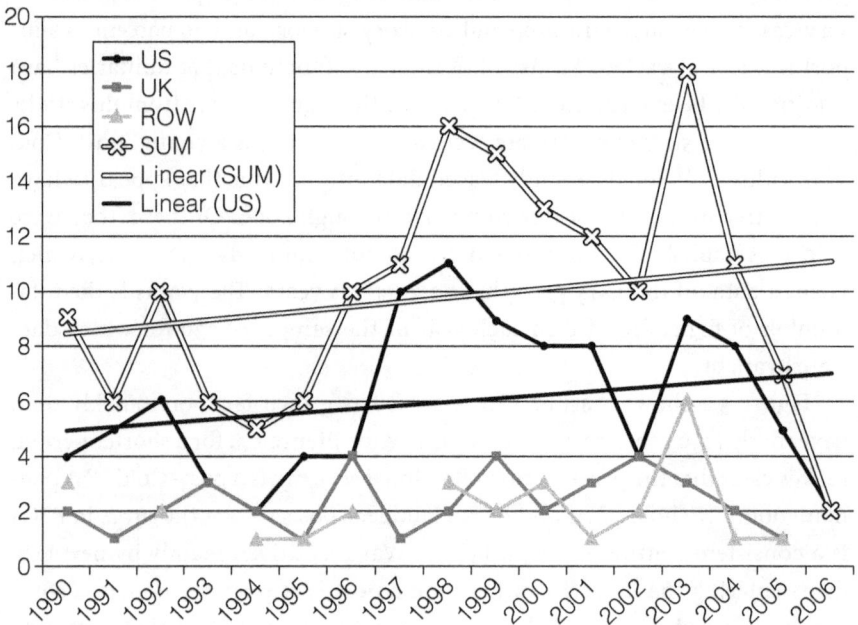

Figure 5.3. PSCs founded, 1990–2006.

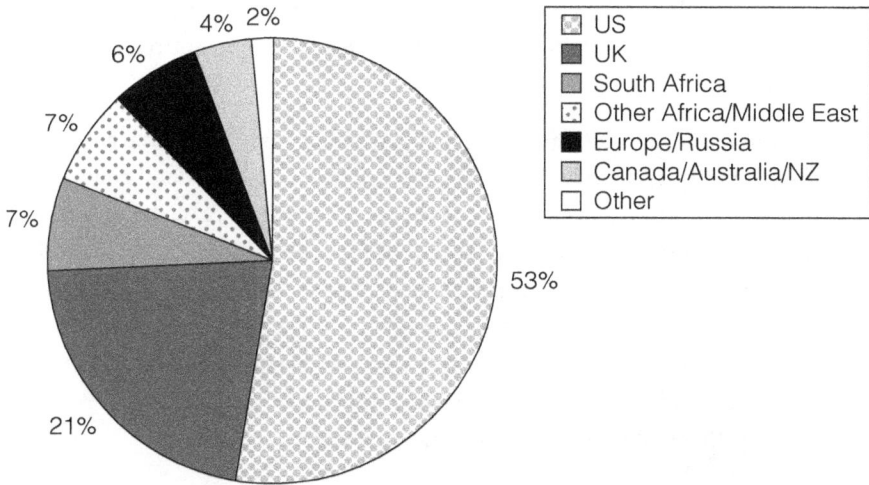

Legend:
- US
- UK
- South Africa
- Other Africa/Middle East
- Europe/Russia
- Canada/Australia/NZ
- Other

Figure labels: 4% 2% 6% 7% 7% 21% 53%

Figure 5.4. Geographical distribution of PSCs.

demonstrates that this is due largely to U.S firms. The researchers found data for over 500 firms, 90 percent of their total population of 550.

As is clear in Figure 5.4, more than 50 percent of the private security contracting industry resides in the United States, while just over 20 percent is in the United Kingdom, by far the nearest competitor. These geographic data are based on over 500 firms, 90 percent of the total population of 550. The tremendous growth in the number of U.S. firms entering the industry after the end of the Cold War has probably changed the international composition of the security contracting sector, making it less evenly cosmopolitan than it was when earlier authors, in the "soldiers of fortune" mode, wrote about it.

In sum, based on the findings of the NPS study, private security contracting is overwhelmingly a U.S.-centric and post–Cold War phenomenon. And it is extremely dynamic. It is no wonder that researchers find it difficult to specify the universe they are attempting to study.

The Drivers of the Contracting Phenomenon

It is important to emphasize, in parallel with the research and findings of the NPS study, that there is a diverse set of "demand drivers" beyond the two or three often listed in studies of the PSCs.[46] Some of these are particularly pertinent to this discussion.

First, the best source to establish a baseline description of the general context for contacting out is the testimony of David M. Walker, U.S. comptroller general, to the House Subcommittee on Readiness in March 2008. Walker offers a list of the factors that have led federal agencies to outsource more and more services:

> . . . limitations on the number of authorized full-time equivalent positions; unavailability of certain capabilities and expertise among federal employees; desire for operational flexibility; and the need for "surge" capacity. According to DOD and armed service officials, several factors have contributed to the department's increased use of contractors for support services: (1) the increased requirements associated with the Global War on Terrorism and other contingencies; (2) policy to rely on the private sector for needed commercial services that are not inherently governmental in nature; and (3) DOD initiatives, such as competitive sourcing and utility privatization programs.[47]

All of these are ongoing and long-term motivations. The issue of competitive sourcing, which sets the context, was already discussed, while inherently governmental functions will be dealt with later in this chapter and in the following chapter.

Second, as Arch Barrett pointed out, "With the all-volunteer force, private security contractors are necessary."[48] At the end of the Cold War, the U.S. Army went from 732,000 active personnel in 1990 to 409,000 in 1997; for the three services, including the Marines, the numbers went from 2,043,705 in 1990 to 1,438,562 in 1997. As of August 2009, with two wars going on, the size of the U.S. Army stood at 552,425.[49] A number of contractor proponents highlighted the personnel shortage to explain the growth of the PSCs.

Third, and specifically with regard to the growth in PSCs, the military cannot provide security protection to personnel who are not members of DoD: "The military provides security to contractors and government civilians only if they deploy with the combat force or directly support the military's mission. . . . As a result, the use of contactors to provide security has increased—a well-publicized and controversial aspect of contractor support in Iraq."[50] A former State Department official explained to me that the use of PSCs happened quickly, pragmatically, and without a plan. The State Department, for example, had asked the Department of Defense for protection for DoS personnel in Afghanistan and for training for the president's security detail. After a time, the DoD refused to do this in Afghanistan, arguing that they didn't have sufficient resources. The DoS, USAID, and others thus had no option but to contract out to meet their security needs in countries whose entire territory was a conflict zone. Ignoring the need for reliable protection was not an option. The Department of State, however, has neither an acquisition corps, which the military has long had, nor a tradition of providing oversight or control over these kinds of private entities.[51] Its Bureau of Diplomatic Security is not set up to handle ongoing operations in war zones. Such problems were equally true for USAID, as well as the many NGOs and private firms working in-country.

Fourth, Secretary of Defense Donald Rumsfeld (2001–2006) wanted to demonstrate that the Iraq invasion and pacification could be accomplished with a lean fighting force and that technology would be a sufficient force multiplier. A success in Iraq would justify his policies that promoted defense "transformation" over a traditional build-up of forces, policies that were encouraged by the vice president in particular. As Richard N. Haass points out in his book, the invasion of Iraq in 2003 was a "war of choice" rather than of necessity as its proponents claimed.[52] Whereas the United States deployed 500,000 troops in the 1991 war against Iraq, in line with the Powell Doctrine premise of using overwhelming force to achieve a clear goal, the 2003 invasion kept troop levels to about 150,000. General Eric Shinseki, Army chief of staff, expressed his disagreement with this policy while being questioned before Congress in 2003. Shortly thereafter, Secretary of Defense Rumsfeld announced Shinseki's replacement, about eighteen months before his scheduled retirement. Rumsfeld ignored military advice on the resources needed to win the war, and other military leaders did not push back.[53] Security contractors will emphasize the very real security vacuum that they have been employed to fill, but the vacuum, at least since the invasion of Iraq, appears to be a result of deliberate policy rather than exigency.

As the NPS data bear out, there are several dimensions to the rapid growth in federal contracting in general and security in particular. As Secretary Rumsfeld's successor, Robert M. Gates, would later state, the numbers and the use of contractors in Iraq, whose numbers "grew willy-nilly after 2003," required study.[54] Now that PSCs have expanded so deeply into areas that previously were the sole responsibility of the uniformed military, it would take a major political effort to redefine this territory; it is here that the concept of "inherently governmental functions" comes to the fore.

The fundamental exception to the policy and process of contracting out was supposed to be those activities deemed inherently governmental functions.[55]

These are defined in a 2003 CRS report, which includes an extensive section on them:

> The primary exception to the policy of contacting-out pertains to an activity which is "inherently governmental." Past definitions have been quite general in nature and were accompanied by numerous examples. The new A-76 [2003] takes a more specific approach in definition, but leaves out the list of examples. The general approach to inherently governmental activities is, also, significantly altered under the revision. The level of discretion required to make a function inherently governmental has been significantly raised. Under the modified circular only activities requiring "*substantial* official discretion in the application of governmental authority and/or in making decisions for the government" would be considered inherently governmental.[56]

Walker discusses A-76 and the Federal Activities Inventory Reform (FAIR) Act as well:

> The Circular reinforces that government personnel shall perform inherently governmental activities. This process does not apply to private sector performance of a new requirement, expanded activity, or continued performance of a commercial activity. As such, this process effectively applies to a small percentage of a commercial activity. Most of the growth in service contracting has occurred outside of the A-76 process. The Federal Activities Inventory Reform (FAIR) Act of 1998 further requires agencies annually to determine and list which government-provided agency activities are not inherently governmental functions. . . . The FAR and OMB also require agencies to provide greater scrutiny and management oversight when contracting for services that closely support the performance of inherently governmental functions. . . . the FAIR Act requires agencies annually to identify government-performed agency activities that are not inherently governmental functions.[57]

Walker goes on to raise warnings and references regarding control over what constitute inherently governmental functions. After illustrating with several examples, Walker states that "in September 2007, we reported than an increasing reliance on contractors to perform services for core government activities challenges the capacity of federal officials to supervise and evaluate the performance of these activities." And, he concludes, "Unless the federal government pays the needed attention to the types of functions and activities performed by contractors, agencies run the risk of losing accountability and control over mission-related decisions."[58]

It is clear to me that PSCs are in fact engaged in "inherently governmental functions." For example, the statutory definitions in the FAIR Act of 1997 seem to indicate this. The FAIR Act, in addition to a short definition, also gives some examples, two of which seem to fit the missions engaged in by the PSCs: "determining, protecting, and advancing U.S. economic, political, territorial, property, or other interests by military or diplomatic action, civil or criminal judicial proceedings, contract management, or otherwise," and "significantly affecting the life, liberty, or property interests of private persons."[59]

During my research, I was fascinated to read a recent handbook on outsourcing, in which Chapter 9 is titled " When Not to Contract: The U.S. Military and Iraq."[60] Yet contracting out in Iraq reached a feverish pace in all mission areas, with the result that by late 2009 there were 25,500 private security contractors engaged in activities that had previously been the responsibility of the uniformed military. The contractors' expansion into missions that were previously fulfilled by uniformed service personnel was a pragmatic decision that came about because: (1) Authority in Iraq was turned over to DoD; (2) there was a serious shortage of troops available due to conscious decisions by civilian policy makers; and (3) the country presented a very dangerous and violent environment. But rather than simply filling an unanticipated need, it is important to recognize that this expansion grew out of the long-term U.S. drive to contract out as many areas of government activity as possible, going back at least to the 1990s. There is a very extensive literature on this topic, and Congressional Research Service reports continually incorporate the latest nuances.[61] Once the PSCs occupied this space, and businesses that depended on federal contracts grew and prospered, a whole industry came into existence that now works diligently at all levels to maintain the activity. The following chapter will analyze the implications of contracting out security, according to the three-part framework developed in the earlier chapters of the book.

6 AN ASSESSMENT OF THE PERFORMANCE OF THE PRIVATE SECURITY CONTRACTORS

This chapter analyzes the results of outsourcing security to private security contractors (PSCs) by applying the three-part framework developed in Chapter 2 and applied to the uniformed military in Chapter 3. While Chapter 3 presented the framework's components in the order of control, efficiency, and effectiveness, however, this analysis will begin with efficiency, a more logical sequence in this case because much of the material for this section is from congressional guidance on oversight and auditing, which is all about efficiency. Furthermore, as some of the factors that influence effectiveness also affect matters of control, it makes sense to discuss effectiveness next, before assessing control.

Using this framework to analyze the PSCs has two major values. First, it allows us to compare and contrast the activities of the uniformed military and the contractors according to those three critical dimensions of performance, which has become increasingly important now that contractors are part of the "total force," have taken on some of the missions that were previously the monopoly of the military, and, as a whole, even outnumber the uniformed military in Iraq and Afghanistan. The resulting analysis will allow us to systematically identify problems in control and effectiveness that have been touched on in other studies of security contracting. The comparisons will be displayed in Chapter 7 in Table 7.1, and the remedies to the challenges will be evaluated in the Conclusion. The second value of this method is that it organizes the prodigious and potentially overwhelming amount of data from government reports and audits in a logical and coherent, and thus more useful, manner.

EFFICIENCY

Efficiency, which in my framework is essentially having in place institutions to investigate and audit where resources go and how they are used, is not currently an insurmountable problem with regard to the private security contractors. That is, the U.S. Congress, the federal government in general, and civil society can get a general idea of what is being done by the contractors and at what economic cost. The federal institutions and mechanisms that carry out audit and investigation functions specifically to monitor the efficiency of PSCs are robust. Mainly due to allegations of waste, fraud, and abuse, Congress created the Special Inspector General for Iraq Reconstruction (SIGIR) in late 2003 and greatly increased oversight of the war effort in general following the November 2006 elections.[1] Among many initiatives geared toward improving transparency in Iraq, Congress directed the Congressional Research Service (CRS) to undertake extensive reporting, including a "Congressional Oversight Manual";[2] the Congressional Budget Office (CBO) to assess budgets and analyze the PSCs' contracts; and the Government Accountability Office (GAO) to study all relevant aspects of the contracting phenomenon; and most importantly and provocatively, Congress kept SIGIR funded despite several efforts by the George W. Bush administration to kill it.[3] With the creation of the Special Inspector General for Afghanistan Reconstruction (SIGAR), every facet of funds and contracting in Afghanistan is under investigation as well.

By February 2009, SIGIR had published twenty quarterly reports, 135 audits, 141 inspections, and four lessons learned. On February 7 and October 2, 2007, the House Committee on Oversight and Government Reform held hearings on PSCs in Iraq.[4] The hearings, and the resultant staff memorandum released by Committee Chair Henry Waxman, drew immediate public and media attention to the PSCs in general and to Blackwater USA in particular.[5] The Nisour Square incident, in which Blackwater employees killed eighteen Iraqi civilians, took place on September 16, 2007, but the media had already focused on Blackwater due to several earlier incidents.[6] Sectors of the think tank and nongovernmental organization (NGO) communities, as well as investigative reporters, also became very active in investigating and reporting on the PSCs after those hearings.

There remains, however, a large gap between what has been mandated by law and the structures and personnel available to meet those mandates. As the Gansler Report states, under the heading of "Audit and Oversight Functions,"

"Today, due to inadequate training and staffing, we have dedicated a greater number of auditors (yet another endangered species in the DoD contracting community) in the USCENTCOM area of operations to review the contract-related problems than should be required."[7] That is, oversight, or auditing, is one thing, and implementation is another.

EFFECTIVENESS

In his statement to Congress on March 11, 2008, Comptroller General David Walker sets the tone for this section on effectiveness:

> DOD's primary challenges have been to provide *effective management and oversight*, including failure to follow planning guidance, an inadequate number of contract oversight personnel, failure to systematically capture and distribute lessons learned, and a lack of comprehensive training for military commanders and contact oversight personnel.[8]

The operations in Iraq and Afghanistan require what is called "expeditionary" or "contingency" contracting. That is, the contract work takes place in problematic, dynamic, and very complicated environments that are in some cases characterized by very high levels of violence. The Gansler Commission Report prefers to call these kinds of operations expeditionary: "The term 'expeditionary' includes both OCONUS and domestic emergency operations. The Commission believes the term 'expeditionary'—rather than 'contingency'—is a broader term that better encompasses any future national defense and national security missions."[9] The commission also notes that "the 'Operational Army' is expeditionary and on a war footing, but does not yet fully recognize the impact of contractors in expeditionary operations and on mission success, as evidenced by poor requirements definition." In other words, while the U.S. Army is on a war footing, the contracting support is not. Under the rubric of "Expeditionary Environment," the Gansler Commission Report notes:

> Expeditionary environments are anticipated to be the norm in the 21st Century. Future military operations will be expeditionary and joint (and, likely, multi-agency) as were Desert Storm, Somalia, the Balkans, Afghanistan, and Iraq. Each situation is unique; and the next national security problem will be different also. However, nearly all warfighters and planners expect the next challenge will be expeditionary and the challenge, by necessity, will heavily involve contractor support. The Army and our Nation need organizations and talent poised to "hit the ground running."[10]

The Gansler Report further notes that the Army has responsibility, as the DoD executive agent, for contracting in Iraq and Afghanistan. Commission Chair Dr. Jacques Gansler confirmed in an interview that, because the Army took the lead for expeditionary operations, some twenty-three of the commission report's forty recommendations for reform are directed specifically to the Army.[11]

The contract is the vehicle and guidance for everything contractors are paid to do. Effectiveness is only as good as the contract and the organizational processes used to plan, award, and administer the contract. Therefore, it is the overall contract management process, not the contractors per se, that must be reviewed, analyzed, and reformed.[12] Chapter 2 argued that effectiveness in the areas of defense planning and implementation required three things: a plan or strategy, coordination as in an interagency process, and adequate resources. Chapter 3 went over problems with the first two of these in the case of U.S. national security and defense policy and its implementation, and Chapter 4 highlighted the attempts between 1986 and today to overcome these problems.

The framework generates key questions that will be addressed in this section: First, is there a plan to coordinate or map out a strategy for the use of contractors in support of military operations? Second, are there institutions to coordinate the contractor management process, and, if so, what are they? And third, what quantity and quality of personnel are in place to award and, even more importantly, monitor the contracts? It will become clear that contract management is weak in all three of these areas.

In this section I again draw heavily on the studies, audits, and testimony from the government agencies that report to Congress. These documents also routinely go to the executive branch, and many include comments by different executive branch agencies. I also make use once more of the many interviews I conducted with officials in GAO, SIGIR, and several congressional committees to better understand and situate these often turgid and tedious documents.[13]

For this discussion, however, I also turn to some different sources to complement or corroborate the findings of those official investigations, audits, and interviews. Two very different recent books by well-respected journalists are particularly useful. First, Suzanne Simons builds her book, *Master of War: Blackwater USA's Erik Prince and the Business of War*, on over 100 hours of interviews with Blackwater founder and CEO Erik Prince and her access to Blackwater's top offices and facilities over eighteen months.[14] Simons repeatedly verifies a remarkable lack of coordination between one of the largest

PSCs in Iraq and the military commanders who were responsible for pursuing U.S. goals in Iraq. A very different book is Linda Robinson's *Tell Me How This Ends: General David Petraeus and the Search for a Way Out of Iraq*.[15] Robinson's focus is on the development and execution of the U.S. military campaign called the "surge," which took place in 2007–2008 to end the escalating internecine violence that had spread across Iraq. Across 363 pages of text she makes perhaps a half dozen brief references to PSCs, but none are mentioned in the list, "Principal Cast of Characters (as of February 2007)," or in the extensive acknowledgments. This is at a time when a CBO report of August 2008 puts the ratio of contractors to military personnel at about one-to-one.[16] Robinson's failure to acknowledge the role of contractors inadvertently demonstrates precisely the argument I develop in the following pages: The contractors, even if they are equal in number to uniformed military personnel in the theater, are not integrated into a plan or within military planning processes and structures. Simons, by contrast, demonstrates quite purposefully that Blackwater USA, which became probably the most infamous PSC in Iraq in the course of its security work for various U.S. non-DoD departments and agencies, was never integrated into planning or even coordinated with by General Ricardo Sanchez, the military commander in Iraq, at the time of her writing.

To set the stage for the discussion in the rest of this chapter, it makes sense to begin with some quotations from GAO on DoD contracts, and contracting in general. One 2009 GAO report notes:

> The Department of Defense (DOD) is the largest buying enterprise in the world. Since fiscal year 2001, DOD's spending on goods and services more than doubled to $388 billion in fiscal year 2008, and the number of weapon system programs has also grown. . . . Since January 2001, GAO has designated strategic human capital management as a government-wide high-risk area. In addition, the DOD acquisition workforce is included in another high-risk area—DOD Contract Management—that GAO designated in 1992.[17]

According to this report, GAO has designated the Defense Department's contracting process, and those involved in managing the contracts, as doubly problematic. "Areas are identified, in some cases, as high risk due to their greater vulnerabilities to fraud, waste, abuse, and mismanagement. GAO also identified high-risk areas needing broad-based transformation to address major economy, efficiency, or effectiveness challenges."[18] It should be noted that the GAO began to categorize certain government areas as high risk in 1990, which means that DoD contract management has been on the list for some nineteen years. These are precisely the structures and processes, and personnel, who are responsible for the PSCs. The GAO report to Congress warns, "The area remains [strategic human capital since 2001] high risk because of a continuing need for a government-wide framework to advance human capital reform. This framework is vital to avoid further fragmentation within the civil service, ensure management flexibility as appropriate, allow a reasonable degree of consistency, provide adequate safeguards, and maintain a level playing field among agencies competing for talent."[19] In other words, the current climate makes it hard to recruit and retain a "capable and committed federal workforce."[20] The same report addresses "Department of Defense Contract Management":

> DOD's reliance on contractors presents several broader management challenges, including determining which functions and activities should be contacted out; developing a total workforce strategy to address the appropriate mix, roles, and responsibilities of contractor, civilian, and military personnel; and ensuring appropriate oversight, including addressing risks, ethics concerns, and surveillance needs. Such issues take on heightened significance in Iraq and Afghanistan, where DOD estimates that more than 230,000-contractor personnel were engaged as of October 2008.[21]

In his 2008 testimony to the House, David Walker noted that DoD contract management is high-risk, "in part due to concerns over the adequacy of the department's acquisition workforce, including contract oversight personnel."[22] The appendix to Walker's testimony lists fifteen "Systemic Acquisition Challenges at the Department of Defense." Together, they make it apparent that the contract management process, as currently structured and populated, cannot result in either control or effectiveness, until and unless major reforms are made.

In his statement, Walker pointed out that "the acquisition of services differs from that of products in several key respects and can be particularly challenging in terms of defining requirements and assessing contractor performance. DOD is by far the largest federal purchaser of service contracts— ranging from housing to intelligence to security."[23] All experts agree that the processes and expertise with regard to contracting for systems and supplies are much more robust than for services, despite the fact that services require much more ability and agility to deal with them effectively. Walker noted earlier that, in FY 2007, the federal government spent about $254 billion on contractor *services*, an amount that has more than doubled over the past decade. DoD obligations on service contracts, expressed in constant FY 2006 dollars, rose from $85.1 billion in FY 1996 to more than $151 billion in FY 2006, a 78 percent increase.[24]

THE CONTRACT PROCESS: PLANNING, IMPLEMENTATION, AND FUNDING

With the preceding picture of the current situation as background, this section will examine contracting in light of each of the three requirements for effectiveness outlined earlier: a plan, institutions to implement the plan, and adequate resources to reach the goal.

Planning the Contract

The first question to ask is, Is there a plan that maps out, coordinates, and implements a strategy for the use of contractors in support of military operations? In his testimony to Congress, Comptroller General Walker made a key point in this regard:

> For example, although DOD estimates that as of the first quarter of fiscal year 2008, 163,590 contractors were supporting deployed forces in Iraq, no one person or organization made a decision to send 163,590 contractors to Iraq. Rather, decisions to send contractors to support forces in Iraq were made by numerous DOD activities both within and outside of Iraq. This decentralized process, combined with the scope and scale of contract support to deployed forces, contributes to the complexity of the problems we have identified in our past work on this topic.[25]

When asked about this, Dr. Rene Rendon, an Associate Professor of Acquisition Management at the Graduate School of Business and Public Policy at the Naval Postgraduate School, noted in his written comments to me that, while procurement planning at both the tactical and strategic levels is done for weapons system contracts, for services contracting, by contrast, there is significantly less planning at the strategic, and sometimes even at the tactical, level.[26] This is despite the fact that, for the first time ever, the contractors are in the same battle space as the troops. Furthermore, while the 2006 QDR considers contractors to be part of the "total force," this does not mean there is a doctrine in place to integrate them into it. (The 2010 QDR will be discussed in the Conclusion to the book). These two points—the unique situation in

Iraq and the lack of doctrine—emerged again and again in interviews with officials, particularly in those agencies responsible for oversight.[27] Even if the combat commander has a strategic vision of how to fight in the theater, as he must, he does not necessarily have control over the contactors operating in the theater or have a way to include them in his strategic vision. As an August 2008 CBO report states:

> Although military commanders can directly control the actions of military personnel and government civilians, their control over individual contractor personnel is less direct. . . . In practice that authority [laws and regulations of the United States] enables the military commander to allocate the personnel under his or her command among any number of tasks those personnel are able and trained to do. The military commander may also request that additional personnel be reassigned from other parts of the government if necessary. By contrast, the duties of contractor personnel are set out in a fixed written contract. . . . The military commander generally lacks the authority either to increase the scope (dollar value) of the contract or to change the contractor's duties except in ways anticipated in the contract language. . . . The military commander has less direct authority over the actions of contractor employees than over military or government civilian subordinates. The contractor, not the commander, is responsible for ensuring that employees comply with laws, regulations, and military orders issued in the theater of operations. Short of criminal behavior by contactor personnel, the military commander has limited authority for taking disciplinary action.[28]

Comptroller General Walker emphasized the failure of DoD to follow what he termed "long-standing planning guidance":[29]

> For example, we noted in 2003 that the operations plan for the war in Iraq contained only limited information on contractor support. However, Joint Publication 4-0, 26 which provides doctrine and guidance for combatant commanders and their components regarding the planning and execution of logistic support of joint operations, stressed the importance of fully integrating into logistics plans and orders the logistics functions performed by contractors along with those performed by military personnel and government civilians. . . . senior military commanders in Iraq told us that when they began to develop a base consolidation plan for Iraq, they had no sources to draw upon to determine how many contractors were on each installation. Limited visibility can also hinder the ability of commanders to make informed decisions

about base operations support (e.g., food and housing) and force protection for all personnel on an installation.[30]

If the commander doesn't even know how many contractors there are, and has no authority over them in any case, then there is little possibility that they can be included in a plan or strategy, even should one exist.

At this time, there is no doctrine that compels integration of the contractors into the military commander's strategy. Professor Cory Yoder, also of the Graduate School of Business and Public Policy at the Naval Postgraduate School, has emphasized this to me a number of times. There are currently efforts by the joint chiefs and DoD to develop both the doctrine and the structures and processes to change this. Once formulated, however, this doctrine will have to be adopted and implemented by the three separate services that individually hold the responsibilities to recruit, train, and equip the armed forces. Yoder estimates that this will take a decade *after* the doctrine is in place. This issue will be updated in the Conclusion.

Institutional Vacuum

An effective security strategy requires institutions to implement a doctrine or plan once it is in place. In the course of showing how planning has lagged far behind the explosion of contracting, the preceding discussion touched on problems with DoD's institutional processes. What kinds of institutions are there, if any, to coordinate the contractors? In her book on Erik Prince and Blackwater USA, Suzanne Simons highlights this issue:

> The coordination of contractors would prove to be a never-ending challenge for Sanchez [General Richard Sanchez, senior U.S. commander in Iraq], one that would lead to ugly confrontations between troops and contractors, many of whom were retired military making more than twice as much as their military counterparts. . . . "This is a question that continues to hound me to this day," said Sanchez. "There was a mind-set that was almost unexplainable about maintaining this separation with the military assets on the ground that permeated just about everything that was going on in the country, from the building of security forces to the actual combat operations and initiatives."[31]

The Gansler Commission report finds problems with complexity, an insufficient focus on postaward contract management, inadequate organization, and inadequate lines of responsibility to facilitate contracting. Under the heading, "Extremely Poor Interagency Operations," the report finds that there is a lack of institutional orientation and functional interagency process in all of the areas previously listed.[32] The following quotations, from this section of the report, elaborate these points, rearranged slightly here to follow the line of my argument:

> In the Cold War environment, it was not envisioned there would be other Departments or Agencies engaged so much on the field of conflict. Today, the military commander who is supported by a "joint" contracting organization actually has a disparate group of well-meaning professionals sitting side-by-side applying different rules to the same situation. . . . While it is recognized that the State Department, Justice, Commerce, Treasury, et al. bring impressive tool kits, which represent some of the most effective tools America has to offer and are critically essential to nation-building, in the Cold War era, these players only entered after the battlefield was relatively secure. They were not the integrated partners which successful expeditionary operations may require.[33]

> General Petraeus, the Commander of the Multi-National Force-Iraq, to whom JCC-I/A reports, only has about 50 percent of the in-theater contracts under him. The lack of integration of the contracting activities is a concern from an accountability, performance, and life-cycle support perspective. There are many independent contracting and management organizations in-theater with no clear responsibility for overall integration, quality, management or oversight. Just the DoD organizations include JCC-I/A, GRD, AFCEE, AMC, CSA, AAA, DLA, Medical Command, and DCMA. Operational commanders should not have to try to figure out who is responsible for acquisitions and management of a particular service or commodity.

> The lines of authority for command versus contracting differ. For Command authority, it flows from Admiral William J. Fallon at Central Command to General David Petraeus Multi National Force-Iraq (MNF-1) commander, to Major General Scott, commander JCC-I/A. For contracting authority it flows from the Head of the Agency to the Senior Acquisition Executive. There are three Army contracting chains of command in Iraq: JCC-I/A, AMC, USACE.[34]

In a jointly written thesis by students in the NPS Acquisition Research program, the authors deal with the problem of coordination, drawing from the SIGIR and Gansler reports. Capt. Kelley Poree, USAF, and colleagues note that "the misalignment of major procurement authorities and funding streams with campaign plan phases. . . . Variations in business practices such as warranting

CCOs to provide contract support during the critical transition from the *dominate phase* to the *stabilize phase* provided for numerous undesired effects not only in the *stabilize phase* but throughout subsequent campaign plan phases."[35]

As the contractors are not under direct control of the commander but are necessary to the success of his plan or strategy, the absence of coordination or an interagency process is especially significant and even dangerous. A key theme, which lead author Capt. Poree highlighted in my interviews with him, is the variation in the recruitment, education, and career tracks of the different services' contracting officers.

The CBO report, "Contractors' Support of U.S. Operations in Iraq," August 2008, conveys a sense of the challenge of coordinating the huge variety of contractors in a number of different areas.[36] For example, with regard to the data the authors have access to, which logically would be all data available, they find that "CBO cannot classify the functions provided by about one-fifth of obligations for contracts performed in the Iraq theater over the 2003–2007 period."[37] Nor can they determine the numbers involved: There are hundreds of firms involved in defense contracting, employing tens of thousands of people of various nationalities; contract work is continuously awarded and completed as requirements dictate; prime contactors may subcontract portions of their contracts to other firms; and subcontracting may run several tiers deep, further decentralizing administration of the workforce and reducing the likelihood of an accurate tally of all contractor personnel.[38] If the CBO cannot even determine the numbers of contractors and personnel obligated to a given contract, how can commanders, with many more pressing responsibilities, hope to coordinate the contractors they have to work with?

What all these sources conclude is that there is no overall plan or strategy within the DoD to integrate the contractors into an effective whole, nor is there an institutional mechanism to coordinate their work. Congressional staffers, academics, and GAO personnel interviewed for this book all emphasized this critical weakness. Several also pointed out the ineffectiveness and limited authority of both the Defense Contract Audit Agency and the Defense Contract Management Agency.[39]

Adequate Resources for the Job

The next question to ask is, What quantity and quality of personnel are in place to award and, even more important, oversee or monitor the contracts? Overall, in the area of acquisitions, DoD is severely handicapped at managing contracts. Rene Rendon demonstrates that the crucial elements for effective oversight are lacking in terms of both the required numbers of personnel and their core competencies, given the complexities of service contracts. The task of formulating the requirements is especially complicated and difficult, and, in Rendon's opinion, the acquisition workforce available doesn't have the skill set and experience to meet the demands of the work.[40] On this point, interviewees, contractors, lobbyists, auditors, and staffers were virtually unanimous.

A member of the permanent staff of the House Armed Services committee referred to the contracting staff, or lack of same, as the "nexus of the issue" of inadequate oversight.[41] This is an institutional issue that is unfortunately very difficult to remedy. The scope of the problem is daunting. The Gansler Commission Report directly addresses the fact that the contract management workforce has not increased despite a *sevenfold* increase in the workload:

> In 1990, the Army had approximately 10,000 people in contracting. This was reduced to approximately 5,500, where it has remained relatively constant since 1996. . . . yet both the number of contract actions (workload) and the dollar value of procurements (an indicator of complexity) have dramatically increased in the past decade while the contracting workforce has remained constant. The dollar value of Army contracts has increased 331 percent from $23.3 billion in 1992 to $100.6 billion in 2006, while the number of Army contract actions increased 654 percent from approximately 52,900 to 398,700 over the same period.[42]

Furthermore, the overwhelming majority of contract managers are civilians; out of a total of 5,800, there are only 279 military personnel doing this job.[43] This is an extremely important point, as military personnel can be deployed much more easily than can civilians, and the report goes into some detail on why it is difficult to deploy civilians.[44] This means that the contract managers are not located in Iraq or Afghanistan, where the contract work is being done, but rather in the United States. In his testimony to the Senate Armed Services Committee in early 2009, Dr. Gansler noted the sharp decrease in the number of Army general officers involved in acquisitions, from five in 1990 to zero in 2007.[45] This is of fundamental importance because, if there are no general officer positions in the Army Contracting Corps, it cannot attract, much less retain, motivated officers who are looking to advance in rank.[46] The background to this situation is found in the reduction of military forces at the end of the Cold War in the 1990s. While overall U.S. Army forces, for example, were reduced 32 percent from 732,000 in 1990 to 499,301 by 2003, the ranks of contracting officers were reduced 45 percent from 10,000 to 5,500, including the elimination of all flag and general officer positions during the same period.[47] Unsurprisingly, the rapid ramp-up in U.S. military operations and security contracting in Iraq, as the Sunni insurgency verged toward civil war, led to a shortage of contracting officers to do the job, particularly within the Iraq theater.

Given this chronic shortage of personnel, who then oversees the fulfillment and completion of the contracts? This is the contracting officer representative, or COR.[48] Rene Rendon emphasized that contracting officers (COs) and their assigned CORs are not interchangeable but are two very different positions on the acquisition project team. The COR is the technical expert for the specific procurement: He or she may be an aircraft maintenance expert who oversees an aircraft maintenance contract, a food service expert for a food service contract, an IT expert for an IT services contract. All of these very different contracts may have the same contracting officer, whose technical expertise is in the government contracting process and regulations, not in aircraft maintenance, food service, or IT services. As such, the CO is the only individual authorized to make changes to the contract and represent the government in contractual matters.

By contrast, the role of the COR is to provide technical guidance to the CO and technical oversight of the contractor's performance; he or she then provides that feedback to the CO. In services acquisition, the CO is typically left to define the requirement (which goes against the FAR) and to lead the project effort, even without a project team. Individuals involved in services acquisition (CORs like the aircraft maintenance expert, the food service expert, and the IT services expert previously mentioned) are not part of the defense acquisition workforce and thus have no training, career development, or priority for COR duties. The problems in expeditionary contracting reflect this lack of a program management approach.

Comptroller General Walker's testimony went into some detail on this point, particularly emphasizing the expeditionary environment: "While this [inadequacy of the acquisition workforce, including oversight] is a DOD-wide problem, having too few contract oversight personnel presents unique difficulties at deployed locations, given the more demanding contracting environment as compared to the United States."[49] He reported that the CORs specifically received little predeployment training on their roles and responsibilities in monitoring contractor performance: "In most cases, deploying individuals were not informed that they would be performing contracting officer's representative duties until after they had deployed, which hindered the ability of those individuals to effectively manage and oversee contractors."[50]

There is agreement among sources on the lack of preparation for CORs and the unreasonable multitasking expected of them. The Gansler Report is very critical of the way CORs are used as an institutional mechanism for oversight:

> Contracting Officer's Representatives (CORs), who are an essential part of contract management, are at best a "pick-up game" in-theater. CORs represent the "last tactical mile" of expeditionary contracting. However, CORs are assigned as contract managers/administrators as an "extra duty," requiring no experience. A COR is often a young Soldier who does not have any experience as a COR. . . . Although being a COR would ideally be a career-enhancing duty, the COR assignment is often used to send a young Soldier to the other side of the base when a commander does not want to have to deal with the person. Additionally, little, if any, training is provided. To further compound matters, generally all COR training is geared for a low-operations, low risk tempo, so it is barely adequate. Despite this, there are still too few CORs. Moreover, COR turnover is high, frequently leaving many gaps in contract coverage.[51]

A more recent SIGIR study concludes that there are major ongoing problems regarding CORs:

> SIGIR identified vulnerabilities in the government's oversight. Generally, the CORs' experience and training was limited, and they had insufficient time available to devote to their oversight responsibilities. This hampered their ability to perform their oversight responsibilities. For example, of 27 CORs responding to SIGIR questions, only 4 CORs said that they had previous contracting experience, 11 said that their training was insufficient to meet their job and requirements, and 6 said that other duties prevented them from conducting adequate oversight.[52]

The report further finds that CORs oversee task orders ranging from $179,000 to $22.2 million.[53] Senior auditors at SIGIR in mid-2009 described one large project for which fifteen different CORs were responsible during a four-year period. They noted that, in many cases, the contractors themselves provided continuity rather than the COR.[54]

An even more serious issue arises from the fact that DoD has contracted out extensively to oversee *its* acquisitions processes. In testimony before the House Oversight and Investigations subcommittee, John K. Needham, director of acquisition and sourcing management for GAO, observed that, at the end of FY 2008, the number of civilian and military personnel in DoD's acquisition workforce totaled nearly 126,000, of which civilian personnel comprised

88 percent.[55] From FY 2001 to FY 2008, the number of civilian and military acquisition personnel had declined by 2.6 percent, which led DoD to contract out contracting functions to augment the in-house workforce. The GAO has found that the number of contract personnel in acquisition-related functions average 37 percent, with ranges from 22 percent in the Army to 47 percent in joint programs.

They have also found that the DoD has no strategy to deal with the problems, and that, rather than saving money as proponents of outsourcing claim, contractors are paid above what government employees receive for equivalent work. In addition to the general issue of the agent overseeing other agents, making them twice removed from the principal, there are important implications for effectiveness in that the contractors doing the oversight of contractors may be working at cross purposes or even involved in conflict of interest.[56] The question of reform is crucial, and this book's conclusion will assess progress by looking at a number of current efforts, all of which are congressionally mandated.

In June 2003, GAO issued a comprehensive analysis of problems with DoD's management and oversight of contactors that support deployed forces and released a follow-on report to Congress in December 2006.[57] In the updated report, William M. Solis, GAO's director of defense capabilities and management, noted that GAO began to report in 1997 on shortcomings in DoD's management and training of contractor support to deployed forces and took on the current study due to the increased use of contractors and ongoing congressional interest: "GAO's objective was to determine the extent to which DOD has improved its management and oversight of contractors supporting deployed force since our 2003 report."[58] The report prefaced its findings with an assessment of ongoing problems:

> DOD continues to face long-standing problems that hinder its management and oversight of contactors at deployed locations. DOD has taken some steps to improve its guidance on the use of contactors to support deployed forces, addressing some of the problems GAO has raised since the mid-1990s. However, while the Office of the Secretary of Defense is responsible for monitoring and managing the implementation of this guidance, it has not allocated the organizational resources and accountability to focus on issues regarding contractor support to deployed forces. Also, while DOD's new guidance is a noteworthy step, a number of problems we have previously reported on continue to pose difficulties for military personnel in deployed locations.[59]

This preface then lists four areas as examples of ongoing problems with contracting, all of which fall within the three analytical dimensions already outlined in the preceding pages: planning, institutions, and resources. What is clear is that the problems identified in the report of June 2003 still applied in December 2006, three and a half years into the Iraq war.[60]

First of all, there is no organization within DOD that collects information on contractors or the services they provide. This means that "senior leaders and military commanders cannot develop a complete picture of the extent to which they rely on contractors to support their operations" and therefore have no basis on which to integrate them into any kind of overall plan or strategy. This is both a strategic and institutional failure that hobbles commanders at both the planning and operational levels.

Without this most basic information and access to any lessons learned that might be derived from it, "as new units deploy to Iraq, they run the risk of repeating past mistakes and being unable to build on the efficiencies other have developed during past operations that involved contractor support."[61] In other words, as of 2006, DoD was not building the institutional foundation or knowledge it needs to make the bloated contracting system work better in the future. Anything that has been learned is being lost. The report also addresses persistent problems with insufficient resources to conduct oversight:

> DOD continues to not have adequate contractor oversight personnel at deployed locations, precluding its ability to obtain reasonable assurance that contractors are meeting contract requirements efficiently and effectively at each location where work is being performed. While a lack of adequate contract oversight personnel is a DOD-wide problem, lacking adequate personnel in more demanding contracting environments in deployed locations presents unique difficulties.[62]

In one case, for example, some facilities never received an inspection from the official responsible for their oversight simply because there were too many on his tour for him to get to. Those contracts, thus, went almost entirely unsupervised over a sixteen-month period.[63] Training is another aspect of the resource dimension:

> Military personnel continue to receive limited or no training on the use of contractors as part of their pre-deployment training or professional military education. The lack of training hinders the ability of military commanders to adequately plan for the use of contractor support and inhibits the ability of

contract oversight personnel to manage and oversee contractors in deployed locations. Despite DOD's concurrence with our previous recommendations to improve such training, we found no standard to ensure information about contractor support is incorporated in pre-deployment training.[64]

Although resources are the main issue in this observation, it also has implications for both planning and institution building, in that, without training to manage and oversee the contractors, a commander and his staff cannot coordinate the contractors' work with the command's actual and evolving needs.

All of the audits and studies that deal with DoD contracting practices come to the same conclusions.[65] At this point, contracting for services still is not included within a national plan or strategy, there is no single responsible institution or interagency process to oversee either the awarding or fulfilling of contracts, and oversight personnel are lacking in both numbers and preparation. The overall process of contract management as it is carried out within DoD, particularly in light of the types of missions the PSCs have assumed since 2003, has serious implications for overall force effectiveness because the uniformed forces rely to a greater and greater extent on contractor support.

CONTROL: WHO GUARDS THE GUARDS?

As discussed in Chapter 5, primarily for reasons of expediency PSCs have assumed activities that were at one time defined as inherently governmental functions, including the use of armed force. Once attention was drawn to PSCs in recent years, due mainly to the disastrous breakdowns in control and oversight reviewed in the preceding section, many government officials, particularly those who had been involved in defining policy, began to raise questions. For example, Allan Burman, prior director of the Office of Federal Procurement Policy in OMB, began to raise questions about contracting out in a series of short articles he wrote in 2008. In one of these, he discussed whether the trend toward contracting out had not gone too far and offered several recommendations on ways to assess the situation. In another, he weighed the kinds of functions assumed by the PSCs in Iraq and Afghanistan against the standard of "inherently governmental functions."[66] The issue was also highlighted by Comptroller General Walker:

> In September 2007, we reported that an increasing reliance on contractors to perform services for core government activities challenges the capacity of federal officials to supervise and evaluate the performance of these activities. . . .

Unless the federal government pays the needed attention to the types of functions and activities performed by contractors, agencies run the risk of losing accountability and control over mission-related decisions.[67]

The GAO's John Needham raised these same issues of control in a more recent GAO report:

> In addition to the risk of paying more than necessary for the work that it needs, is the risk of loss of government control over and accountability for mission-related policy and program decisions when contractors provide services that closely support inherently governmental functions, which require discretion in applying government authority or value judgments in making decisions for the government. The closer contractor services come to supporting inherently governmental functions, the greater the risk of their influencing the government's control over and accountability for decisions that may be based, in part, on contractor work.[68]

These reports, among others, illustrate the emergence of an increasingly widely shared sense that the PSCs have been allowed to expand their activities into what were previously considered inherently governmental functions. This theme emerged in many personal interviews, including with very senior policy makers such as Burman and Gansler. The issue was also taken up by the U.S. Congress during the last months of 2008, where the ensuing political battle over the definition of "inherently governmental" exposed some of the different powers and funding sources of different sectors of the security contracting realm. It also became obvious that contracting out, especially with the PSCs, was not merely a technical or commercial issue. The result, although not the political battle that preceded it, is captured well in a CRS report of February 2009, which examines the key issues relevant to this topic and reviews extensive elements of the FY 2009 National Defense Authorization Act.[69] Key among these is:

> Section 832 which is a "Sense of Congress" provision that security operations in "uncontrolled or unpredictable high-threat environments" should ordinarily be performed by the military forces; that private security contractors should not perform inherently governmental functions in the area of combat operations, but that it should be in the "sole discretion of the commander of the relevant combatant command" to determine whether such activities should be delegated to individuals not in the chain of command.[70]

That legislative debate, and the fact that the new administration coming into office on January 20, 2009 included not only President Barack Obama but also Secretary of State Hillary Clinton, both of whom had weighed in as senators in that debate on the side of tightening up the definition of inherently governmental functions, meant that the issue would continue to have a high profile. Consequently, in mid-2009, the OMB was tasked with delimiting inherently governmental functions by October 14, 2009, for which it held a public discussion in June. That same June, the CRS published a valuable background report to inform members and staffers in Congress, and other interested parties on the debate, about issues and options up to that point.[71] The crucial effort to find a clear definition, with all its implications for Iraq, Afghanistan, and future warfare, was being fought out across the bitter political divide of the 111th Congress.[72]

This political battle is readily comprehensible within the context of New Institutionalism, the analytical approach that informs this book. The U.S. political system is a marketplace, not just of ideas, but also of financial profit and loss, thanks to laws that allow corporations, including contractors, to lobby lawmakers and make unlimited campaign donations.[73] By condoning a vague and ambiguous definition of what activities are inherently governmental, those agencies of the U.S. government with oversight responsibility have allowed the market, including the lobbying that is a hallmark of our political marketplace, to spread into tasks, roles, and missions that were previously considered the purview of the federal government. Now that PSCs have taken on the missions that were previously inherently governmental, and developed clienteles within the federal bureaucracy through the use of campaign funds and lobbyists, it is extremely difficult to turn the trend around.

If an area of governmental responsibility that originally was considered to be inherently governmental has been opened up to the PSCs, then what kind of control can be exerted to be sure they are acting in the best interests of the country? Given the reports and testimony I have quoted on the paucity of resources, institutions, and oversight for contractors, this question only becomes more important with time. It certainly is not the robust set of institutions, oversight, and professional norms that apply to the uniformed military—they do not apply even to those contractors who carry out what seem to be military functions. Some experts, especially non-U.S. sources, look to legal controls through enforcement of or changes to existing law.[74] While this appears promising in theory, in fact the legal basis for reigning in the PSCs is problematic.

Legal Control

In her book on Erik Prince and Blackwater USA, Suzanne Simons quotes at length an exchange at the Johns Hopkins University in April 2006, in which President George W. Bush tried, and failed, to answer the question: "What law governs contractors?" Secretary of Defense Donald Rumsfeld had earlier been unable to answer this same question, despite the fact that he had been a strong proponent of contracting both before and during his time in office.[75] The legal bases on which to regulate and control the PSCs are dealt with in studies by the CBO, CRS, GAO, and by contract law specialists. The issue of legal status is important for the degree of control that the government can exert over the PSCs but also for the degree of control the PSCs can exercise over their own employees. This latter point was highlighted in an interview with Michael J. Heidingsfield, a retired long-time professional police officer who went to work for DynCorp, where he spent fourteen months overseeing a large, $487 million police training program in Iraq. He managed some 1,000 people there, 550 of them former U.S. police officers, which gives his experience some weight. Heidingsfield noted that there was only a flimsy legal basis for control over the personnel he hired to administer the program and carry out the training and that he had few means by which to ensure they were doing the jobs as they were expected to under the terms of their contract. Aside from reprimanding and sending them home, he had no other means to stimulate, reward, or penalize their behavior.[76]

It is very difficult to determine the current legal status of contractors, including the PSCs. This situation is quickly evolving because of the rapid departure of the U.S. military from Iraq, the tendency for members of Congress to attempt to exert control over contractors through legislation, and the nature of U.S. law, which is developed on the basis of precedent.[77] As a 2008 CRS report to Congress states, "Contractors to the coalition forces in Iraq operate under three levels of legal authority: (1) the international order of the laws and usages of war and resolutions of the United Nations Security Council; (2) U.S. law; and, (3) Iraqi law, including orders of the CPA [Coalition Provisional Authority] that have not been superseded."[78] Under international law, contractors and other civilians working with the military are classified as civilian noncombatants. The application of international laws of armed conflict, including under the 1977 Protocol I to the Geneva Convention on mercenaries, however, is ambiguous, according to this CRS report and others.[79]

Before adoption of the Security Agreement of November 17, 2008, between the United States and the government of Iraq, the relevant guidance stated that: "Under CPA Order Number 17, as revised June 27, 2004, contractors are exempt from Iraqi laws for acts related to their contracts."[80] In other words, if a contractor could claim he had committed an act such as killing a civilian while carrying out his contractual duties, the Iraqi government had no power to prosecute him. At one point, for example, after a large number of what appeared to be wrongful civilian deaths at the hands of Blackwater employees, the government in Baghdad tried to expel Blackwater USA from the country. It never succeeded in exerting its authority to do so; only international pressure compelled the U.S. government to restrain Blackwater's scope of action and eventually to attempt to prosecute six employees.[81]

Under U.S. law, "U.S. contractor personnel and other U.S. civilian employees in Iraq may be subject to prosecution in U.S. courts. Additionally, persons who are 'employed by or accompanying the armed forces' overseas may be prosecuted under the Military Extraterritorial Jurisdiction Act of 2000 (MEJA) or, in some cases, the Uniform Code of Military Justice (UCMJ)."[82] But even with this statutory authority, some contractors "might fall outside the jurisdiction of U.S. criminal law, even though the United States is responsible for their conduct as a matter of state responsibility under international law and despite that such conduct might interfere with the ability of the Multi-National Forces in Iraq to carry out its U.S. mandate."[83] Despite its attempts at clarification, the ensuing discussion in this CRS Report leaves the reader with a great sense of ambiguity.

Military lawyer Marc Lindemann, writing in 2007, discusses Congress's expansion of UCMJ jurisdiction to the contractors, without congressional debate, by inserting five words into the 2007 Defense Authorization bill: "in time of *declared* war *or a contingency operation*."[84] Lindemann points out that, previously, both the UCMJ and MEJA had virtually no impact on civilian contractors, but the insertion of those five words meant that "the expansion of the UCMJ's jurisdiction now provides a means of regulating contractor behavior, whatever the contracting company's missions is in the combat zone. In doing so, the 2007 legislation has fundamentally changed the military-civilian relationship in stability operations."[85] He concludes, "The amendment has turned the concept of civilian control of the military on its head, as Congress has, in effect, placed more than 100,000 civilians under the jurisdiction of military courts."[86] In the course of his discussion, Lindemann makes it obvious that, as with much else in the U.S. legal system, the actual ramifications of this seemingly minor change remain to be seen. Based on interviews with "industry" lawyers in October 2009, it appears that the UCMJ will not in fact be applied to civilian contractors, while the MEJA applies only to U.S. contractor personnel who work for the DoD.

One would have expected that, with the November 2008 Security Agreement between the United States and Iraq, the legal situation would be clearer. While similar to a Status of Forces Agreement (SOFA), however, a CRS report on this topic notes that "the Security Agreement contains other rules and requirements that have traditionally not been found in SOFAs concluded by the United States, including provisions addressing combat operations by U.S. forces."[87] The same report also notes that there is controversy over this agreement, which was entered into on behalf of the United States by the Bush administration without the participation of Congress.[88] A more recent CRS report reviews these issues but finds that things have become no clearer, in actual fact, regarding the contractors, despite the fact that Congress was extensively involved in changing both the MEJA and UCMJ in 2008.[89]

One legal analysis specifically concerned with the contractors finds large gaps in the SOFA regarding their status. It concludes that contractors seem to have few protections under the SOFA and apparently are required to comply with Iraqi civil and regulatory codes.[90] Jeff Green, who was counsel to the Committee on Armed Services in the U.S. House of Representatives and is now president of his own lobbying firm, and Doug Brooks, president of the International Peace Operations Association (IPOA, since 2010 named the International Stability Operations Association), concurred with this assessment when interviewed in mid-June 2009. Brooks noted that while initially he and the members of IPOA were concerned with the SOFA, its implementation has worked out better than expected. Another expert on this issue, however, concluded, "Thus, it appears that Congress's action may have again failed to fully address the need for PMC [private military contractor] accountability."[91] The only thing that becomes apparent from these sources is that, at present, clear control is exercised over the PSCs by neither international nor U.S. law. Because the latter system is based on precedent, cases such as the Blackwater shootings will have to work their way through the appellate courts and the Supreme Court to reach some determination of how existing laws apply and possibly to point the way toward additional legislation. As previously mentioned, Iraqi law is thought now to apply to foreign contractors, but until recently this has not been a problem for the contractors. A civil wrongful-death suit related to the failed U.S. prosecution of the Blackwater employees, however, is going forward in Iraq and may also provide some clarification of jurisdiction.[92] Thus, although MEJA, UCMJ, and even the SOFA could offer legal bases for the oversight and control of PSCs, when practical considerations of sovereignty, jurisdiction, diplomacy, and resources come into account, there is in fact no existing mechanism to do so.[93]

CONCLUSION

For a number of reasons, as noted in the previous chapter, the U.S. government, including the Department of Defense, has chosen to contract out many formerly military security functions. This trend has been accelerated by pragmatic demands for protection in the face of pervasive insecurity in Iraq. The PSCs were encouraged to assume missions previously fulfilled by U. S. armed forces, in large part thanks to a proprivatization ideology pervasive within government and facilitated by fluctuating and vague interpretations of what constitutes "inherently governmental functions." Since public and official attention was drawn to undesirable outcomes of this policy, and the Democratic Party took over control of Congress in 2007, there have been several efforts in different areas of government to clarify the policy and legal frameworks within which the PSCs operate. This process is ongoing. Unlike the uniformed military, for whom the "control" dimension of the three-part analytical framework presented in this book is not an issue, the research on which this chapter is based finds there is little control over PSCs from any branch of government. Control through U.S. law is nascent. Under Iraqi law, it is also tentative and subject to interference from U.S. interests due to weak Iraqi sovereignty. Effectiveness is also problematic in terms of what contracting as a system is providing. The only dimension of the three-part framework that is robust with regard to security contracting is the efficiency, or oversight, element, which provides comprehensive and current information to Congress and has resulted in a number of laws, mandates, and guidance intended to remedy the identified problems of control and effectiveness. The concluding chapter to this volume, which follows, will analyze and update these dimensions and the status of the proposed remedies.

7 SUMMARY AND CONCLUSION

The primary purpose of this book is to analyze the formulation and implementation of national security and defense policy in the United States through the prism of civil–military relations. It is intended to fill a gap in the literature on the use of military force by the United States and on the relationship between the military and the democratically elected civilian leadership. The first question this analysis asks is, Who is in charge? That is, who makes the policy decisions, and who is responsible for their implementation? It thus mainly concerns political power. Until now, the literature on civil–military relations has contributed nothing to the analysis of the current operations in Afghanistan and Iraq. While there has been an explosion of material recently on defense contractors, particularly the private security contractors, or PSCs, none of it so far has been grounded in an analysis of civil–military relations, which means that it cannot help us situate PSCs within the context of national defense policy. This is especially true now that PSCs have taken on missions that were previously the responsibility of the uniformed military, and 90 percent of their funding in Iraq comes from the Department of Defense. Clearly the increasing use of contractors to carry out what were formerly military duties holds broad implications for U.S. security and the country's credibility abroad.

The civil–military relations framework used in this book was developed in the course of my work at the Center for Civil–Military Relations and in interactions with civilians and officers from around the world since 1994. It became obvious over years of study that the analysis of civil–military relations cannot be limited to achieving democratic control over the military. While this is the central issue in newer democracies, attention ultimately turns to whether the armed forces, along with other security forces, can in fact achieve the goals set for them by their civilian leadership. Closely tied to the assessment of effectiveness is the issue of cost: Is the nation buying the security it needs at a cost it can afford? To better understand the true nature of civil–military relations across countries, I developed a framework that, by asking these questions, seeks to capture what civilians and the security forces are in fact increasingly concerned with in most countries.

The framework is applied in this volume to the PSCs as well as to the uniformed military, to achieve an integrated analysis that gives us a more complete and accurate picture of U.S. national security and defense in the twenty-first century. The most important national security reform initiatives concerning the uniformed military were treated in Chapter 4. Chief among them is the Goldwater-Nichols Defense Reorganization Act of 1986, which was implemented almost a quarter-century ago and has served as the model for most reform efforts since that time. Indeed, the head of the current major reform effort, one that culminates decades of work since Goldwater-Nichols, is James R. Locher III, who was a key figure in writing and winning passage of the 1986 law. Because the phenomenon of contracting out security operations, by contrast, is very new and its scope, organization, and implications are only partially known, it is not possible to assume the same level of knowledge as with the uniformed military and defense reform. Of the reform initiatives reviewed in Chapter 4, only the PNSR even mentions the contractors as an issue. Chapter 5 described the political basis for the PSCs and fit often alarming popular perceptions about them into the more prosaic reality of the security contracting business in the U.S. government, while Chapter 6 then held them up to the analytical framework of control, effectiveness, and efficiency. With this practical basis for comparison in hand, it is now possible to assess the likely impact of current national security reforms. This chapter therefore will first summarize the findings of the earlier chapters and then evaluate the probability that current reform initiatives aimed at both the uniformed military and the PSCs will be successful enough to make a real difference to the security of the United States.

SUMMING UP THE CHAPTERS

Chapter 1 demonstrates that the current academic literature on U.S. civil–military relations is not very useful for analyzing the current state of U.S. security or how well the uniformed military and its civilian leadership work together, nor does it provide many insights for policy makers. Control is simply not an issue for the U.S. armed forces, and yet it is almost the exclusive focus in the academic literature.

The main journal in the field, *Armed Forces & Society*, is not robust in several areas, including sources and analytical rigor, which limits its utility for policy makers. Of greatest concern about *AF&S*, and by extension the field of civil–military relations in general, are its very short historical perspective, which makes it unsuitable for applying the useful analytical tools of New Institutionalism, and its lack of primary-source interview material and official government data. These fundamental weaknesses together severely undermine the potential analytical rigor of the premier journal in the field, which in my view should aspire at least to the minimal standards of the discipline of comparative politics.

Chapter 2 develops a framework for understanding civil–military relations that incorporates the three dimensions of control, effectiveness, and efficiency. The emphasis of the chapter is on the institutions that implement policy and are responsible for outcomes in all three dimensions. It compares and contrasts this framework to security sector reform and concludes that what is valuable in SSR is already included in this approach to civil–military relations. It then illustrates the framework's usefulness by applying it to information on the new democracies in Latin America and finds that, whereas there is a great deal of attention to, and thus material on, democratic civilian control, there is almost nothing on effectiveness and efficiency with which to assess the actual state of national security in these countries.

Chapter 3 moves to the United States and applies the framework to show that the norm of democratic civilian control over the armed forces pervades virtually all aspects of American politics and society. There is also a very large and robust set of institutions within both the executive and legislative branches of government, and in civil society as well, that carry out continual investigation, auditing, and oversight of the military. The presence and functioning of these mechanisms constitutes the analytical dimension of efficiency in the use of resources. There is general agreement among policy makers and outside observers that the main challenge for the U.S. security sector is effectiveness in fulfilling roles and missions. The analysis in Chapter 3 highlights both the general failure of security actors to develop a useful national plan or strategy, even though mandated by Congress, and the weakness of interagency coordination. There are substantial resources available, but their application, including to contractors, is problematic. Claus Offe suggests several functions that institutions fulfill, of which the two most relevant to this discussion are their formative impact on actors, by rewarding compliance with institutional norms, and continuity—that is, the propensity of institutions to "solidify" themselves and resist change.

Chapter 4, which examines several national security and defense reform initiatives, beginning with Goldwater-Nichols in 1986, reinforces the findings of Chapter 3 on the problematic dimension of effectiveness. None of these reform initiatives, from Goldwater-Nichols through the Project on National Security Reform (PNSR), gives any attention to civilian control. Efficiency is touched on to a limited degree, but the overwhelming emphasis in all of the reform initiatives is on effectiveness. The Goldwater-Nichols Act focused on reforming defense sector organizations and promoting jointness as the best means to make the armed forces more effective in combat. The 9/11 Commission promoted organizational changes intended to increase the effectiveness of the intelligence community. Other reform initiatives, culminating in the PNSR, have dealt with different aspects of how to increase effectiveness. The posited requirements for effectiveness—a plan or strategy, institutions for coordination, and resources— all figure centrally in these efforts at defense reform. It becomes clear from this study that the main impediment to reform is the inertia of established structures and processes, which can be overcome only with major political commitments in either the legislature (as was the case with Goldwater-Nichols) or, as the PNSR intends, the executive branch. The challenge of implementing targeted change to increase effectiveness is readily explained by referring again to three of Offe's posited functions of institutions. These are congruent preference formation, by which institutions provide a stable and predictable structure in which actors can function; frictionless self-coordination, through opportunities and incentives; and, again, continuity. The five obstacles to reform that James Locher highlighted in my last interview with him in the fall of 2009,which are also reviewed in the PNSR's progress report, easily correlate with these three functions of institutions, which in this case act as impediments to the reform of national security.[1]

Chapter 5 introduces the topic of security contractors and specifically the issues surrounding their use. It begins by discussing the causes behind the polemical tone of most studies concerning the use of contractors in the contingency or expeditionary environment, which arises from the long-entrenched assumption that nation-states should have a monopoly on the use of force. In contrast to the situation facing previous authors, since about 2006 the amount of credible data available to understand the scope, causes, and implications of contracting out has dramatically increased. As with research into any private enterprise, much less one for which secrecy is a routine part of operations, there remain significant challenges to gathering reliable data on the firms themselves. What has changed with regard to information on the contractors is the number of studies undertaken by the Congressional Research Service (CRS), the Government Accountability Office (GAO), the Special Inspector General for Iraq Reconstruction (SIGIR), the Gansler Commission, and the Commission on Wartime Contracting. This may be the first academic study on this topic to utilize these very rich research resources; I can only hope it will not be the last. These materials, along with extensive research by professors and students in the Graduate School of Business and Public Policy at the Naval Postgraduate School, help describe the scope and causes of the explosion in the numbers of contractors, particularly in Iraq. The chapter breaks out the PSCs, currently numbering 20,738 in Iraq, from the larger universe of contractors and demonstrates that they have assumed missions, including many that potentially involve the use of deadly force, previously exclusive to the uniformed military.[2] Two of Offe's functions of institutions are clearly at work here: the formative impact on actors, reflected in the drive within the U.S. government to privatize many of its functions; and economizing on transaction costs, which has always been privatization's chief justification. The numbers and scope of the PSCs in Iraq can be understood only in the context of the huge push in Washington to contract out government activities. Private firms were prepared and eager to move into the area of security contracting once they had established themselves and were seeking to expand their businesses.

Chapter 6 completes the picture by analyzing the institutional structures of contracting out security in terms of the three-dimensional civil–military relations framework, which helps clarify their status in comparison to the uniformed military. There is no doubt that there are mechanisms to oversee the efficiency of the PSCs. This is, however, the only dimension of the framework in which the institutions that oversee PSCs are assessed positively. The effectiveness dimension, measured just as for the uniformed military by the character of the strategy, institutions, and resources that go into them, is very weak when applied to the PSCs. The evidence, gathered from the same rich collection of public and private sources, clearly and consistently shows that the use of PSCs in Iraq, as a whole, is not effective. There is no strategy and minimal doctrine by which to incorporate the PSCs into military operations or campaign plans.

Undoubtedly the greatest weakness concerns the contracting officers and the contracting officer representatives, who tend to be too few, too poorly trained, and too overtasked to do their jobs well. The number, location, preparation, and utilization of these vital personnel, all experts and investigators agree, are major impediments to the effectiveness of the PSCs. Despite the fact that PSCs have expanded into areas that were previously regarded as "inherently governmental," there are only minimal institutional controls in place similar to those pertaining to the uniformed armed forces. Any legal controls are in the process of development and remain relatively weak. Clearly, the continuity function of institutions, among those cited by Offe, pertains here. By this time, the private security industry is ingrained within the government's approach to achieving security, thanks to a strong lobby, and within the armed forces, whose reliance on contractors is fairly well set and will not be easily changed.

There is admittedly a perhaps exaggerated but nevertheless intentional emphasis in this book on the institutional dimensions of civil–military relations and contracting out, to correct a persistent lack of consideration of institutions and the generally weak analysis in the current literature. The popular media tend to zero in on personalities rather than the institutions in which they function, whether to demonize them, as with Eric Prince, or to canonize them, as with General David Petraeus. The contention of this book is that the problems we are encountering with PSCs lie not with personalities or even professions but in the institutional bases of politics, governance, and society.[3]

When I compared my extensive research of government documents, and interviews with officials in oversight agencies, with documents on PSCs and interviews with employees of contracting firms, their lobbyists, and lawyers, I discovered a great deal of agreement on the nature of the issues of control and effectiveness. The U.S. government has gone wholeheartedly for privatization and contracting out, which is specified in excruciating detail in the Federal Acquisition Regulation (FAR), so it is important to remember that the PSCs as such are not engaged in illegal activity. They are private businesses, which, like other businesses, exist to make a profit. Due to the security vacuum in Iraq and the inability of either the scaled-down DoD or the DoS to protect all the people and facilities operating there, the PSCs were hired to fulfill a spectrum of armed missions traditionally the responsibility of the U.S. armed forces.

Table 7.1. Institutional dimensions of public and private national security and defense.

	Efficiency	Control	Effectiveness
Civil–military relations	Monitoring and oversight by full spectrum of institutional mechanisms	Control exercised by full spectrum of institutions, oversight mechanisms, and professional education	Problematic due to lack of strategy and weakness of interagency institutions
Private security contractors	Same as above	Minimal control due to uncertain concept of inherently governmental functions and sketchy legal controls	Problematic due to lack of doctrine to include PSCs and absence or shortage of contracting officers and CORs

Once the private firms moved into this domain and began to make very good money at it, it is not surprising that they lobby to keep the interpretation of what are inherently governmental functions limited. This is part of the American political process. The contractors have moved into an area where they make a profit and have developed interests and elaborated strategies to gain more, which is what one would expect in line with a New Institutionalist approach. This dynamic is not very different from what initiatives to reform the uniformed armed forces, such as the PNSR, confront. Of Offe's five functions of institutions, in both cases the last, continuity, is predominant.

In Table 7.1, I compare the institutional dimensions that affect the uniformed military, under the rubric of civil–military relations, with those that currently apply to the PSCs. While civilian control of the uniformed military in the United States is not a concern, for the PSCs it most definitely is. The effectiveness of the uniformed military, due to institutional gaps or weaknesses at the national or strategic level, is problematic. But it is for the PSCs as well, once we consider them not as a single entity, let alone a single contractual obligation, but rather in terms of the overall contract management process.

UPDATE ON THE KEY REFORM ISSUES

With the issues highlighted in the previous pages in mind, with a rough draft of the book completed, and to better understand the status of reform initiatives seeking remedies, I returned to Washington, DC, in the fall of 2009 for more interviews with officials involved in defense reform. Since that time I have continued to collect all available documentation, followed news items in the press, and communicated regularly with interviewees and specialists. In addition, CCMR research assistant Kristyn Admire went to Washington, DC, in late August 2010 to conduct a further series of interviews.[4] The most important indicators of the state of progress in reform, based on my findings, are: (1) the status of the PNSR and the reforms it advocates; (2) the (re)definition of what are to be considered inherently governmental functions, which was directed by Congress in the National Defense Authorization Act of 2009; (3) developments and clarifications in the legal status of contractors; and (4) the implementation of guidance from the Congress to DoD relating to doctrine, coordination, and personnel.

PNSR

The PNSR released a hefty progress report on September 30, 2009.[5] The comprehensive vision and scope of the project, and the thoroughness with which it is being executed, are impressive. When asked about progress during our September 2009 meeting, project head James Locher responded that he anticipated a ten-year project. He had begun work on PNSR in January 2006 and brought the other main figures on board in December 2006. Progress has indeed been difficult, at least from an outsider's perspective, particularly in light of the several impediments discussed in Chapter 4. To put the PNSR in the institutional context where real reform takes place, Locher pointed out that "nobody owns all of the space which is encompassed in the project. If anyone should own it, it is the National Security advisor, but his position is weak and without a budget." In other words, the very ambitious project still lacks a sponsor with real clout in the executive or legislative branches. In the meantime, Locher and his team are working diligently to develop support, convince allies of PNSR's importance, and broaden a network of change advocates.[6]

Inherently Governmental Functions

This book has made clear that the definition of inherently governmental functions is fundamental to the legal use of PSCs in expeditionary operations. As discussed in Chapter 5, the U.S. Congress directed that the OMB devise a single, coherent, definition of the term *inherently governmental.*[7] In a memorandum dated March 4, 2009, President Barack Obama announced his administration's priorities in contracting policy, one of which focused on "ensuring that functions considered to be inherently governmental are not contracted out."[8] Secretary of Defense Robert Gates elaborated on President Obama's statement in his budget announcement, dated April 6, 2009, which commits DoD to reduce the number of support service contractors and replace them with new civil servants.[9] As part of the process of developing an official definition of inherently governmental functions, OMB held a public meeting "on the Presidential Memorandum on Government Contracting," on June 18, 2009. It was scheduled to release the official definition on October 14, and on March 31, 2010, a proposed policy letter on "Work Reserved for Performance by Federal Government Employees" was posted for public comment.[10] As noted in Chapter 6, the contractors and their lobbyists want no single definition of what is inherently governmental or, failing that, to have it remain as vague as the current one.[11] On the other side, some in the executive and legislative branches want a clear definition that can be used to delineate what should and should not be contracted out. By June 1, 2010, when the comment period for the policy letter closed, more than 100 individuals and organizations had offered public comments. As the title of the article by Robert Brodsky in *Government Executive* reads: "Inherently Governmental Rule Sparks Little Consensus."[12] One interviewee on the Senate permanent staff emphasized that the scope of the PSC is very hard to resolve legislatively because the issue is highly political and complicated by a number of considerations. Another staffer interviewee, this time on the House permanent staff, reiterated how important that definition can be in determining what can be contracted out. As things stand, until and unless that definition is tightened up and published, contracting out security functions in war zones will remain wide open, with little government oversight or accountability.[13] The Office of Federal Procurement Policy reviewed the comments and issued on March 31, 2010 a "proposed policy letter" to be included in the Federal Acquisition Regulation. I reviewed the proposed policy letter and conferred with my contacts with background in the OMB. My conclusion has now been captured in an authoritative manner in a CRS Report in the following terms. "However, neither the proposed policy letter nor the notice from OFPP introducing it indicates whether or how the Obama Administration would amend the definitions of 'inherently governmental function' in the Federal Acquisition Regulation, OMB Circular A-76, or other executive branch regulations and policy documents."[14]

Legal Control or Accountability?

The common term to describe the hierarchical relationship democratically elected civilians have with the armed forces is *control*. I have demonstrated here that, due to the flimsiness of the concept of what is, or is not, an inherently governmental function, the control mechanisms described in Chapter 3 do not apply to the PSCs. The other possible avenue for control would be via the legal system. In interviews with lawyers working with the PSCs, however, I began to hear them use the term *accountability* rather than *control*. There are critical differences in these terms and in the concepts behind them. On the one hand, *control* has come to mean, at least in the United States, the type of robust, multilayered system described in Chapter 3. *Accountability*, on the other hand, does not imply any relationship beyond the personal accountability of the employee to the firm holding the contract. This is certainly legally accurate, but a relationship of personal accountability does not equal one of institutional control. When asked directly about the legal framework, a lawyer who worked for a contracting firm on issues involving PSCs admitted that "nobody has a clue," a statement that pretty well captures the current situation. International law is not enforceable; the Military Extraterritorial Jurisdiction Act (MEJA) could apply, the Uniform Code of Military Justice (UCMJ) probably will not apply, and the Status of Forces Agreement does indeed turn over jurisdiction concerning PSCs to the Iraqi government. Baghdad, however, still lacks the institutional framework to implement legal control over the contractors, and, although U.S. prosecutors could do much more, they still face limiting factors, including jurisdiction, diplomacy, and resources. I do not, therefore, foresee a legal framework coming into force that will provide the institutional basis for control over private contractors in a way that approximates the U.S. system's oversight of the uniformed military. Recent studies and developments support this conclusion. A December 2009 working paper by Richard Fontaine and John Nagl, of the Center for a New American Security, states: "The legal framework governing ES&R [expeditionary, stabilization, and reconstruction contractors] in wartime is complicated, features overlapping jurisdictions, and is somewhat ambiguous."[15] The interest of at least some in the U.S. Congress in this topic is evident in CRS reports in December 2009 and January 2010, which come to identical conclusions:[16]

> Despite the amendment to the UCMJ to subject military contractors supporting the Armed Forces during contingency operations to court-martial jurisdiction, and despite the extension of MEJA to cover certain non-DOD contractors working with the military overseas, some private security contractors may remain outside the jurisdiction of U.S. courts, civil or military, for improper conduct in Iraq or Afghanistan. As the courts begin to interpret and apply these statutes, and as the effects of the new contractual require-

ments are implemented, Congress may be called on to review and amend the existing statutory framework.[17]

The most telling court action in the United States was the decision by Judge Ricardo M. Urbina of Federal District Court in Washington, DC, on December 31, 2009, to dismiss charges against five of the six Blackwater employees who allegedly opened fire on Iraqi civilians in Baghdad's Nisour Square in September 2007. Judge Urbina's memorandum opinion seems to question whether any case against PSCs abroad could stand up in the U.S. court system.[18] Not surprisingly, Iraqis were outraged by the decision, and, aside from the civil suit that is going forward there, Iraqi legislators are said to be working on a law to regulate the legal status of PSCs in Iraq; one of the main points will be to apply any new legislation retroactively to such incidents as the Nisour Square shootings. It remains to be seen whether the law will pass and whether the Iraqi government can in fact implement it.[19]

While the focus in this book has been on Iraq, recent events in Afghanistan, where combat operations intensified throughout 2010, require some attention. During the week of August 16, 2010, Afghan President Hamid Karzai stated his intention to abolish private security contractors in his country within four months. From all that we could determine through interviews in Washington, DC, the following week, this statement has about as much credibility as Iraqi control of PSCs through the SOFA—that is, not much. Developments in the intervening period, up to early 2011, don't give me any sense that this will soon change.

DoD Implementation of Guidance from Congress
Regarding Doctrine, Coordination, and Personnel

Section 862 of the National Defense Authorization Act for Fiscal Year 2008 gives extensive guidance to the executive branch on the topic of "contractors performing private security functions in areas of combat operations."[20] I had two meetings, in mid-June and mid-September 2009, and Kristyn Admire had one meeting on August 24, 2010, with lead personnel in the Office of the Secretary of Defense Assistant Deputy Undersecretary (Logistics & Material Readiness/Program Support), the main office in DoD responsible for acting on the guidance. The staff did a very thorough job of reviewing the issues with contracting, discussed in Chapter 6, that have resulted in poor control and effectiveness.[21] This office had been created on the recommendation of the GAO in October 2006, to assign responsibility in one office in the Pentagon for the implementation of congressional guidance regarding the PSCs.[22]

At these meetings, the staff highlighted two areas of progress toward remedying what are defined here as problems of effectiveness. First is a July 2009 Department of Defense instruction that provides guidance to DoD on the use of PSCs in contingency operations.[23] Second is an "Interim final rule" that "establishes policy, assigns responsibilities and provides procedures for the regulation of the selection, accountability, training, equipping, and conduct of personnel performing private security functions under a covered contract during contingency operations."[24] This document provides guidelines for all of the U.S. government and is very complete, at least in its text.

These initiatives go some way toward improving coordination of the PSCs with military planning and operations in the field. They are a beginning step toward fixing some of the worst problems commanders face when they try to integrate PSCs into their planning. The incremental progress they offer is recognized in a recent SIGIR report: "Field commanders and CONOC officials generally believe that the new PSC control and coordination procedures have been effective in ensuring that such activities *are not inconsistent with* ongoing combat operations."[25]

Nevertheless, there is still little doctrine to integrate the PSCs into combat operations. The current guidance, issued by the Joint Staff, remains sketchy.[26] It is supposed to be replaced by a Department of Defense instruction, which was in the staffing process in mid-November 2009 and is still in process in March 2011. Among other requirements, this document calls for the development of contractor oversight plans and adequate military personnel to oversee the contracts.[27] There are ongoing efforts, as illustrated in the Joint Chiefs' Dependence on Contractors Task Force, to determine and define how to integrate contractors into the force in Afghanistan, based on lessons learned from Iraq.[28] The office of the assistant deputy undersecretary of defense (supply chain integration) has joint responsibility with the joint chiefs of staff to develop training for the armed forces on the use of PSCs, but by the end of 2009 this training had not taken place. Rather, a course had been developed, by a contractor at that, for commanders in contingency environments, but it had not been made a requirement for their education as of late 2010.[29]

In sum, the DoD is implementing to some degree the guidance they have received from Congress included in the National Defense Authorization Act of FY 2008. There are organizations whose purpose is to manage defense contracting, including the Joint Contracting Command–Iraq and the Defense Contract Audit Agency, and there are efforts to build the contractors into the military capability. As highlighted in the Gansler Report and reiterated in several interviews, however, the military is resistant to full recognition and thus incorporation of contractors into a contingency environment, and the personnel requirements for overseeing the implementation of contracts in this environment remain unmet. Basic to all this is the fact that Title 10 of the U.S. Code gives the armed services the authority to organize, train, supply, equip, and maintain their particular department of armed service. Thus, while the Department of Defense, the joint chiefs of staff, and the combatant commanders can issue directives, cajole, even threaten in their efforts to bring the services line with congressional direction, it is up to the services to do whatever is necessary to somehow incorporate contractors within their doctrine and operations. In the meantime, various "solutions" can be sought in an attempt to provide oversight.[30]

As noted in the Introduction to this volume, contractors were included in the Quadrennial Defense Review of February 6, 2006, as a fourth "element" of the total force. The February 2010 Quadrennial Defense Review Report also includes contractors but in fairly cautious terms:

> The services provided by contractors will continue to be valued as part of a balanced approach that properly considers both mission requirements and overall return. In keeping with the Administration's goal of reducing the government's dependence on contractors, the Department introduced its in-sourcing initiative in the FY 2010 budget. Over the next five years, the Department will reduce the number of support service contractors to their pre-2001 level of 26 percent of the workforce (from the current level of 39 percent) and replace them, if needed, with full-time government employees.[31]

The Obama administration's 2011 budget submission has the federal acquisition workforce growing significantly, some 5 percent, and also proposes investments in training, certification management, and technology for the contracting staff.[32] There is, however, a disparity between federal civil service pay and the average wage or salary in the private sector, something that must be considered when assessing the likelihood of hiring, and retaining, the staff who will supervise contractors. According to a recent CRS report, average wages among all workers in the economy have risen by 632 percent since 1969; salaries for federal employees have increased by 428 percent during the same period.[33] This gap, which signifies a lack of incentives to enter the federal service, was a theme in many of my interviews. This is extremely important because, as noted in the previous chapter, the overwhelming majority of contract managers are civilians; of a total of 5,800, there are only 279 military personnel doing this job.

The government will need very talented lawyers, contract writers, and contract overseers to craft a reliable system in which contractors can safely be entrusted with sensitive functions. Some of those interviewed pointed out that the disparity between federal and private sector pay has three consequences: First, a lot of very good people do not enter federal service in the first place because they can do so much better financially in the private sector; second, those who do become federal employees often leave after only a few years' service; and, third, those who leave frequently use the experience gained in the government to "outsmart" government restrictions when they deal with them from the private sector. In his compelling analysis of the multiple causes for the U.S. government's inability to faithfully execute the laws, Paul Light highlights, among other factors, "the clear incentives that make a contract or grant job more attractive than a civil service position."[34] In short, there are real, and continuing, structural problems that are likely to impede the administration's current, and much needed, reform efforts.[35]

Commission on War Time Contracting
In recognition that much is yet to be resolved regarding the PSCs, the Commission on War Time Contracting continues its work and issued an interim report in June 2009. In interviews with the staff, the authors reported progress on some of the issues, as already noted, but also have a sense of skepticism regarding how much reform can be implemented regarding the PSCs. Their due date for the final report has been extended to July 30, 2011. Based on the outcomes of reform efforts since Goldwater-Nichols in 1986, and the ongoing problems with the PSCs, it will require a reform effort with the planning, broad-based support, and rigorous implementation of Goldwater-Nichols to deal with the unending problems with the PSCs.[36]

SOME FINAL THOUGHTS
Utilizing the three-part analytical framework posited in this book, which I found appropriate to organize the wealth of credible and relevant data available on PSCs, including extensive and repeated personal interviews with experts, I was able to reach a number of conclusions on the topic. Efficiency, in

terms of monitoring and oversight, is not at issue because Congress makes extensive use of existing institutions such as CBO, CRS, and GAO; where closer oversight was needed, it created SIGIR, and then SIGAR, to oversee Iraq and Afghanistan, respectively. Effectiveness remains a deficient area and is gradually being addressed through implementation of congressional directives by DoD. Still, no single entity, office, or department has assumed control over PSCs. Control also remains a serious problem, in that the concept of inherently governmental functions remains so broad and vague that PSCs have successfully appropriated a broad range of work that seems to be crossing a line into the military domain, while the legal framework for control over contractors is extremely rudimentary. The Office of Federal Procurement Policy within OMB did not resolve anything when it came up with its definition of inherently governmental functions. Ultimately, I believe, the most serious weakness will probably be found in the shortage of qualified government employees who could in fact exercise this putative control.

The federal government has spent twenty years downsizing the civil service according to one view of economic orthodoxy, in the belief that privatizing as many government functions as possible would introduce private-sector efficiencies. Oversight, however, has not kept up with rampant privatization, nor has there been a methodical, long-term, and in-depth study of the effects and outcomes of contracting out. The wars in Iraq and Afghanistan have taken contracting to a whole new level, where we have private security contractors, often vilified in the popular press as mercenary armies, taking on missions that until recently were assumed to be the rightful responsibility of the U.S. military. Crimes such as the prisoner torture at Abu Ghraib and the alleged shooting of unarmed civilians in Baghdad have shone a spotlight on the contractors and revealed a dangerous lack of basic control and accountability. Reforms are being discussed and researched, but until Congress and the White House are ready to acknowledge that this is an issue critical to the country's defense and security, until the Department of Defense is able to change the way it does business, and until lawmakers can pass, and enforce implementation of, the needed legislation, we are likely to continue dealing with the confusion, ineffectiveness, and inefficiency of private security contracting as it is today.

REFERENCE MATTER

APPENDIX 1
PRESIDENT BARAK OBAMA'S MEMORANDUM
FOR HEADS OF DEPARTMENTS AND
AGENCIES, MARCH 4, 2009

THE WHITE HOUSE

Office of the Press Secretary

For Immediate Release   March 4, 2009

March 4, 2009

MEMORANDUM FOR THE HEADS OF EXECUTIVE DEPARTMENTS
AND AGENCIES

SUBJECT: Government Contracting

The Federal Government has an overriding obligation to American taxpayers. It
should perform its functions efficiently and effectively while ensuring that its actions
result in the best value for the taxpayers.

Since 2001, spending on Government contracts has more than doubled, reaching
over $500 billion in 2008. During this same period, there has been a significant
increase in the dollars awarded without full and open competition and an increase
in the dollars obligated through cost-reimbursement contracts. Between fiscal years
2000 and 2008, for example, dollars obligated under cost-reimbursement contracts nearly doubled, from $71 billion in 2000 to $135 billion in 2008. Reversing
these trends away from full and open competition and toward cost-reimbursement
contracts could result in savings of billions of dollars each year for the American
taxpayer.

Excessive reliance by executive agencies on sole-source contracts (or contracts with a limited number of sources) and cost-reimbursement contracts creates a risk that taxpayer funds will be spent on contracts that are wasteful, inefficient, subject to misuse, or otherwise not well designed to serve the needs of the Federal Government or the interests of the American taxpayer. Reports by agency Inspectors General, the Government Accountability Office (GAO), and other independent reviewing bodies have shown that noncompetitive and cost-reimbursement contracts have been misused, resulting in wasted taxpayer resources, poor contractor performance, and inadequate accountability for results.

When awarding Government contracts, the Federal Government must strive for an open and competitive process. However, executive agencies must have the flexibility to tailor contracts to carry out their missions and achieve the policy goals of the Government. In certain exigent circumstances, agencies may need to consider whether a competitive process will not accomplish the agency's mission. In such cases, the agency must ensure that the risks associated with noncompetitive contracts are minimized.

Moreover, it is essential that the Federal Government have the capacity to carry out robust and thorough management and oversight of its contracts in order to achieve programmatic goals, avoid significant overcharges, and curb wasteful spending. A GAO study last year of 95 major defense acquisitions projects found cost more overruns of 26 percent, totaling $295 billion over the life of the projects. Improved contract oversight could reduce such sums significantly.

Government outsourcing for services also raises special concerns. For decades, the Federal Government has relied on the private sector for necessary commercial services used by the Government, such as transportation, food, and maintenance. Office of Management and Budget Circular A-76, first issued in 1966, was based on the reasonable premise that while inherently governmental activities should be performed by Government employees, taxpayers may receive more value for their dollars if non-inherently governmental activities that can be provided commercially are subject to the forces of competition.

However, the line between inherently governmental activities that should not be outsourced and commercial activities that may be subject to private sector competition has been blurred and inadequately defined. As a result, contractors may be performing inherently governmental functions. Agencies and departments must operate under clear rules prescribing when outsourcing is and is not appropriate.

It is the policy of the Federal Government that executive agencies shall not engage in noncompetitive contracts except in those circumstances where their use can be fully justified and where appropriate safeguards have been put in place to protect the taxpayer. In addition, there shall be a preference for fixed-price type contracts. Cost-reimbursement contracts shall be used only when circumstances do not allow the agency to define its requirements sufficiently to allow for a fixed-price type contract. Moreover, the Federal Government shall ensure that taxpayer dollars are not spent on contracts that are wasteful, inefficient, subject to misuse, or otherwise not well designed to serve the Federal Government's needs and to manage the risk associated with the goods and services being procured. The Federal Government must have sufficient capacity to manage and oversee the contracting process from start to finish, so as to ensure that taxpayer funds are spent wisely and are not subject to excessive risk. Finally, the Federal Government must ensure that those functions that are inherently governmental in nature are performed by executive agencies and are not outsourced.

I hereby direct the Director of the Office of Management and Budget (OMB), in collaboration with the Secretary of Defense, the Administrator of the National Aeronautics and Space Administration, the Administrator of General Services, the Director of the Office of Personnel Management, and the heads of such other agencies as the Director of OMB determines to be appropriate, and with the participation of appropriate management councils and program management officials, to develop and issue by July 1, 2009, Government-wide guidance to assist agencies in reviewing, and creating processes for ongoing review of, existing contracts in order to identify contracts that are wasteful, inefficient, or not otherwise likely to meet the agency's needs, and to formulate appropriate corrective action in a timely manner. Such corrective action may include modifying or canceling such contracts in a manner and to the extent consistent with applicable laws, regulations, and policy. I further direct the Director of OMB, in collaboration with the aforementioned officials and councils, and with input from the public, to develop and issue by September 30, 2009, Government-wide guidance to:

(1)   govern the appropriate use and oversight of sole-source and other types of noncompetitive contracts and to maximize the use of full and open competition and other competitive procurement processes;

(2)   govern the appropriate use and oversight of all contract types, in full consideration of the agency's needs, and to minimize risk and maximize the value of Government contracts generally, consistent with the regulations to be promulgated pursuant to section 864 of Public Law 110-417;

(3)   assist agencies in assessing the capacity and ability of the Federal acquisition workforce to develop, manage, and oversee acquisitions appropriately; and

(4)   clarify when governmental outsourcing for services is and is not appropriate, consistent with section 321 of Public Law 110-417 (31 U.S.C. 501 note).

Executive departments and agencies shall carry out the provisions of this memorandum to the extent permitted by law. This memorandum is not intended to, and does not, create any right or benefit, substantive or procedural, enforceable at law or in equity by any party against the United States, its departments, agencies, or entities, its officers, employees, or agents, or any other person.

The Director of OMB is hereby authorized and directed to publish this memorandum in the *Federal Register*.

BARACK OBAMA

APPENDIX 2
LETTER TO OFPP OF OMB, BY
CONTRACTING INDUSTRY REPRESENTATIVES,
DATED JUNE 8, 2009

Ms. Julia Wise
Office of Federal Procurement Policy
Office of Management and Budget
Washington, DC

**Re: Multi-Association Comments on the President's Memorandum
on Government Contracting**

Dear Ms. Wise:

The undersigned organizations submit this letter for the record at the June 18, 2009
public meeting on implementation of Section 321 of the National Defense Authorization Act (NDAA) for Fiscal Year 2008. We supported the enactment of this provision
of the NDAA and offer this letter and its attachments to support its implementation
by OMB. Congress concluded that the patchwork of guidance for determining what
government employees must do, i.e., "inherently governmental functions," and what
constitutes "functions closely related to inherently governmental functions" and
commercial activities excepted by the Competitive Sourcing Official under OMB
Circular A-76, fails to adequately guide agencies in making these key, total work
force, decisions.

In the attached material, we propose a definition of "inherently governmental" that
relates to the existing OMB guidance and the examples in FAR 7.503(c). We also offer
definitions of "critical functions and positions." We do not, and we respectfully urge
the Executive Branch not, to suggest examples of critical functions and positions.
While we considered FAR 7.503(d) in making our recommendations, we consciously
decided that critical functions and positions were in some cases broader and in some

cases narrower, than the examples in FAR 7.503(d). As FAR 7.503(d) itself states, it provides, "examples of functions generally not considered inherently governmental functions . . . [but] may approach being in that category because of the nature of the function, the manner in which the contractor performs the contract, or the manner in which the Government administers contractor performance." The examples of functions listed thus depends upon at least the circumstances listed in the FAR itself. This important consideration of interrelated circumstances has at times been lost in the use of this FAR provision to "define" the phrase "functions closely associated with inherently governmental functions."[1] To follow FAR 7.503(d) too closely in implementing Section 321 would perpetuate this fundamental flaw in the current framework.

As we analyzed the history of this issue, the congressional purpose behind the enactment of Section 321, and alternatives to meet the congressional direction in that section, we adopted the decision tree in figure 1 to help address these issues.

We tried to carefully distinguish between a function—an activity that an employee performs—and the position that the employee holds. A position can perform and be responsible for many functions. Likewise many positions may perform the same function. The threshold issue is whether an activity is so "intimately related to the public interest" that a public employee must perform it, and thus it becomes an "inherently governmental" function. Inherently governmental functions will be the uniformly applicable no matter the agency, i.e. an inherently governmental function at one agency will be an inherently governmental function at every other agency. Thus, in every agency, all "inherently governmental" functions will be performed by government[2] employees.

Critical functions, in contrast, are those that are so important to the agency's missions or its operations that the function must be controlled by government employees. Furthermore, what constitutes a "critical function" may vary from agency to agency depending on each agency and its missions. Moreover, not every critical function must be performed exclusively by government employees as long as the agency maintains control of functions by having government employees fill supervisory positions that can control the function, i.e., critical positions.

We also agree that there are positions that need to have sufficient government employees to learn and gain experience to fill vacated positions exercising inherently governmental functions and vacated critical positions. We do not envision this requiring that all persons needed to fill positions exercising inherently governmental functions or critical positions be government employees. In fact, only using government employees to fill all of these positions would be unwise as it discourages bringing new ideas and perspectives to governmental service. But it would likewise be unwise to rely solely on the private sector to fill all such positions.

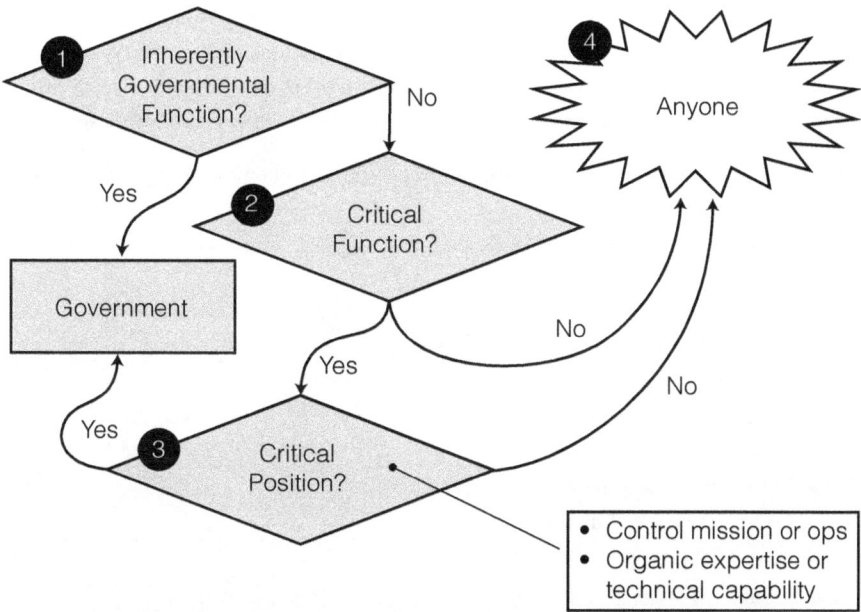

Figure 1. Industry View of Decision Tree Regarding Performance of Functions by Government Employees or Others

Stepping through this decision tree:

1. Inherently governmental functions must be assigned to government employees.

2. If a function is not critical, that function can be performed by either government employees or the private sector.

3. If a function is critical, the agency must ensure that government employees fill critical positions to oversee that function. "Criticality" is determined by the function or position's impact on agency missions or operations. A position may also be treated as critical if it is needed to provide the agency with organic expertise and technical capability.

Note: No positions are reserved or presumed to be filled by contractor employees.

Each agency will face different circumstances and decisions when seeking to get the remaining work done, and these circumstances will also change over time. In the vast majority of cases, the work will involve neither inherently governmental functions nor critical positions. We believe that perhaps the best guidance that can be presented for purposes of determining who should do this remaining work is to offer a list of factors that may be pertinent to the workforce decision. We do not believe any factor in the following list (with a few possible exceptions such as the type of funding) will always require either government employees or contractor employees to fill the position in question. We also do not believe this list to be all inclusive.

We offer the following factors (in *no* order of priority) as a beginning point for consideration:

- Congressional personnel ceilings
- The types of available funding
- Duration of services
- Available qualified, government employees
- Ability to timely hire qualified government employees
- Management flexibility
- Costs
- Operational requirements
- Ability to control quality
- Need for innovation/change
- Higher quality
- Public perceptions
- Statutes or treaty obligations
- Existing sources of the services
- BRAC impacts
- Budget stability
- Agency business models - large contractor work force versus small contractor work force
- Past practices
- Mission imperatives
- Statutory or other deadlines for implementation

As GAO observed in 1991,[3] concerns about contractors performing inherently governmental functions is not new. The current framework does not mention the key to these debates—does the government through its elected and appointed officials and through its employees maintain control of governmental missions and operations. The addition of critical functions and position analysis with total manpower planning will improve each agency's ability to ensure it controls its missions and operation. These new tools are a vast improvement over mandates to increase or decrease government employees to address such concerns. Nonetheless, no one should assume that this or any other approach will be the proverbial panacea that will forever put to rest these debates because the problems are complex, interrelated and change with time, technology and our collective views on what government and the private sector do best.

Aerospace Industries Association
American Council of Engineering Companies
International Peace Operations Association
National Defense Industrial Association
Professional Services Council
TechAmerica
U.S. Chamber of Commerce

New Definitions of Inherently Governmental Function, Critical Functions
and Critical Positions

A.   **Inherently Governmental Functions**. "Inherently governmental function"
means a function that is so intimately related to the public interest as to mandate
performance by Government employees. A function is a task or action that an
individual performs. An inherently governmental function includes functions that
require either the exercise of significant[4] discretion in applying Government authority, or making decisions for the Government that require significant value judg-
ments. Inherently governmental functions normally fall into two categories: the act
of governing, *i.e.*, the substantial discretionary exercise of Government authority or
of significant monetary transactions and entitlements.

(1) An inherently governmental function involves, among other things, the
interpretation and execution of the laws of the United States so as to—

(i) Bind the United States to take or not to take some action by contract,
policy, regulation, authorization, order, or otherwise through the exercise of significant judgment;

(ii) Determine, protect, and advance United States economic, political, territorial, property, or other interests by military or diplomatic action, civil or criminal
judicial proceedings, contract management, or otherwise;

(iii) Significantly affect the life, liberty, or property of private persons;

(iv) Commission, appoint, direct, or control officers or employees of
the United States performing inherently governmental functions or in critical
positions; or

(v) Exert ultimate control over the acquisition, use, or disposition of the
property, real or personal, tangible or intangible, of the United States, including the
collection, control, or disbursement of Federal funds.

(2) Inherently governmental functions do not normally include gathering information for or providing advice, opinions, recommendations, or ideas to Government
officials or project specific services (such as technical planning, analysis and development of documentation and strategies required for decision making by Government officials, design, or construction). They also do not include functions that are
primarily ministerial and internal in nature.

(3) The following examples of inherently governmental functions are not all inclusive:

(i) Directing the conduct of criminal investigations for the government.

(ii) Controlling prosecutions by the government and issuing decisions on behalf of the US government.

(iii) Commanding any military personnel of the United States, especially the leadership of military personnel who are members of the combat, combat support, or combat service support role.

(iv) Conducting foreign relations and the determination of foreign policy.

(v) Determining agency policy through determining the content and application of regulations, statements of policy binding on persons employed by the agency or otherwise, or directing agency action when no policy applies, among other things.

(vi) Determining Federal program priorities for budget requests.

(vii) Directing or controlling of Federal employees who are in critical positions as determined under guidelines issued by the Office of Management and Budget.[5]

(viii) Directing or controlling intelligence and counter-intelligence operations.

(ix) Selecting or rejecting individuals for Federal Government employment, when the decision involves discretionary exercise of hiring authority.

(4) The approval of position descriptions and performance standards for Federal employees performing inherently governmental functions or in critical positions.

(5) Determining what Government property is to be disposed of and on what terms when that determination involves the discretionary exercise of disposal or sale authority.

(6) In Federal procurement activities with respect to prime contracts—

(i) Determining what supplies or services the Government will acquire if doing so involves discretionary exercise of authority to set government requirements;

(ii) Participating as a voting member on any source selection boards;

(iii) Providing final approval to any contractual documents, to include documents defining requirements, incentive plans, and evaluation criteria that will bind the Government;

(iv) Making contract award decisions and signing contractual documents committing the Government;

(v) Administering contracts (including decision making and signing contractual documents, ordering changes in contract performance or contract quantities, taking action based on evaluations of contractor performance, and accepting or rejecting contractor products or services) when the administration involves the discretionary exercise of contractual authority;

(vi) Terminating contracts; and

(vii) Determining finally whether contract costs are reasonable, allocable, and allowable; and

(viii) Participating as a voting member on performance evaluation boards.

(6) Approving agency responses to Freedom of Information Act requests (other than routine responses that, because of statute, regulation, or agency policy, do not require the exercise of judgment in determining whether documents are to be released or withheld), and the approval of agency responses to the administrative appeals of denials of Freedom of Information Act requests.

(7) Conducting administrative hearings to determine the eligibility of any person for a security clearance, or involving actions that affect matters of personal reputation or eligibility to participate in Government programs except as to alternative dispute resolution procedures.

(8) Approving Federal licensing actions and inspections when the approval involves the discretionary application of licensing criteria.

(9) Determining budget policy, guidance, and strategy.

(10) Collecting, controlling, and disbursing of fees, royalties, duties, fines, taxes, and other public funds that require the discretionary application of criteria to these activities or that are not controlled by defined processes and procedures to minimize risk of misuse, unless authorized by statute, such as 31 U.S.C. 952 (relating to private collection contractors) and 31 U.S.C. 3718 (relating to private attorney collection services). Examples of defining processes and procedures that have adequate controls include but are not limited to —

(i) Collection of fees, fines, penalties, costs, or other charges from visitors to or patrons of mess halls, post or base exchange concessions, national parks, and similar entities or activities, or during other monetary exchanges, where the amount to be collected is easily calculated or predetermined and the funds collected can be easily controlled using standard cash management techniques; and

(ii) Routine voucher and invoice examination.

(11) Controlling treasury accounts.

(12) Administration of public trusts.

(13) Approving agency Congressional testimony, responses to Congressional correspondence, or responses to audit reports from the Inspector General, the Government Accountability Office, or other Federal audit entity.

B.   **Critical Functions and Positions**. Critical functions are not inherently governmental functions but are so important to ensuring an agency achieves its missions or operates in accordance with its policy that the function must be controlled by government employees. A critical position[6] is a position, job or billet that oversees a critical function, but not necessarily in a direct supervisory role. Each agency using reasonable judgment determines what positions are critical to it based on its missions; how it operates, e.g., extensive organic staff vs. extensive use of service or other contractors overseen by the agency; and any pertinent laws or regulations. To effectively control a critical function, the person filling the critical control position must either have the requisite subject matter expertise to rigorously evaluate the work of those performing the pertinent critical function, or government staff, or contractor staff acting independently from those contractors performing the work that can supply requisite expertise. Having organic government staff is the preferred approach. Contractor employees can perform critical functions but not fill critical positions.

(1) Critical functions are often tasks that require exercising judgment and discretion to provide advice that those performing an inherently governmental function will consider in performing that function. For example, a critical position may be a subject matter expert who either oversees or evaluates the work product of a contractor providing advice or studies that the agency may rely upon in performing its mission, altering it operations, formulating regulations or providing agency positions to other agencies or other branches of government.

(2) Critical positions oversee contractors who:

(i) are working where a reasonable person might assume that they are agency employees or representatives, or:

(ii) interpret agency policies,

(3) A function is critical if the function involves more than ministerial services or more than the compilation of objective facts or data, *and* the work product could also significantly influence:

(i) budgets;

(ii) agency missions, operations or potential reorganization;

(iii) requirements definition, planning, evaluation, award or management of agency contracts;

(iv) evaluating, mediating or otherwise facilitating arbitration or alternative dispute resolution; or

(v) legal advice to other than the agency office of legal counsel.

(4) A function may also be considered critical if:

(i) those performing the function have access to health information, personally identity information, confidential business information or to other sensitive information submitted to the government, or;

(ii) the performance of the function exposes individuals to immediate physical harm if performed improperly, e.g., armed security activities, prisoner detention, or supporting interrogations.

C.   **Organic expertise and technical capability**. In accordance with total workforce plans, positions should also be identified to ensure the agency has adequate in-house expertise and capability to fill positions exercising inherently governmental functions and critical positions. Consideration of directly hiring personnel to fill inherently governmental functions and critical positions should balance the benefit of varied technical experience against internal agency experience.

APPENDIX 3
THE NATIONAL DEFENSE AUTHORIZATION ACT
FOR FISCAL YEAR 2008

SEC. 862,
THE NATIONAL DEFENSE AUTHORIZATION ACT
FOR FISCAL YEAR 2008,
PUBLIC LAW 110-181 (DECEMBER 5, 2007):
CONTRACTORS PERFORMING PRIVATE SECURITY FUNCTIONS
IN AREAS OF COMBAT OPERATIONS

(a) REGULATIONS ON CONTRACTORS PERFORMING PRIVATE
SECURITY FUNCTIONS.—

(1) IN GENERAL.—Not later than 120 days after the date of the enactment
of this Act, the Secretary of Defense, in coordination with the Secretary of State,
shall prescribe regulations on the selection, training, equipping, and conduct of
personnel performing private security functions under a covered contract in an
area of combat operations.

(2) ELEMENTS.—The regulations prescribed under subsection (a) shall,
at a minimum, establish—

(A) a process for registering, processing, accounting for, and keeping
appropriate records of personnel performing private security functions in an
area of combat operations;

(B) a process for authorizing and accounting for weapons to be carried by,
or available to be used by, personnel performing private security functions in
an area of combat operations;

(C) a process for the registration and identification of armored vehicles, helicopters, and other military vehicles operated by contractors performing private security functions in an area of combat operations;

(D) a process under which contractors are required to report all incidents, and persons other than contractors are permitted to report incidents, in which—

(i) a weapon is discharged by personnel performing private security functions in an area of combat operations;

(ii) personnel performing private security functions in an area of combat operations are killed or injured; or

(iii) persons are killed or injured, or property is destroyed, as a result of conduct by contractor personnel;

(E) a process for the independent review and, if practicable, investigation of—

(i) incidents reported pursuant to subparagraph (D); and

(ii) incidents of alleged misconduct by personnel performing private security functions in an area of combat operations;

(F) requirements for qualification, training, screening (including, if practicable, through background checks), and security for performing private security functions in an area of combat operations;

(G) guidance to the commanders of the combatant commands on the issuance of—

(i) orders, directives, and instructions to contractors performing private security functions relating to equipment, force protection, security, health, safety, or relations and interaction with locals;

(ii) predeployment training requirements for personnel performing private security functions in an area of combat operations, addressing the requirements of this section, resources and assistance available to contractor personnel, country information and cultural training, and guidance on working with host country nationals and military; and

(iii) rules on the use of force for personnel performing private security functions in an area of combat operations;

(H) a process by which a commander of a combatant command may request an action described in subsection (b)(3); and

(I) a process by which the training requirements referred to in subparagraph (G)(ii) shall be implemented.

(3) AVAILABILITY OF ORDERS, DIRECTIVES, AND INSTRUCTIONS.—. The regulations prescribed under subsection (a) shall include mechanisms to ensure the provision and availability of the orders, directives, and instructions referred to in paragraph (2)(G)(i) to contractors referred to in that paragraph, including through the maintenance of a single location (including an Internet website, to the extent consistent with security considerations) at or through which such contractors may access such orders, directives, and instructions.

(b) CONTRACT CLAUSE ON CONTRACTORS PERFORMING PRIVATE SECURITY FUNCTIONS.—

(1) REQUIREMENT UNDER FAR.—Not later than 180 days after the date of the enactment of this Act, the Federal Acquisition Regulation issued in accordance with section 25 of the Office of Federal Procurement Policy Act (41 U.S.C. 421) shall be revised to require the insertion into each covered contract (or, in the case of a task order, the contract under which the task order is issued) of a contract clause addressing the selection, training, equipping, and conduct of personnel performing private security functions under such contract.

(2) CLAUSE REQUIREMENT.—The contract clause required by paragraph (1) shall require, at a minimum, that the contractor concerned shall—

(A) comply with regulations prescribed under subsection (a), including any revisions or updates to such regulations, and follow the procedures established in such regulations for—

(i) registering, processing, accounting for, and keeping appropriate records of personnel performing private security functions in an area of combat operations;

(ii) authorizing and accounting of weapons to be carried by, or available to be used by, personnel performing private security functions in an area of combat operations;

(iii) registration and identification of armored vehicles, helicopters, and other military vehicles operated by contractors and subcontractors performing private security functions in an area of combat operations; and

(iv) the reporting of incidents in which—

(I) a weapon is discharged by personnel performing private security functions in an area of combat operations;

(II) personnel performing private security functions in an area of combat operations are killed or injured; or

(III) persons are killed or injured, or property is destroyed, as a result of conduct by contractor personnel;

(B) ensure that all personnel performing private security functions under such contract are briefed on and understand their obligation to comply with—

(i) qualification, training, screening (including, if practicable, through background checks), and security requirements established by the Secretary of Defense for personnel performing private security functions in an area of combat operations;

(ii) applicable laws and regulations of the United States and the host country, and applicable treaties and international agreements, regarding the performance of the functions of the contractor;

(iii) orders, directives, and instructions issued by the applicable commander of a combatant command relating toequipment, force protection, security, health, safety, or relations and interaction with locals; and

(iv) rules on the use of force issued by the applicable commander of a combatant command for personnel performing private security functions in an area of combat operations; and

(C) cooperate with any investigation conducted by the Department of Defense pursuant to subsection (a)(2)(E) by providing access to employees of the contractor and relevant information in the possession of the contractor regarding the incident concerned.

(3) NONCOMPLIANCE OF PERSONNEL WITH CLAUSE.—The contracting officer for a covered contract may direct the contractor, at its own expense, to remove or replace any personnel performing private security functions in an area of combat operations who violate or fail to comply with applicable requirements of the clause required by this subsection. If the

violation or failure to comply is a gross violation or failure or is repeated, the contract may be terminated for default.

(4) APPLICABILITY.—The contract clause required by this subsection shall be included in all covered contracts awarded on or after the date that is 180 days after the date of the enactment of this Act. Federal agencies shall make best efforts to provide for the inclusion of the contract clause required by this subsection in covered contracts awarded before such date.

(5) INSPECTOR GENERAL REPORT ON PILOT PROGRAM ON IMPOSITION OF FINES FOR NONCOMPLIANCE OF PERSONNEL WITH CLAUSE.—Not later than March 30, 2008, the Inspector General of the Department of Defense shall submit to Congress a report assessing the feasibility and advisability of carrying out a pilot program for the imposition of fines on contractors for personnel who violate or fail to comply with applicable requirements of the clause required by this section as a mechanism for enhancing the compliance of such personnel with the clause. The report shall include—

(A) an assessment of the feasibility and advisability of carrying out the pilot program; and

(B) if the Inspector General determines that carrying out the pilot program is feasible and advisable—

(i) recommendations on the range of contracts and subcontracts to which the pilot program should apply; and

(ii) a schedule of fines to be imposed under the pilot program for various types of personnel actions or failures.

(c) AREAS OF COMBAT OPERATIONS.—

(1) DESIGNATION.—The Secretary of Defense shall designate the areas constituting an area of combat operations for purposes of this section by not later than 120 days after the date of the enactment of this Act.

(2) PARTICULAR AREAS.—Iraq and Afghanistan shall be included in the areas designated as an area of combat operations under paragraph (1).

(3) ADDITIONAL AREAS.—The Secretary may designate any additional area as an area constituting an area of combat operations for purposes of this section if the Secretary determines that the presence or potential of combat

operations in such area warrants designation of such area as an area of combat operations for purposes of this section.

(4) MODIFICATION OR ELIMINATION OF DESIGNATION.—The Secretary may modify or cease the designation of an area under this subsection as an area of combat operations if the Secretary determines that combat operations are no longer ongoing in such area.

(d) EXCEPTION.—The requirements of this section shall not apply to contracts entered into by elements of the intelligence community in support of intelligence activities.

NOTES

Introduction

1. Cited in *The Economist* (June 13, 2009): 21. According to the Stockholm International Peace Research Institute (SIPRI), the FY 2008 U.S. defense budget reached $661 billion and is projected to reach $710 billion in 2010. In 2008, the U.S. share, at 4.3 percent of GDP, was 43 percent of the world total. "Media Background—Military Expenditure SIPRI Yearbook 2010," SIPRI, Stockholm, June 2, 2010: 3, 8. Available at www.sipri.org/media/pressreleases/pressreleasetranslations/storypackage_milex.

2. Project on National Security Reform. "Forging a New Shield: Executive Summary." Washington, DC: Author, November 2008: i. The PNSR website contains a wealth of comprehensive and detailed material: www.pnsr.org/.

3. Commission on Wartime Contracting in Iraq and Afghanistan. "At What Cost? Contingency Contracting in Iraq and Afghanistan Interim Report." Commission on Wartime Contracting in Iraq and Afghanistan, Washington, DC: Author, June 2009: 21.

4. The most egregious known incident to date took place on September 16, 2007, when private security contractors working for Blackwater USA were conducting an armed convoy through the Nisoor Square neighborhood of Baghdad. For reasons as yet unclear, the contractors stopped the convoy and began a shooting barrage that resulted in the deaths of seventeen and the wounding of twenty-four Iraqi civilians. In a Memorandum Opinion on December 31, 2009, U.S. District Judge Ricardo M. Urbina dismissed criminal charges against the former Blackwater security guards. For Judge Urbina's ninety-page ruling, go to http://letterofapology.com/wp-content/uploads/2009/12/blackwateropinion.pdf.

5. Commission on Army Acquisition and Program Management in Expeditionary Operations (the Gansler Commission). "Urgent Reform Required: Army Expeditionary Contracting." Washington, DC: Author. October 31, 2007.

6. Government Accountability Office, GAO-08-572T, March 11, 2008: 1. The comptroller general is the head of GAO and is confirmed through a joint executive-legislative selection and appointment process for a fifteen-year term of office.

7. Quadrennial Defense Review Report, Office of the Secretary of Defense, February 6, 2006: 75; available at www.defenselink.mil/qdr/report/Report20060203.pdf.

8. See "Report of the Defense Science Board Task Force on Institutionalizing Stability Operations Within DoD," Office of the Under Secretary of Defense for Acquisition, Technology, and Logistics, Washington, DC, September 2005: 14, 31, 33, 38, 49; available at www.acq.osd.mil/dsb/reports/2005-09-Stability_Final.pdf.

9. See: "Army Strategic Guidance 2005": 6, 15, available at www.army.mil/references/ APSG14Jan05.doc; and "Air Force Strategic Plan 2006–2008": 17, available at www.au .af.mil/au/awc/awcgate/af/af_strat_plan_06-08.pdf .

10. See the bibliography for full information on these authors' books. Leading academic presses, including Cambridge, Cornell, Oxford, and Yale, have published a number of books on contractors. It should also be noted that major think tanks and nongovernmental organizations are actively involved in researching and publishing on the topic of the contractors. These include the Bonn International Center for Conversion, Brookings Institution, Center for a New American Security, Geneva Center for the Democratic Control of Armed Forces, Human Rights First, New America Foundation, RAND Corporation, and Stockholm International Peace Research Institute.

11. For a review of the public debate on contracting out, see John R. Luckey, Valerie Bailey Grasso, and Kate M. Manuel, "Inherently Governmental Functions and Department of Defense Operations: Background, Issues, and Options for Congress," Congressional Research Service (CRS) Report for Congress, Washington, DC, September 14, 2009: 4–7. On the continuity from one administration to another, I am much influenced by the works of Paul C. Light. His most recent book is *A Government Ill-Executed: The Decline of the Federal Service and How to Reverse It* (Cambridge, MA: Harvard University Press, 2008).

12. The traditional civil–military concern with "controlling the guardians" is, however, a serious issue in most, if not all, newer democracies. See Thomas C. Bruneau and Scott D. Tollefson, eds., *Who Guards the Guardians and How: Democratic Civil–Military Relations* (Austin: University of Texas Press, 2006).

13. A good sample of these works includes: Risa A. Brooks and Elizabeth A. Stanley, eds., *Creating Military Power: The Sources of Military Effectiveness* (Stanford, CA: Stanford University Press, 2007); Michael C. Desch, *Power and Military Effectiveness: The Fallacy of Democratic Triumphalism* (Baltimore: The Johns Hopkins University Press, 2008); Stephen Biddle and Stephen Long, "Democracy and Military Effectiveness," *Journal of Conflict Resolution* 48, 4 (August 2004): 525–546; and Risa A. Brooks, *Shaping Strategy: The Civil–Military Politics of Strategic Assessment* (Princeton, NJ: Princeton University Press, 2008).

14. "Partnership Action Plan on Defence Institution Building," NATO, June 7, 2004; available from the NATO website at www.nato.int/cps/en/SID-38020F1A-2CF2CA8E/ natolive/topics_50083.htm.

15. "Government Performance Results Act of 1993," Office of Management and Budget, Washington, DC: Section 2 "Findings and Purposes," a. 2, January 5, 1993.

16. "Report to the Ranking Minority Member, Committee on Governmental Affairs, U.S. Senate, Status of Achieving Outcomes and Addressing Major Management Challenges," U.S. General Accounting Office, GAO-01-783, June 2001: 2.

17. Only the book by Eliot Cohen, *Supreme Command: Soldiers, Statesmen, and Leadership in Wartime* (New York: The Free Press, 2002) figures on any of the lists for the four U.S. armed services. Also see Judith Hicks Stiehm, "Civil–Military Relations in War College Curriculum," *Armed Forces & Society* 27, 2 (Winter 2001): 273–294.

18. Quoted in Arthur L. Stinchcombe, *Constructing Social Theories* (New York: Harcourt, Brace & World, 1968): v.

19. Peter A. Hall and Rosemary C. R. Taylor, "Political Science and the Three New Institutionalisms," *Political Studies*, XLIV (1996): 936–957; and Kathleen Thelen, "Historical Institutionalism in Comparative Politics," *Annual Review of Political Science* (1996): 369–404.

20. Hall and Taylor, "Political Science and the Three New Institutionalisms," 938.

21. Claus Offe, "Political Institutions and Social Power: Conceptual Explorations" in Ian Shapiro, Stephen Skowronek, and Daniel Gavin, eds., *Rethinking Political Institutions: The Art of the State* (New York: New York University Press, 2006): 9.

22. Ibid.: 14–18.

23. Most of the recent analyses of security issues by academics use the concepts of New Institutionalism in one form or another. In the bibliography, see, for example, Avant, 1994; Brooks, 2008; and Zegart, 2007.

24. The list of interviewees is included as a separate section in the bibliography.

25. See the list of abbreviations for definitions.

26. For a breakdown of the data, go to the Freedom House website at www .freedomhouse.org/.

Chapter 1

1. Things are no more stable today, in early 2011. The International Crisis Group still regularly features Nepal, along with Somalia, Bosnia, and other nations facing intractable political situations. See www.crisisgroup.org/home.

2. The best-known of Huntington's works on civil–military relations is *The Soldier and the State: The Theory and Politics of Civil-Military Relations* (Cambridge, MA: Belknap Press, 1981; originally published in 1957).

3. Peter D. Feaver, "Civil–Military Relations," *Annual Review of Political Science* 2 (1999): 211–241; on the renaissance, see 236–238.

4. The contributions I have in mind include the following: Risa A. Brooks and Elizabeth A. Stanley, eds., *Creating Military Power: The Sources of Military Effectiveness* (Stanford, CA: Stanford University Press, 2007); Michael C. Desch, *Power and Military Effectiveness: The Fallacy of Democratic Triumphalism* (Baltimore: Johns Hopkins University Press, 2008); Stephen Biddle and Stephen Long, "Democracy and Military Effectiveness," *Journal of Conflict Resolution* 48, 4 (August 2004): 525–546; and Risa A. Brooks, *Shaping Strategy: The Civil–Military Politics of Strategic Assessment* (Princeton, NJ: Princeton University Press, 2008).

5. See the Bibliography for the complete references.

6. Paul Bracken, "Reconsidering Civil–Military Relations," in Don M. Snider and Miranda A. Carlton-Carew, eds., *U.S. Civil-Military Relations in Crisis or Transition?* (Washington, DC: Center for Strategic & International Studies, 1995), 145.

7. Ibid., 146.

8. Peter D. Feaver, *Armed Servants: Agency, Oversight, and Civil-Military Relations* (Cambridge, MA: Harvard University Press, 2003), 7.

9. John Allen Williams, "Political Science Perspectives on the Military and Civil–Military Relations," in Giuseppe Caforio, ed., *Social Sciences and the Military: An Interdisciplinary Overview* (London and New York: Routledge, 2007), 93.

10. Eliot A. Cohen, *Supreme Command: Soldiers, Statesmen, and Leadership in Wartime* (New York: The Free Press, 2002). Cohen debunks this "normal" theory throughout his book.

11. The annual Senior Conference, U.S. Military Academy at West Point, May 31–June 2, 2007. The book from the conference was published in late 2009. See Suzanne C. Nielsen and Don M. Snider, eds., *American Civil–Military Relations: The Soldier and the State in a New Era* (Baltimore: Johns Hopkins University Press, 2009). The most recent book is Mackubin Thomas Owens, *US Civil–Military Relations after 9/11: Renegotiating the Civil–Military Bargain* (New York: Continuum, 2011).

12. It must be noted that Cohen, in *Supreme Command*, Feaver in *Armed Servants*, and several authors in Nielsen and Snider find very serious fault with Huntington's formulation. Yet, as Cohen and Feaver observe, it remains the "normal," and thus dominant, theory in the field.

13. Bengt Abrahamsson, *Military Professionalization and Political Power* (Beverly Hills and London: Sage Publications, 1972), 159.

14. Feaver, *Armed Servants*, 38.

15. Ibid., 18.

16. Samuel E. Finer, *The Man on Horseback: The Role of the Military in Politics* (New Brunswick, NJ: Transaction Publishers, 2002; originally published in 1962), 25–30.

17. Alfred Stepan, "The New Professionalism," in Alfred Stepan, ed., *Authoritarian Brazil: Origins, Policies, and Future* (New Haven, CT: Yale University Press, 1973); see the table on p. 52.

18. Ibid., 47–65. See also Alfred Stepan, *The Military in Politics: Changing Patterns in Brazil* (Princeton, NJ: Princeton University Press, 1971).

19. Brian McAllister Linn, *The Echo of Battle: The Army's Way of War* (Cambridge, MA: Harvard University Press, 2007).

20. Ibid., 41.

21. Huntington, *The Soldier and the State*, 3.

22. Feaver, "Civil–Military Relations," 211.

23. Dale R. Herspring, *The Pentagon and the Presidency: Civil–Military Relations from FDR to George W. Bush* (Lawrence: University Press of Kansas, 2005), xii.

24. Bracken states this issue well:

> The central role that civilian control has played in civil–military relations is understandable. But in its raw form it is a trivial problem because under nearly any conceivable set of arrangements civilian control is assured. To over-concentrate on it when it is inappropriate to do so will only elevate a host of ordinary misunderstandings and differences into a high political arena where they do not belong. Moreover, it will distract attention from other important dimensions that characterize the relationship of the military to the state."

Bracken, "Reconsidering Civil–Military Relations," 163.

25. Richard H. Kohn, "The Erosion of Civilian Control of the Military in the United States Today," *Naval War College Review* 55, 3 (Summer 2002).

26. Several of those papers have been posted on the FPRI website. Papers from the conference can also be found in *Orbis* 52, 2 (Spring 2008).

27. Thomas S. Szayna, Kevin F. McCarthy, Jerry M. Sollinger, Linda J. Demaine, Jefferson P. Marquis, and Brett Steele, "The Civil–Military Gap in the United States: Does It Exist, Why, and Does It Matter?" No. MG-379-A. Santa Monica, CA: RAND Corporation, 2007: xvi–xvii.

28. Bracken, 146; emphasis in the original. For further analysis of this issue, see the very useful article by Deborah Avant, "Conflicting Indicators of 'Crisis' in American Civil–Military Relations," *Armed Forces & Society*, 24, 3 (Spring 1998): 375–388.

29. See the special issue of *Armed Forces & Society* 27, 2 (Winter 2001), on the issue of "a cultural gap between the military and American society."

30. Feaver, *Armed Servants*, 292. Feaver suggests the relevance of his approach to the analysis of other countries but doesn't actually carry out such an analysis in any publications that I am aware of.

31. The Third Wave of democracy, as Sam Huntington termed it in his book with the same title, began on April 25, 1974, when a small group of junior officers in Portugal overthrew the country's dictatorship in a remarkably peaceful coup known as the "Carnation Revolution" and eventually instituted full democratic rule.

32. For more on these points, see in Bruneau and Tollefson, *Who Guards the Guardians*, especially the Introduction; and Thomas C. Bruneau and Florina Cristiana Matei, "Towards a New Conceptualization of Democratization and Civil–Military Relations," *Democratization* 15, 5 (December 2008): 909–913. For a strong appeal to improve theoretical approaches to civil–military relations, see David Pion-Berlin, ed., *Civil–Military Relations in Latin America: New Analytical Perspectives* (Chapel Hill: University of North Carolina Press, 2001), 1–35.

33. Among Olmeda's many publications are several on civil–military relations. Of particular note is his edited volume, *Democracias fragiles: las relaciones civiles-militares en el mundo iberoamericano* (Valencia, Spain: Tirant lo Blanch, 2005). For another meta-analysis of a smaller sample from *AF&S*, see Arjana Olldashi, "Civil–Military Relations in Emerging Democracies as Found in the Articles of *Armed Forces & Society*," Political Science Department, Texas State University-San Marcos, 2002; available at http://ecommons.txstate.edu/arp/54/.

34. Feaver, "Civil–Military Relations," 211.

35. Gerardo L. Munck and Richard Snyder, "Debating the Direction of Comparative Politics: An Analysis of Leading Journals," *Comparative Political Studies* 40, 1 (January 2007): 5–31. Their data set codes 319 articles from three journals: *Comparative Political Studies*, *Comparative Politics*, and *World Politics* (only articles relevant to comparative politics), from several years between 1989 and 2004. The analysis was based on twenty-nine variables, a description of which can be found on the authors' faculty web pages at, respectively, www-rcf.usc.edu/~munck/ or http://brown.edu/polisci/people/snyder/.

36. Munck and Snyder, "Debating the Direction of Comparative Politics," 8–10.

37. The other 400-plus articles in *the sample time frame* deal with a variety of issues, particularly concerning the military profession.

38. *Armed Forces & Society* data set (1989–2007) (*N* = 103).

39. Munck and Snyder, "Debating the Direction of Comparative Politics," 10.

40. The data are drawn from the variable "time" subset, of the *Armed Forces and Society* data set.

41. Munck and Snyder, "Debating the Direction of Comparative Politics," 10.

42. This is based on the definitions from Munck and Snyder:

A theory is understood to consist of a proposition or set of propositions about how or why the world is as it is. An empirical analysis is understood to consist of an inquiry based on observable manifestations of a concept or concepts. Thus, empirical analysis is not restricted to causal hypothesis testing. In turn, the term *descriptive* is not used, as is common, in a critical fashion, as when a work is characterized as being *merely descriptive*. Here, the term is used in a positive manner, as referring to accounts about what the state of the world is, that are differentiated from causal accounts that seek to explain why the state of the world is as it is." (Ibid., 11)

43. Ibid., 11.

44. Ibid., 18–19.

45. Munck and Snyder, "Debating the Direction of Comparative Politics," 21.

46. Ibid., 22.

47. In his introduction to the journal, Janowitz wrote, "Its contents should, at the same time, be of interest to political and administrative leaders, persons concerned with public affairs, and journalists among others. . . . Therefore, a special section on policy papers will endeavor to explore the implications of scholarly research for public policy." "Armed Forces and Society: An Interdisciplinary Journal," *Armed Forces & Society* 1, 1 (Fall 1974): 3–4.

48. Munck and Snyder, "Debating the Direction of Comparative Politics," 12. The reference is to T. Skocpol, "Doubly Engaged Social Science: The Promise of Comparative Historical

Analysis," in J. Mahoney and D. Rueschemeyer, eds., *Comparative Historical Analysis in the Social Sciences* (New York: Cambridge University Press, 2003), 407–428.

49. Ibid., 26.

Chapter 2

1. Samuel P. Huntington, *The Third Wave: Democratization in the Late Twentieth Century* (Norman: University of Oklahoma Press, 1991).

2. Thomas C. Bruneau and Alex MacLeod, *Politics in Contemporary Portugal: Parties and the Consolidation of Democracy* (Boulder, CO: Lynne Rienner Publishers, 1986); and Felipe Agüero, *Soldiers, Civilians and Democracy: Post-Franco Spain in Comparative Perspective* (Baltimore: Johns Hopkins University Press, 1995).

3. Juan J. Linz and Alfred Stepan, *Problems of Democratic Transition and Consolidation: Southern Europe, South America, and Post-Communist Europe* (Baltimore: Johns Hopkins University Press, 1996). For the application of a broad conceptual model to newer democracies in Latin America, which takes consideration of the global environment, see Michael C. Desch, *Civilian Control of the Military: The Changing Security Environment* (Baltimore: The Johns Hopkins University Press, 2001).

4. Adam Przeworski, *Democracy and the Market: Political and Economic Reforms in Eastern Europe and Latin America* (New York: Cambridge University Press, 1991); and Philippe Schmitter, "The Consolidation of Political Democracies: Processes, Rhythms, Sequences, and Types," in G. Pridham, ed., *Transitions to Democracy* (Aldershot, UK: Dartmouth, 1995).

5. Felipe Agüero, "Democratic Consolidation and the Military in Southern Europe and South America," in Richard Gunther, Nikiforos Diamandouros, and H. Pulhe, eds., *The Politics of Democratic Consolidations in Southern Europe* (Baltimore: The Johns Hopkins University Press, 1995); Andrew Cottey, Timothy Edmunds, and Anthony Forster, eds., *Democratic Control of the Military in Postcommunist Europe:*

Guarding the Guards (New York: Palgrave, 2002); David Pion-Berlin, *Through Corridors of Power: Institutions and Civil–Military Relations in Argentina* (University Park: Pennsylvania State University Press, 1997); David Pion-Berlin, ed., *Civil–Military Relations in Latin America: New Analytical Perspectives* (Chapel Hill: University of North Carolina Press, 2001); Alfred Stepan, *Rethinking Military Politics: Brazil and the Southern Cone* (Princeton, NJ: Princeton University Press, 1988); and Harold A. Trinkunas, *Crafting Civilian Control of the Armed Forces in Venezuela: A Comparative Perspective* (Chapel Hill: University of North Carolina Press, 2006).

6. See Kiernan Williams and Dennis Deletant, *Security Intelligence Services in New Democracies: The Czech Republic, Slovakia and Romania* (Basingstoke, UK: Palgrave, 2001); Thomas C. Bruneau and Steven C. Boraz, eds., *Reforming Intelligence: Obstacles to Democratic Control and Effectiveness* (Austin: University of Texas Press, 2007); and Stuart Farson, Peter Gill, Mark Phythian, and Shlomo Shpiro, eds., *PSI Handbook of Global Security and Intelligence; National Approaches*, Volumes 1 and 2 (Westport, CT: Praeger Security International, 2008).

7. There are two exceptions. One is Timothy Edmunds, "What Are Armed Forces For? The Changing Nature of Military Roles in Europe," *International* Affairs 82, 6 (2006): 1059–1075; and a working paper by Felipe Agüero, "The New 'Double Challenge': Simultaneously Crafting Democratic Control and Efficacy Concerning Military, Police and Intelligence," Geneva Centre for the Democratic Control of Armed Forces (DCAF), April 2005.

8. I am encouraged to see that the importance of effectiveness is forcefully advocated in a recent article by the eminent British scholar of strategy, Hew Strachan. See Hew Strachan, "Making Strategy: Civil–Military Relations after Iraq," *Survival* 48, 3 (Autumn 2006): 59–82, especially 66.

9. The literature has focused exclusively on the armed forces and national defense; this focus, while appropriate for armed conflict, is less useful when analyzing other roles and missions and other security instruments. See, for example, Risa A. Brooks and Elizabeth A. Stanley, eds., *Creating Military Power: The Sources of Military Effectiveness* (Stanford, CA: Stanford University Press, 2007).

10. Chester Barnard, *The Functions of the Executive* (Cambridge, MA: Harvard University Press, 1962; originally published in 1938), 55.

11. Juan J. Linz, *The Breakdown of Democratic Regimes: Crisis, Breakdown, and Reequilibration* (Baltimore: The Johns Hopkins University Press, 1978), 20, 22.

12. Herbert A. Simon, *Administrative Behavior* (New York: Macmillan Company, 1961), 179. Italics in the original.

13. Arthur M. Okun, *Equality and Efficiency: The Big Tradeoff* (Washington, DC: The Brookings Institution, 1975), 2.

14. The classic, which is still used today, is Charles J. Hitch and Roland N. McKean, *The Economics of Defense in the Nuclear Age* (New York: Atheneum, 1978; originally published 1960); see especially Chapter 7, "Efficiency in Military Decisions," 105–132.

15. I have consistently found, especially in newer democracies, that only the war-fighting role is focused on. In addition to the pragmatic reason for not admitting any reconsideration, lest a decision is made to abolish the armed forces (as with Costa Rica and Panama), the argument of Carl H. Builder in *The Masks of War: American Military Styles in Strategy and Analysis* (Baltimore: The Johns Hopkins University Press, 1989) on "enduring personalities" is persuasive.

16. As Samuel E. Finer notes, "Instead of asking why the military engage in politics, we ought surely ask why they ever do otherwise. For at first sight the political advantages of the military vis-à-vis other and civilian groups are overwhelming. The military possess vastly superior organization. And they possess *arms*." Samuel E. Finer, *The Man on Horseback: The Role of the Military in Politics* (New Brunswick, NJ: Transaction Publishers, 2002; originally published in 1962), 5.

17. The most useful sources on "mandates" are: William J. Durch, *UN Peace Operations and the "Brahimi" Report*, Washington, DC: The Henry L. Stimson Center, revised October 2001; and Victoria K. Holt and Tobias C. Herkman, *The Impossible Mandate? Military Preparedness, the Responsibility to Protect and Modern Peace Operations* (Washington, DC: The Henry L. Stimson Center, 2006); see Chapter 5, "From the Council to the Field: Navigating Mandates and Rules of Engagement." The most concrete and current discussion of "caveats" is found in Paul Gallis, "NATO in Afghanistan: A Test of the Transatlantic Alliance." Washington, DC: Congressional Research Service (CRS) Report for Congress (updated October 23, 2007).

18. A similar point is made by David Pion-Berlin and Harold Trinkunas, "Democratization, Social Crisis and the Impact of Military Domestic Roles in Latin America," *Journal of Political and Military Sociology* 33, 1 (Summer 2005): 5–24. One expert forcefully insists, "When one includes consideration of the possibilities offered by foreseeable security environments in Latin America, the suggestion of completely divorcing the military from domestic law enforcement activities appears unworthy." Geoffrey B. Demarest, "The Overlap of Military and Police Responsibilities in Latin America," *Low Intensity Conflict & Law Enforcement* 4, 2 (Autumn, 1995): 252.

19. See Bruneau and Tollefson, *Who Guards the Guardians*; and Bruneau and Boraz, *Reforming Intelligence*. CCMR has recently analyzed the role of national security councils in improving the effectiveness of the security sector. See Thomas C. Bruneau, Florina Cristiana Matei, and Sak Sakoda, "National Security Councils: Their Potential Functions in Democratic Civil–Military Relations," *Defense & Security Analysis* 25, 3 (September 2009): 255–269.

20. For more on different formal oversight mechanisms see, for example, Table 3.1, "Summary of Oversight Mechanisms in Ascending Order of Intrusiveness," in Peter D. Feaver, *Armed Servants: Agency, Oversight, and Civil–Military Relations* (Cambridge, MA: Harvard University Press, 2003), 86. For a comprehensive (149-page) listing of all imaginable legislative oversight mechanisms, see Frederick Kaiser, Walter Oleszek, T. J. Halstead, Morton Rosenberg, and Todd Tatelman, "Congressional Oversight Manual," CRS Report for Congress, Washington, D.C., updated January 2, 2007.

21. The challenge of professionalizing international peacekeeping troops is serious and increasingly recognized. On a proposed solution to this topic, see Nina M. Serafino, "The Global Peace Operations Initiative: Background and Issues for Congress." Washington, DC: CRS Report for Congress, updated October 3, 2006.

22. Some obvious successes in the improvement of military effectiveness include the Goldwater-Nichols Defense Reorganization Act of 1986, which compelled U.S. military forces to work more jointly and thus more effectively; Colombian President Álvaro Uribe's Democratic Security Strategy, which began in 2003 and has resulted in increased security through a wide variety of measures; Romania's successful transition to a smaller, more professional force, now operating in Afghanistan, Iraq, and elsewhere, and its effective reformation of the intelligence system; and Mongolia's transition from a territorial defense strategy during the Cold War to deploying effective peacekeeping forces in Afghanistan, Iraq and ten U.N.-mandated missions.

23. Hew Strachan, "The Lost Meaning of Strategy," *Survival* 47, 3 (Autumn 2005): 52.

24. The Federal Acquisition Regulations include various preferences: prisoners (FAR 8.6), the blind and severely handicapped (FAR 8.7), and "small disadvantaged businesses, and women-owned small business concerns," (FAR 19.7); available at www.acquisition.gov/far/.

25. Hitch and McKean, *The Economics of Defense in the Nuclear Age.*

26. Sharon Caudle, "Homeland Security: Approaches to Results Management," *Public Performance & Management Review* 28, 3 (March 2005): 18; quoted from the manuscript version.

27. Feaver, *Armed Servants*, 86.

28. A good discussion of the GAO, which includes information on other countries' "supreme audit institutions" is in Frederick M. Kaiser, "GAO: Government Accountability Office and General Accounting Office." Washington, DC: CRS Report for Congress, updated June 22, 2007.

29. It should be noted that the GAO works with other countries to strengthen their supreme audit institutions. See the website for the International Organization of Supreme Audit Institutions (SAIs), which serves as the umbrella organization of the 189 SAIs worldwide: www.intosai.org.

30. The "official" document, fourteen pages long, is entitled "Security Sector Reform" with the emblems of the U.S. Agency for International Development, U.S.

Department of Defense, and the U.S. Department of State. It is undated, but it was compiled in 2009; there is no place of publication. Official U.S. adherence to the SSR approach follows from U.S. participation in, and adherence to, the Organisation for Economic Co-Operation and Development (OECD), Development Assistance Committee on SSR. See "Security System Reform and Governance," DAC Guidelines and Reference Series. Paris: OECD, 2005.

31. The concept of security sector reform was first publicized in a 1998 speech by Clare Short, first minister for international development in Britain's newly created (1997) Department for International Development. It emerged from several European development assistance programs, U.N. agencies, and other international organizations. See Timothy Edmunds, *Security Sector Reform in Transforming Societies: Croatia, Serbia and Montenegro* (Manchester, UK: Manchester University Press, 2007), especially Chapter 2, "Security Sector Reform: A Framework for Analysis," 15–50. This is the clearest and most straightforward discussion on SSR.

32. Mirolsav Hadzic, "The Concept of Security Sector Reform," in Philipp Fluri and Miroslav Hadzic, eds., "Sourcebook on Security Sector Reform: Collection of Papers." Geneva and Belgrade: DCAF, March 2004, 11–22; available at www.dcaf.ch/publications/.

33. Hans-Georg Ehrart and Albrecht Schnabel, *Security Sector Reform and Post-Conflict Peacebuilding* (Tokyo: United Nations University Press, 2005).

34. For proposals on their inclusion see the following: Roberto Perito, "The Private Sector in Security Sector Reform: Essential but Not Yet Optimized," U.S. Institute of Peace, January 2009, available at www.usip.org/files/resources/USIP_0109.PDF; and Anna Richards and Henry Smith, "Addressing the Role of Private Security Companies within Security Sector Reform Programmes," *Journal of Security Sector Management* 5, 1 (May 2007): 1–14.

35. Timothy Edmunds, "Defining Security Sector Reform," in "Civil–Military Relations and Security Sector Reform in the 21st Century," *CMR Network*, 3 (October 2001).

36. Ibid. SSR may include nonstatutory security force institutions (liberation armies, guerrilla armies, and private security companies); see also Martina Fischer, Hans J. Gießmann, and Beatrix Schmelzle, eds., *Berghof Handbook for Conflict Transformation* (Berlin: Berghof Research Center for Constructive Conflict Management, updated 2009); available only on the web at www.berghof-handbook.net/uploads/download/dialogue2_wulf.pdf.

37. Search for Common Ground, "Resource Guide on Security Sector Reform," Washington, DC: Author, December 21, 2005; available at www.sfcg.org/programmes/ilr/security1.pdf.

38. More than a dozen definitions of SSR can be found in Edmunds, *Security Sector Reform*. David Chutter defines it as "the efficient and effective provision of state

and human security within a framework of democratic governance" in "Understanding Security Sector Reform," *Journal of Security Sector Management* 4, 2 (2006); Malcolm Chalmers, Christopher Cushing, Luc van de Goor, and Andrew McLean, "Implementation Framework for Security System Reform (IF-SSR)," draft manuscript for the Organization for Economic Cooperation and Development, Development Assistance Committee, SSR Practitioner's Workshop, Ghana, December 2005, available at www.africansecurty.org; the Institute for Security Studies, Pretoria, available at www.iss.co.za; "Security Sector Reform," paper for the regional conference, Special Coordinator of the Stability Pact for South Eastern Europe, Working Table III, Security and Defence Issues, Bucharest, 25–26 October 2001, available at www.stabilitypact.org/reg-conf/011015-ssr.doc; Michael Brzoska, "The Concept of Security Sector Reform in Security Sector Reform," Briefing Paper Number 15, Bonn International Center for Conversion, Bonn, 2000: 9-11; "Resource Guide on Security Sector Reform," Search for Common Ground, Washington, DC, available at www.sfcg.org/programmes/ilr/security1.pdf; Norwegian Initiative on Small Arms Transfers, Oslo; and "Security Sector Reform and Governance: Policy and Good Practice," OECD Development Assistance Committee, Paris, 2004, available at www.oecd.org/dataoecd/8/39/31785288.pdf.

39. Mark Sedra, "European Approaches to Security Sector Reform: Examining Trends through the Lens of Afghanistan," *European Security* 15, 3 (September 2006): 323–338.

40. Ibid.

41. Ibid. These are called "partial programs."

42. Albrecht Schnabel and Hans-Georg Ehrhart, "Post-Conflict Societies and the Military: Challenges and Problems of Security Sector Reform," in Ehrhart and Schnabel, *Security Sector Reform*, 7–8.

43. Heiner Hänggi, "Conceptualising Security Sector Reform and Reconstruction," in Alan Bryden and Heiner Hänggi, eds., "Reform and Reconstruction of the Security Sector," Geneva: DCAF, 2004: 4–9; available at www.dcaf.ch/publications/bm_ssr_yearbook2004.cfm; and

44. In his book on the Western Balkans, Timothy Edmunds uses a narrow definition of SSR. In personal communication with the author on January 18, 2010, he reported that this was probably due to his sense that it was simply impossible to make the wider, all-encompassing SSR definitions work in practice, whether empirically or analytically. See Edmunds, *Security Sector Reform*, especially Chapter 2, "Security Sector Reform: A Framework for Analysis," 15–50.

45. Pete Cornell of the U.S. Defense Security Cooperation Agency provided me a copy of a Department of Defense document from 2009 on "Statutory Authorities for Department of Defense Foreign Affairs Related Activities" that is seventeen pages long and averages seven different authorities per page. Virtually all of these legal authorities require coordination with other U.S. government agencies.

46. Red de Seguridad y Defensa de América Latina [RESDAL], *A Comparative Atlas of Defence in Latin America* (Buenos Aires: Author, 2008). Also published in Spanish and French. See www.resdal.org.

47. Facultad Latinoamericana de Ciencias Sociales [FLACSO]. *Report on the Security Sector in Latin America and the Caribbean* (Santiago, Chile: Author, 2007, English edition, 2008). See www.flacso.cl.

48. The FLACSO study also generated twenty-five country reports, in English or Spanish, which can be found at www.flacso.cl. The newest RESDAL Atlas was published in November 2010.

49. FLACSO: 19–20, 21–22, 28.

50. Ibid., 44–52.

51. Ibid., 53.

52. Ibid., 126–127.

53. RESDAL, 42–46 and 88–89.

54. FLACSO, 127.

55. The average percent of GDP committed to defense in the sixteen countries of the study is 1.36 percent. The Stockholm International Peace Research Institute (SIPRI) data on military expenditure as a share of GDP, which lists a total of thirty-eight countries that spent more than 4 percent in any of the years 1998–2003, includes only Colombia from Latin America; available at www.sipri.org/databases/milex.

56. FLACSO, 38.

57. Ibid., 53.

58. In a personal communication on January 12, 2010, Marcela Donadio of RESDAL commented that this fact is largely due to the different sources for defining roles and missions. In some, such as Honduras, it is the constitution; in others it is in laws; and in others so-called white books.

59. RESDAL, 50.

60. Ibid., 52.

61. FLACSO, 24. See Table 1.9 on p. 25, Budget Control Mechanisms.

62. FLACSO, 25–27.

Chapter 3

1. Specifically, there are 552,425 personnel in the Army; 330,703 in the Navy; 204,261 in the Marines; and 334,342 in the Air Force. The source for this data is the Department of Defense (DoD) Personnel and Procurement Statistics: Personnel and Procurement Reports and Data Files, as of August 2009, available at http://siadapp .dmdc.osd.mil/personnel/MILITARY/miltop.htm; the data on civilians are from the Defense Manpower Data Center in Monterey, California, as of September 2009, available at http://wiadapp.dmdc.osd.mil/personnel/civilian/civtop.html; and for the Na-

tional Guard, see Michael Waterhouse and JoAnne O'Bryant, "National Guard Personnel and Deployments: Fact Sheet," Congressional Research Service (CRS) Report for Congress, updated May 1, 2008. For further data on the armed services, see "Population Representation in the Military Services," Office of the Undersecretary of Defense, Personnel and Readiness, Fiscal Year 2005, available at http://prhome.defense.gov/poprep2005/index.html. It should be noted that data on the reserves are not included in these numbers listed in this latter document.

2. Information on the executive structure of the federal government is available at www.whitehouse.gov/our_government/executive_branch/.

3. The full text of the Constitution, its amendments, and other founding documents are available at www.house.gov/house/Educate.shtml.

4. Claus Offe, "Political Institutions and Social Power: Conceptual Explorations," in Ian Shapiro, Stephen Skowronek, and Daniel Gavin, eds., Rethinking Political Institutions: The Art of the State (New York: New York University Press, 2006), 14.

5. Ibid., 18.

6. Attributed to James Madison, The Federalist No. 51: "The Structure of the Government Must Furnish the Proper Checks and Balances between the Different Departments," originally published in the Independent Journal, Wednesday, February 6, 1788, and available at www.constitution.org/fed/federa51.htm.

7. Ibid.

8. Richard H. Kohn, ed., The United States Military under the Constitution of the United States, 1789–1989 (New York: New York University Press, 1991). See also Joseph E. Goldberg, "Executive Prerogatives, the Constitution, and National Security," in Howard E. Shuman and Walter R. Thomas, eds., The Constitution and National Security: A Bicentennial View (Washington, DC: National Defense University Press, 1990).

9. Kohn, The United States Military, 71.

10. Ibid., 77.

11. Ibid., 80.

12. The continuing relevance of this observation was highlighted to me in a review article by Walter Isaacson in the New York Times on Sunday, January 24, 2010, in which he discusses the contrasting perspectives on executive versus legislative powers in John Yoo, Crisis and Command: The History of Executive Power from George Washington to George W. Bush (New York: Kaplan Publishing, 2010), and Garry Wills, Bomb Power: The Modern Presidency and the National Security State (New York: Penguin Press, 2010).

13. See a comparison of the remarkable number of think tanks in the United States versus the rest of the world at the Foreign Policy Research Institute website, available at http://thinktanks.fpri.org/.

14. See, for example, Thomas E. Ricks, a contributor to Foreign Policy online, available at http://ricks.foreignpolicy.com.

15. "Men in society act with and against each other on the basis of their material and ideal interest." Reinhard Bendix, *Max Weber: An Intellectual Portrait* (New York: Anchor Books, 1962), 80.

16. On joint education see, for example, Representative Ike Skelton, *Whispers of Warriors: Essays on the New Joint Era* (Washington, DC: National Defense University Press, 2004). Skelton, a leading advocate in Congress for the armed services, and chairman of the House Armed Services Committee between 2007 and 2011, comments on the importance and implications of "jointness."

17. Arch Barrett, interview with author in Austin, Texas, December 8–9, 2008.

18. ROTC graduates constitute 56.6 percent of the Army, 11.7 percent of the Marine Corps, 20.7 percent of the Navy, and 41.6 percent of Air Force officers, a combined 39 percent of all active duty officers in DoD. Those who attend the three service academies make up 15.9 percent of Army, 12.6 percent of Marine, 19.4 percent of Navy, and 19.3 percent of Air Force officers, a combined 17.7 percent of all active duty officers in DoD. "Population Representation in the Military Services: Active Component Officers," Office of the Undersecretary of Defense, Personnel and Readiness, Washington, DC; available at www.defenselink.mil/prhome/poprep2004/officers/commission.html.

19. R. Eric Petersen, "Congressional Nominations to U.S. Service Academies: An Overview and Resources for Outreach and Management," CRS Report for Congress, December 29, 2005.

20. Rep. Robert Wittman, press release on appointment to the U.S. Naval Academy Board of Visitors, U.S. Naval Academy, Washington, DC, July 27, 2009.

21. See Amy Zegart, *Flawed by Design: The Evolution of the CIA, JCS, and NSC* (Stanford, CA: Stanford University Press, 1999), Chapters 2 to 5 regarding the National Security Council and Joint Chiefs of Staff. This section on Goldwater-Nichols draws from the prominent literature on the topic, including Peter J. Roman and David W. Tarr, "The Joint Chiefs of Staff: From Service Parochialism to Jointness," *Political Science Quarterly* 113, 1 (1998): 91–111; Dennis J. Quinn, ed., *The Goldwater-Nichols DOD Reorganization Act: A Ten-Year Retrospective* (Washington, DC: National Defense University Press, 1999); and James R. Locher, *Victory on the Potomac: The Goldwater Nichols Act Unifies the Pentagon* (College Station: Texas A&M University Press, 2004). Thanks also to Arch Barrett for providing me with copies of the bills and other materials relating to the Goldwater-Nichols legislation.

22. James Locher affirmed in our interview (Arlington, Virginia, February 23, 2009) that the purpose of Goldwater-Nichols was to improve effectiveness rather than control. Regarding the goals of Goldwater-Nichols and how they will be met, Locher wrote, "First, to leave no doubt as to the defense secretary's authority, report language declares, 'The secretary has sole and ultimate power within the Department of Defense on any matter on which the secretary chooses to act.'" Locher, *Victory on the Potomac*, 438.

23. Roman and Tarr, "The Joint Chiefs of Staff," 101.

24. Ibid., 102.

25. Locher, *Victory on the Potomac*, 448.

26. Roman and Tarr, "The Joint Chiefs of Staff," 102, 109.

27. See Richard F. Grimmett, "War Powers Resolution: Presidential Compliance," CRS Report to Congress, September 23, 2009; James A. Baker III and Warren Christopher, cochairs, "The National War Powers Commission Report," Miller Center for Public Affairs, University of Virginia, July 2008. See also James A. Nathan, "Revising the War Powers Act," *Armed Forces & Society*, 17, 4 (Summer 1991): 513–543.

28. On the use of military force, see Richard F. Grimmett, "Instances of Use of United States Armed Forces Abroad, 1798–2008," CRS Report for Congress, Washington, DC, February 2, 2009.

29. The attacks of September 11, 2001, further exacerbated competition between the executive and the legislative branches in the broader areas of national security and defense. The literature on "executive privilege," for example, is extensive; some examples include Morton Rosenberg, "Presidential Claims of Executive Privilege: History, Law, Practice and Recent Developments" CRS Report for Congress (RL30319), Washington, DC, updated July 5, 2007; Charlie Savage, *Takeover: The Return of the Imperial Presidency and the Subversion of American Democracy* (New York: Little, Brown and Company, 2007), especially on signing statements; and Frederick A. O. Schwarz Jr. and Aziz Z. Huq, *Unchecked and Unbalanced: Presidential Power in a Time of Terror* (New York: The New Press, 2007). The power of the purse as a control mechanism is described in "Congressional Use of Funding Cutoffs since 1970 Involving U.S. Military Forces and Overseas Deployments," CRS Report (RS 20775), Washington, DC, updated January 16, 2007. More on the powers of Congress can be found in Richard F. Grimmett, "Declarations of War and Authorizations for the Use of Military Force: Historical Background and Legal Implications," CRS Report for Congress, Washington, DC, updated August 11, 2006. It must be stressed that the CRS Reports are produced for the use of Congress and thus tend to reflect current interests among the members and professional staff. This is particularly apparent when control of Congress shifts between parties.

30. Grimmett, "War Powers Resolution," 1.

31. Ibid., 1.

32. Ibid., Summary (which is the page before the table of contents and text in CRS Reports).

33. Baker and Christopher, "The National War Powers Commission Report," 4.

34. Ibid., 10.

35. According to U.S. Code 10, # 163, the president may "direct that communications between the President or the Secretary of Defense and the commanders of the

unified and specified combatant commands be transmitted through the Chairman of the Joint Chiefs of Staff."

36. For details, see, for example, the chapters on Ministries of Defense, Legislatures, and Budgets in Thomas C. Bruneau and Scott D. Tollefson, eds., *Who Guards the Guardians and How: Democratic Civil-Military Relations* (Austin: University of Texas Press, 2006).

37. For more on the extent of this oversight see, for example, Frederick M. Kaiser, "GAO: Government Accountability Office and General Accounting Office," CRS Report for Congress, Washington, DC, updated June 22, 2007; and Frederick M. Kaiser, "Statutory Offices of Inspector General: Past and Present," CRS Report for Congress, Washington, DC, updated September 25, 2008.

38. Interview with Arch Barrett, December 8–9, 2008.

39. See Karen Guttieri, "Professional Military Education in Democracies," in Bruneau and Tollefson, *Who Guards the Guardians and How*, for extensive details on the U.S. system of PME.

40. This information on the officer promotion process comes from my work with retired flag and general officers and congressional staffers in CCMR programs. Most of the officers have served on promotion boards, while the staffers have reviewed the lists for Senate approval.

41. See, for example, Eliot A. Cohen and John Gooch, *Military Misfortunes: The Anatomy of Failure in War* (New York: Vintage Books, 1990). In a recent example, analyses of the intelligence community's inability, despite credible warnings, to prevent a Nigerian suicide bomber from getting on a plane in December 2009 were being made public within days of the incident. Mike Mazzetti and Eric Lipton, "Spy Agencies Failed to Collate Clues on Terror," *New York Times* online, December 30, 2009.

42. Lewis Carroll, *Alice's Adventures in Wonderland* and *Through the Looking Glass* (London: Penguin Classics, 2003), 50–59.

43. Office of the President, Republic of Colombia, "Democratic Security and Defence Policy," Casa de Narino, Bogota, June 16, 2003.

44. See the Ministry of National Defense, Republic of Colombia, website on the policy and measures of effectiveness (in Spanish); available at www.mindefensa.gov .co/index.php?page=451.

45. These include directing the president to submit an annual report on national security strategy, instructing the JCS chairman to prepare fiscally constrained strategic plans and requiring the defense secretary to provide written policy guidance for the preparation and review of contingency plans, with assistance from the undersecretary of defense for policy. Locher, *Victory on the Potomac*, 441.

46. Catherine Dale, "National Security Strategy: Legislative Mandates, Execution to Date, and Considerations for Congress," CRS Report for Congress, Washington, DC, updated September 23, 2008, 3.

47. Ibid.

48. Ibid., 4.

49. Goldwater-Nichols Department of Defense Reorganization Act of 1986, Title VI, Section 603.

50. U.S. Congress, Report of the Panel on Military Education of the 100th Congress, Committee on Armed Services, House of Representatives, 101st Congress, 1st session, April 21, 1989; Barrett interview.

51. National Defense Authorization Act (NDAA) for FY 2000 that amended Title 10 of the U.S. Code to this effect.

52. Dale, "National Security Strategy," 5–8.

53. The National Military Strategy is mandated in Title 10, U.S. Code, as amended by the NDAA for FY 2004.

54. Ibid., 8.

55. Ibid., 10. Congress also mandates other strategy documents, in areas including National Strategy for Combating Terrorism, homeland security, and intelligence. See list of legislative mandates for strategy documents see on p. 11, plus note 29 on this same page.

56. Ibid., 18–19; see 16–21 for Dale's general discussion on options.

57. LTC Nathan Freier, "The Strategy Deficit," Op-ed, Strategic Studies Institute, U.S. Army War College, Washington, DC, March 20, 2008: 2; available at www.strategicstudiesinstitute.army.mil/pdffiles/PUB863.pdf and quoted in Dale, "National Security Strategy," note 61.

58. See Michèle A. Flournoy and Shawn W. Brimley, "Strategic Planning for National Security: A New Project Solarium," *Joint Forces Quarterly* 41 (2nd quarter 2006): 80. This is not to say that that the planning process serving the CJCS is not effective in developing classified national military strategy and contingency plans. For the GAO Report under Flournoy's leadership, see GAO, "Quadrennial Defense Review," April 30, 2010; GAO 10–575R.

59. See Grimmett, "War Powers Resolution," 5–7, regarding the United States and Iraq in the context of the War Powers Resolution.

60. Frier, "The Strategy Deficit," 2.

61. Thomas Ricks, *Fiasco: The American Military Adventure in Iraq* (New York: Penguin Press, 2006); Bob Woodward, *Plan of Attack* (New York: Simon & Schuster, 2004) and The *War Within: A Secret White House History 2006–2008* (New York: Simon & Schuster, 2008); Thomas Ricks, *The Gamble: General David Petraeus and the American Military Adventure in Iraq, 2006–2008* (New York: Penguin Press, 2009); and James Stephenson, *Losing the Golden Hour: An Insider's View of Iraq's Reconstruction* (Dulles, VA: Potomac Books, 2007).

62. See, for instance, George Packer, who wrote of the postcombat occupation, "I came to believe that those in positions of highest responsibility for Iraq showed

a carelessness about human life that amounted to criminal negligence." Packer, *The Assassins' Gate: America in Iraq* (New York: Farrar, Straus and Giroux, 2005), 448; Michael R. Gordon and General Bernard E. Trainor, *Cobra II: The Inside Story of the Invasion and Occupation of Iraq* (New York: Pantheon Books, 2006), which reviews five grievous errors made by President Bush and his team (Epilogue, 497–504); and Joseph J. Collins, "Choosing War: The Decision to Invade Iraq and Its Aftermath," Occasional Paper 5, Institute for National Strategic Studies. Washington, DC: National Defense University Press, April 2008, which lists ten errors ("Decisionmaking and Execution," 16–28).

63. Ricks, *Fiasco*, 115.

64. Ibid., 127–128.

65. Ibid., 129.

66. Ibid., 185.

67. Woodward, *The War Within*, 53.

68. Ibid., 59.

69. The book by Richard N. Haass, *War of Necessity, War of Choice: A Memoir of Two Iraq Wars* (New York: Simon & Schuster, 2009), deals at length with the issue of missing, or incoherent, strategy. Referring to the draft document Haass wrote on formulating the national security strategy, which he turned over to Secretary of State Colin Powell in December 2001, he recalled, "He signed it out and sent it over to Condi without changing a word. It would be months before we heard back, and not until the summer of 2002 that we saw a new and much-changed document" (201). The document that was published, in September 2002, included preemptive war against Iraq, which was a new policy decision indicating that, for Haass, "the national security process was deeply flawed" (220).

70. Ricks, *The Gamble*, 9. See also Linda Robinson, *Tell Me How This Ends: General David Petraeus and the Search for a Way Out of Iraq* (New York: Public Affairs, 2008).

71. We have elaborated on this general point, comparing the United States with seven other democracies, in Thomas C. Bruneau, Florina Cristiana Matei, and Sak Sakoda, "National Security Councils: Their Potential Functions in Democratic Civil-Military Relations," *Defense & Security Analysis* 25, 3 (September 2009): 255–269.

72. Ricks, *Fiasco*, 4.

73. Woodward, *The War Within*, 123.

74. Ibid., 21.

75. Ibid., 49. This account is verified by my interviews with officials in the Bush administration at that time.

76. Nora Bensahel, "Mission Not Accomplished: What Went Wrong with Iraqi Reconstruction," *The Journal of Strategic Studies* 29, 3 (June 2006), 470. For the full RAND Report, which makes for shocking reading, see Nora Bensahel, Olga Oliker,

Keith Crane, Richard R. Brennan Jr., Heather S. Gregg, Thomas Sullivan, and Andrew Rathmell, *After Saddam: Prewar Planning and the Occupation of Iraq* (Santa Monica: RAND, Arroyo Center, 2008.)

77. Michèle A. Flournoy and Shawn W. Brimley, "Strategic Planning for National Security: A New Project Solarium," *Joint Forces Quarterly* 41 (2nd quarter 2006): 81.

78. Ibid., 82.

79. Cody M. Brown, "The National Security Council: A Legal History of the President's Most Powerful Advisers," report for the Project on National Security Reform, Washington, DC, December 2008). James Locher noted that providing recommendations to the president's national security advisor, General Jim Jones, is a top priority of the PNSR. Author interview with James Locher on June 15, 2009, in Arlington, Virginia.

80. Joseph J. Collins, "Choosing War: The Decision to Invade Iraq and Its Aftermath," Occasional Paper 5, Institute for National Strategic Studies, National Defense University Press, Washington, DC, April 2008: 27.

81. Catherine Dale, Nina Serafino, and Pat Towell, "Organizing the U.S. Government for National Security: Overview of the Interagency Reform Debates," CRS Report for Congress (RL 34455), April 2008; and Richard A. Best Jr., "The National Security Council: An Organizational Assessment," CRS Report for Congress (RL 30840), June 8, 2009. Several recent books on the U.S. NSC indicate that serious change is necessary. See Bruneau et al., "National Security Councils"; and Haass, *War of Necessity, War of Choice.*

82. Dale et al., "Organizing the U.S. Government," Summary page.

83. Ibid.

84. "Active Duty Military Personnel Strengths by Regional Area and by Country (309A)," DoD Military and Personnel Casualty Statistics, March 31, 2008; available at http://siadapp.dmdc.osd.mil/.

85. Barrett interviews, December 8–9, 2008.

86. After the Democrats took over both houses of Congress in early 2007, they requested, and received, a comprehensive review of their oversight authorities, processes, and instruments. See Frederick M Kaiser, Walter J. Oleszek, T. J. Halstead, Morton Rosenberg, and Todd B. Tatelman, "Congressional Oversight Manual," CRS Report for Congress, updated January 3, 2007, which contains 149 pages of detailed information on all imaginable aspects of oversight, including a list of eight videos to illustrate and explain some aspects of oversight. Of fundamental importance here is Section V, pages 114–145, which provides extensive details on "Oversight Information Sources and Consultant Services."

87. Statutory Inspectors General exist in more than sixty federal departments and agencies; see Vanessa K. Burrows and Frederick M. Kaiser, "Statutory Inspectors General: Legislative Developments and Legal Issues," CRS Report for Congress, September

18, 2007. They were established by legislation in 1976, which was continued with the passage of the 1978 Inspector General Act, and modified in 1988. IGs have four principal responsibilities: (1) to conduct and supervise audits and investigations relating to the programs and operations of the agency; (2) to provide leadership and coordination and recommend policies to promote the economy, efficiency, and effectiveness of these programs and operations; (3) to prevent and detect waste, fraud, and abuse; and (4) to keep the agency head and Congress fully and currently informed about problems, deficiencies, and recommended corrective action. Frederick M. Kaiser, "Statutory Offices of Inspector General: Past and Present," CRS Report for Congress, September 25, 2008: 1–2. See also Frederick M. Kaiser, "GAO: Governmental Accountability Office and General Accounting Office," CRS Report for Congress, updated June 22, 2007.

88. "Department of Defense: Status of Achieving Outcomes and Addressing Major Management Challenges," GAO report (GAO-01-783), June 2001, 2, "Results in Brief."

Chapter 4

1. The reform initiatives reviewed in this chapter are what I would term "mainstream." I am not dealing with the more polemic "military reform movement." For an excellent review by two of the main participants in this movement, see Winslow T. Wheeler and Lawrence J. Korb, *Military Reform: A Reference Handbook* (Westport, CT: Praeger Security International, 2007). According to Kathleen H. Hicks, *Invigorating Defense Governance: A Beyond Goldwater-Nichols Phase 4 Report* (Washington: D.C.: Center for Strategic & International Studies, March 2008), 67-68, there have been twenty-one defense reform initiatives between Goldwater-Nichols and March 2008.

2. Catherine Dale, Nina Serafino, and Pat Towell, "Organizing the U.S. Government for National Security: Overview of the Interagency Reform Debates," CRS Report for Congress, April 18, 2008, 3.

3. Ibid., Summary.

4. Ibid., 2n3.

5. Ibid.

6. Thomas H. Kean, Commission Chair, "How to Do It Different? A Different Way of Organizing the Government," The 9/11 Commission Report: Final Report of the National Commission on Terrorist Attacks Upon the United States (Washington, DC: U.S. Government Printing Office, July 22, 2004), 13.1; available at http://govinfo.library .unt.edu/911/report/index.htm.

7. Office of the Director of National Intelligence. "Intelligence Community Directive Number 601. Human Capital: Joint Intelligence Community Duty Assignments" (Washington, DC: Author, May 2006, amended in September 2009). In his testimony to the U.S. Senate, Dr. Ronald Sanders, associate director of national intelligence for human capital, refers to "joint duty" in intelligence. Sanders, "National Security Reform: Implementing a National Security Service Workforce," testimony before the

Senate Subcommittee on Oversight of Government Management, the Federal Work-force, and the District of Colombia, Washington, DC, April 30, 2009; available at: www.dni.gov/testimonies/20090430_testimony.pdf.

8. In his retrospective on Goldwater-Nichols, General Jones says the following: "Arch single-handedly kept the subject alive for a major part of the 4-1/2 years to en-actment. There would not be a Goldwater-Nichols without him. . . . Again a staffer, Jim Locher, was absolutely essential to success. His outstanding study of the problems convinced many, and there would not be a Goldwater-Nichols without him, also." David C. Jones, "Reform: The Beginnings," in Dennis J. Quinn, *The Goldwater-Nichols DOD Reorganization Act: A Ten-Year Retrospective* (Washington, DC: National De-fense University Press, 1999), 7.

9. Clark A. Murdock, lead investigator, "Beyond Goldwater-Nichols: Defense Re-form for a New Strategic Era," Phase 1 Report (Washington, DC: Center for Strategic and International Studies, March 2004), 12.

10. Author interviews with Arch Barrett in Austin, Texas, December 8 and 9, 2008.

11. Archie D. Barrett, *Reappraising Defense Organization: An Analysis Based on the Defense Organization Study of 1977–1980* (Washington, DC: National Defense Uni-versity Press, 1983).

12. At that hearing, General Jones stated: "It is not sufficient to have just resources, dollars and weapon systems; we must also have an organization which will allow us to develop the proper strategy, necessary planning, and the full warfighting capability." Quoted in Locher, *Victory on the Potomac*, 34. Incidentally, General Jones wrote the introduction to Barrett's book, *Reappraising Defense Organization*.

13. Locher, *Victory on the Potomac*.

14. These are Locher, *Victory on the Potomac*, and Quinn, *The Goldwater-Nichols DOD Reorganization Act*.

15. My thanks to Arch Barrett and Jim Locher for their time, invaluable insights, and help clarifying the issues. Barrett also has provided me with several useful docu-ments, which include "Goldwater-Nichols Act Readings: Legislative Activities and Documents Leading to the Passage of the Goldwater-Nichols Department of Defense Reorganization Act of 1986." This is in two photocopied volumes, for course purposes, NPS, May 2001; and "Report of the Panel on Military Education," Committee on the Armed Services, House of Representatives, 101st Congress, First Session. Washington, DC: U.S. Government Printing Office, April 21, 1989.

16. Locher, *Victory on the Potomac*, 29.

17. Arch Barrett's 1983 book (*Reappraising Defense Organization*) is a remarkable effort to analyze the institutional problems of defense organization and to review ef-forts to resolve them. He demonstrates that there had been no significant change, or reform, between 1958 and when he published the book in 1983.

18. On the importance of General Jones's testimony see Locher, 2002, 34–37. On why joint chiefs of staff must change, see Murdock, "Beyond Goldwater-Nichols," Phase 1 Report.

19. James R. Locher , briefing slides for a course at the Naval Postgraduate School May 29, 2002: slide 30. The title of the briefing is the same as his 2002 book, *Victory on the Potomac: The Goldwater-Nichols Act Unifies the Pentagon.*

20. Ibid., slides 40–41.

21. Arch Barrett emphasized to me the important role played by Les Aspin, who became HASC chairman at the same time Goldwater became SASC chairman (1985). It was under Aspin's leadership in 1985, and at his request, that Nichols rewrote and strengthened his weaker 1983 JCS bill. It was under Aspin's leadership, and at his request, that Nichols held hearings and reported a bill in early 1986 that reorganized other parts of DOD, the unified commands, military departments, and defense agencies.

22. Author interview with Arch Barrett, Austin, Texas, December 8 and 9, 2008.

23. Locher deals with the past opposition in Congress and how it came around to oppose the Pentagon, in promoting the reform, in Quinn, *The Goldwater-Nichols DOD Reorganization Act*, 1–22.

24. Murdock, "Beyond Goldwater-Nichols," Phase 1 Report: 12.

25. See "Goldwater-Nichols Department of Defense Reorganization Act of 1986," Public Law 99-433-1, October 1986.

26. Locher, briefing: slides 42–43.

27. Catherine Dale, "National Security Strategy: Legislative Mandates, Execution to Date, and Considerations for Congress," CRS Report for Congress, Washington, DC, updated September 23, 2008, 3. Italics in the original.

28. Murdock, "Beyond Goldwater-Nichols," Phase 1 Report, 15.

29. These opinions are amply cited in Locher, *Victory on the Potomac*; Quinn, *The Goldwater-Nichols DOD Reorganization Act*; and Peter J. Roman and David W. Tarr, "The Joint Chiefs of Staff: From Service Parochialism to Jointness," *Political Science Quarterly* 113, 1 (1998).

30. Murdock, "Beyond Goldwater-Nichols," Phase 1 Report.

31. Ibid., 15–17, 18.

32. For an authoritative source on this widely recognized point, see Sam C. Sarkesian, John Allen Williams, and Stephen J. Cimbala, *U.S. National Security: Policymakers, Processes, & Politics*, 4th edition (Boulder, CO: Lynne Rienner Publishers, 2008), 300–305.

33. See Thomas C. Bruneau and Steven C. Boraz, eds., *Reforming Intelligence: Obstacles to Democratic Control and Effectiveness* (Austin: University of Texas Press, 2007), for a discussion of intelligence and its reform, as a civil–military relations challenge; and the National Commission on Terrorist Attacks (the 9/11 Commission), *The*

9/11 Commission Report: Final Report of the National Commission on Terrorist Attacks upon the United States (New York: W. W. Norton & Company, 2004).

34. Zegart is associate professor of public policy at the University of California, Los Angeles. Amy B. Zegart, *Flawed by Design: The Evolution of the CIA, JCS, and NSC* (Stanford, CA: Stanford University Press, 1999), 11. Her analysis of the fiasco leading up to 9/11 is required reading for anyone interested in U.S. intelligence. For this analysis, see Amy Zegart, *Spying Blind: The CIA, the FBI, and the Origins of 9/11* (Princeton, NJ: Princeton University Press, 2007).

35. See Bruneau and Boraz, *Reforming Intelligence*, for case studies. See also Thomas C. Bruneau, "Democracy and Effectiveness: Adapting Intelligence for the Fight against Terrorism," *International Journal of Intelligence and Counterintelligence* 21, 3 (Fall 2008), 448–460.

36. Richard A. Best Jr., "Proposals for Intelligence Reorganization, 1949–2004," CRS Report for Congress, Washington, DC, July 29, 2004, Summary.

37. Michael Warner and J. Kenneth McDonald, "U.S. Intelligence Community Reform Studies since 1947" (Washington, DC: Center for the Study of Intelligence, April 2005). Richard Betts, in *Enemies of Intelligence: Knowledge & Power in American National Security* (New York: Columbia University Press, 2007), identifies between fifteen and twenty sets of official proposals for "reorganization" of the intelligence community. See p. 143.

38. Warner and McDonald, 43.

39. *The 9/11 Commission Report*, 348.

40. Kenneth Kitts, *Presidential Commissions & National Security: The Politics of Damage Control* (Boulder, CO: Lynne Rienner, 2006); on page 133 he has a table of these proposals; see page 137 regarding how the commission became possible. See also Ernest R. May, "When Government Writes History: A Memoir of the 9/11 Commission," *The New Republic* (May 23, 2005), 30–35.

41. Kitts, *Presidential Commissions*, 140. See also, "Piloting a Bipartisan Ship: Strategies and Tactics of the 9/11 Commission" (C15-05-1813.0) (Cambridge, MA: Kennedy School of Government Case Program, 2005).

42. Philip Shenon, *The Commission: The Uncensored History of the 9/11 Investigation* (New York: Twelve Publishers, 2008). See also Kitts, *Presidential Commissions*, for a case study of 9/11. See also May, "When Government Writes History," for a critique by an insider.

43. Intelligence Reform and Terrorism Prevention Act of 2004 (Public Law 108-458), 108th Congress, December 17, 2004; Richard F. Grimmett, Coordinator, "9/11 Commission Recommendations: Implementation Status," CRS Report for Congress, Washington, DC, December 4, 2006, 2.

44. Dale, "National Security Strategy," 14–16. Grimmett, "9/11 Commission Recommendations"; and Thomas H. Kean, commission chair, "Final Report on 9/11 Com-

mission Recommendations, December 5, 2005." 9/11 Public Discourse Project, available at www.9-11pdp.org.

45. Ibid., 11.

46. For an update on this issue, see "Intelligence Community Joint Duty Program Highlighted in Nationwide Public Television Series," Office of the Director of National Intelligence News Release No. 24-09, Washington, DC, June 30, 2009, available at: www.odni.gov/press_releases/20090630_release.pdf.

47. The FAS website lists an impressive collection of studies and reports under the Publications heading: www.fas.org.

48. The former figure is from the *New York Times* of October 31, 2007, and the latter is from a news release from the Office of the Director of National Intelligence, ODNI News Release No. 33-09, dated October 30, 2009. Whereas Public Law 110-53 requires the DNI to disclose the aggregate amount, there is no requirement that any further details be released. It is estimated that in 2010 the budget will increase by $2 billion.

49. See Richard A. Best Jr. and Alfred Cumming, "Director of National Intelligence Statutory Authorities: Status and Proposals," CRS Report for Congress, updated April 17, 2008, concerning efforts to strengthen the powers of the Director of National Intelligence.

50. For example, if one reviews the Senate testimony of Dr. Ronald Sanders, there is not a single mention of education. Arch Barrett, working with Congressman Ike Skelton, quickly realized that joint education would be crucial to ensuring joint thinking and operations. Sanders, "National Security Reform."

51. See, for example, Eric Lipton, Eric Schmitt, and Mark Mazzetti, "Review of Jet Bomb Plot Shows More Missed Clues," *New York Times*, January 18, 2009.

52. Statement for the Record of Dennis C. Blair, director of national intelligence, and Michael E. Leiter, director of the National Counterterrorism Center, "Intelligence Reform: The Lessons and Implications of the Christmas Day Attack," Senate Homeland Security and Governmental Affairs Committee, 111th Congress, 2nd session, January 20, 2010, available at: http://hsgac.senate.gov/public/index.cfm?FuseAction= Hearings.Home. See also "Summary of the White House Review of the December 25, 2009, Attempted Terrorist Attack," January 7, 2010, available at www.whitehouse.gov/ sites/default/files/summary_of_wh_review_12-25-09.pdf.

53. For the directive, go to www.whitehouse.gov/sites/default/files/potus_directive_ corrective_actions_1-7-10.pdf.

54. Murdock, "Beyond Goldwater-Nichols," Phase 1 Report, 6. In fact, there is also a Phase 4 Report, published in March 2008. See Kathleen H. Hicks, *Invigorating Defense Governance: A beyond Goldwater-Nichols Phase 4 Report* (Washington, DC: Center for Strategic & International Studies, March 2008).

55. Ibid.

56. Ibid., 20.

57. Ibid., 18.

58. Ibid., 20.

59. Ibid., 26–74.

60. Ibid., 75–77.

61. Clark A. Murdock and Michèle A. Flournoy, lead investigators, "Beyond Goldwater-Nichols: Defense Reform for a New Strategic Era," Phase 2 Report, CSIS, July 2005, 6–12.

62. Ibid., 131.

63. Ibid., 139.

64. Ibid., 140.

65. Ibid.

66. Arch Barrett, Report of the Panel on Military Education of the One Hundredth Congress of the Committee on Armed Services, House of Representatives, 101st Congress, 1st session, April 21, 1989, 11.

67. In my interviews with Barrett and Locher, they were adamant that Goldwater-Nichols and other reform initiatives were not concerned with asserting civilian control but with problems of effectiveness. Author interviews with Barrett and with James R. Locher III, Arlington, Virginia, February 23, June 15, and September 16, 2009. There could also be some confusion in a quick glance at Kathleen H. Hicks, *Invigorating Defense Governance*, in that one of the key words is "Civil–Military Relations—United States" and on p. xii a title is "Civilian control of the military is a paramount value." However, in further reading that title it states: "As the president's representative, the secretary of defense should have appropriate tools and mechanisms to exercise authority and control over the defense establishment and U.S. military forces." In sum, the focus, in terms of my framework, is on effectiveness and not control.

68. These initiatives are very nicely summarized in Murdock and Flournoy, "Beyond Goldwater-Nichols," Phase 2, 139–145.

69. Ibid., 150.

70. Nor in the later, Kathleen H. Hicks, *Invigorating Defense Governance: A Beyond Goldwater-Nichols Phase 4 Report* (Washington, DC: Center for Strategic & International Studies, March, 2008), 69–72, is there any mention at all of contracting out in the twenty-nine recommendations. The term *contractor* is mentioned once in the seventy-three-page document.

71. Richard L. Armitage and Joseph S. Nye, Jr., cochairs, "CSIS Commission on Smart Power: A Smarter, More Secure America," final report, Washington, DC: CSIS, November 6, 2007.

72. Ibid., 1.

73. In my discussions with a former State Department official, a strong proponent of this commission's work, the official emphasized the background and motivation for this CSIS initiative. The U.S. engagements in Afghanistan and Iraq in the post-combat phase, Phase 4, were disastrous because the only significant instrument the United States used was military force. Other tools of "smart power," including at a minimum the State Department (DoS) and USAID, were too anemic. Military power is not intended or set up for reconstruction and nation building. The argument was, then, to complement military force with other instruments, which would make U.S. policy "smart."

74. Armitage and Nye, "CSIS Commission on Smart Power," 19–20.

75. Ibid., 6.

76. Ibid., 7.

77. Ibid., 8.

78. Ibid., 9.

79. Ibid., 61.

80. Ibid. This section is titled "Implementation Challenges" and extends from page 62 through page 65.

81. Ibid., 64.

82. Ibid., 65

83. Interview with former State Department official.

84. For the general theme of "smart power," see U.S. Department of State, *Leading through Civilian Power: The First Quadrennial Diplomacy and Development Review.* Washington, DC: 2010. There are a large number of studies and reports on the issue of the balance between DoD and other agencies, especially DoS on foreign policy and foreign assistance. See for example, Nina M. Serafino, coordinator, "The Department of Defense Role in Foreign Assistance: Background, Major Issues, and Options for Congress," CRS Report for Congress, Washington, DC, December 9, 2008. Gordon Adams provides ongoing commentary on these issues at: http://budgetinsight.wordpress.com/.

85. This section, on the most important national security reform effort in a generation, is relatively brief for two reasons. First, it is ongoing, and the interim prospects for success will be reviewed in the Conclusion to this book. Second, the output of the Project on National Security Reform is huge, and all of it can be readily accessed on the continually updated website, www.pnsr.org.

86. See Defence Reform Commission, "The Path to Partnership for Peace: Report of the Defence Reform Commission" (Sarajevo, Bosnia and Herzegovina: Defence Reform Commission, September 25, 2003).

87. For more information on this project, see "Forging a New Shield," Project on National Security Reform (PNSR), December 2008; "Case Studies," Vol. 1: 1–632; and "The National Security Council: A Legal History of the President's Most Powerful Advisers," 1–129. All of this material, and much more, can be found at www.pnsr.org.

88. Author interview with James R. Locher III in Arlington, Virginia, on February 23, 2009. At that time, he insisted that I use the term *national security reform* when describing the PNSR project.

89. PNSR, "Forging a New Shield," Executive Summary, November 2008, i.

90. Ibid., vii.

91. Ibid., x–xiv.

92. PNSR, "Forging a New Shield," Full Report, November 2008, 86.

93. Ibid., 500–503.

94. Ibid., 265.

95. The PNSR website updates the members of the founding coalition who have entered the Obama Administration: www.pnsr.org.

96. Dale et al., "Organizing the U.S. Government for National Security," 2, note 3.

97. These include: Designing the National Security Staff for the 21st Century; Engagement with the National Counterterrorism Center; Developing the "Next Generation" State Department; Strengthening Intergovernmental Coordination for Homeland Security; Matching Resources to Strategy; and hosting a set of Global Roundtables. Locher reviewed these with me on June 15 and provided me with a list. At our September 16 meeting, the list was expanded to include assisting the NSC staff with a strategy directorate and initiating the use of modern IT technology by the NSC staff to improve collaboration and system response speed.

98. These five challenges are listed in PNSR, "Turning Ideas into Action:" Executive Summary, ii.

99. Ibid., vii.

Chapter 5

1. Author interview with James R. Locher III, Arlington, Virginia, February 23, 2009.

2. Author interview with Christopher Lamb, director of research for PNSR, National Defense University, Washington, DC, January 8, 2009.

3. With regard to roles and missions, please refer back to Table 2.1 in Chapter 2. Simply stated, roles and missions refer to what the armed forces and other security instruments, including the police and intelligence agencies, do. See also Paul Shemella, "The Spectrum of Roles and Missions of the Armed Forces," in Thomas C. Bruneau and Scott D. Tollefson, eds,, *Who Guards the Guardians and How: Democratic Civil–Military Relations* (Austin: University of Texas Press, 2006), 122–142.

4. See Robert Young Pelton, *Licensed to Kill: Hired Guns in the War on Terror* (New York: Three Rivers Press, 2006); Steve Fainaru, *Big Boy Rules: America's Mercenaries Fighting in Iraq* (Cambridge, MA: Da Capo Press, 2008); Jeremy Scahill, *Blackwater: The Rise of the World's Most Powerful Mercenary Army* (New York: Nation Books, 2007); and Simon Chesterman and Chia Lehnardt, eds., *From Mercenaries*

to Market: The Rise and Regulation of Private Military Companies (New York: Oxford University Press, 2007).

5. Max Weber, *Economy and Society: An Outline of Interpretive Sociology*, edited by Gunther Roth and Claus Wittich (Berkeley: University of California Press, 1978), 56.

6. See for example the very influential work by Theda Skocpol in *States and Social Revolutions: A Comparative Analysis of France, Russia and China* (New York: Cambridge University Press, 1979), 29–32, 285.

7. In this regard, Samuel P. Huntington, *The Soldier and the State: The Theory and Politics of Civil–Military Relations* (Cambridge, MA: Harvard University Press, 1957), is useful. See especially Chapter 2 (19–58), on "The Rise of the Military Profession in Western Society."

8. For a very useful discussion on the theme of "state authority and the private military companies," see, for example, Anna Leander, *Eroding State Authority? Private Military Companies and the Legitimate Use of Force* (Rome: Rubbettino Editore, 2006).

9. Niccolo Machiavelli, "On Different Kinds of Troops, Especially Mercenaries," Chapter XII in *The Prince*, translated and edited by Robert M. Adams (New York: W. W. Norton & Company, 1977, originally written in 1513), 35.

10. Steve Fainaru captures the friction in his title, *Big Boy Rules*. He writes, "The mercs policed themselves under their own unwritten code. 'Big Boy Rules,' they called it. The military couldn't drink in Iraq; troops had to leave the country just to have a beer. Triple Canopy had its own bar, the Gem, which was located inside the company 'man-camp' behind the blast walls of Baghdad's Green Zone." Fainaru, *Big Boy Rules*, 19.

11. See, for example, Pelton, *Licensed to Kill*.

12. Peter W. Singer, "Can't Win with 'Em, Can't Go to War without 'Em: Private Military Contractors and Counterinsurgency," Policy Paper Number 4, Brookings Institution, Washington, DC, September 2007. Unfortunately, the same phenomenon is occurring in Afghanistan. The *New York Times* reported in July 2010 that "a crowd of hundreds of Afghans rioted after a sports utility vehicle carrying American Embassy contractors struck a car of Afghans . . . The crowd chanted 'Death to America' and 'Death to foreigners.'" "July's Toll Worst for U.S. Troops in Afghanistan," *New York Times*, July 31, 2010, A-8.

13. See Federal Acquisition Regulation (FAR 15.4), "Contract Pricing."

14. A succinct and objective statement of the pro argument is found in Steven L. Schooner, "Why Contractor Fatalities Matter," *Parameters* 38, 3 (Autumn 2008), 78–91, especially 82–83. The most recent Quadrennial Defense Review Report, of February 2010, also includes the contractors: "The services provided by contractors will continue to be valued as part of a balanced approach that properly considers both mission requirements and overall return." This formulation will be returned to in the Conclusion. For the report, go to www.defense.gov/qdr/QDR%20as%20of%2026JAN10%200700.pdf.

15. For an easily accessible "industry" view, see the *Journal of International Peace Operations*, which appears six times per year and is published both in paper and on-line. See also Patrick Cullen and Peter Ezra Weinberger, *POI Report: Reframing the Defense Outsourcing Debate: Merging Government Oversight with Industry Partnership* (Washington, DC: Peace Operations Institute, 2007). IPOA's new name, from 2010, is International Stability Operations Association.

16. For a very useful review of the issues, see Kevin R. Kosar, "Privatization and the Federal Government: An Introduction," CRS Report for Congress (Washington, DC, December 26, 2008), which was published some six weeks after the elections that gave the Democrats control both houses of Congress. In my interviews with Allan V. Burman, who had been head of the Office of Federal Procurement Policy at OMB in the late 1980s and early 1990s, he noted that there was a strong push for "competitive sourcing" through the Office of Federal Procurement Policy in OMB, under Deputy Director of Management Clay Johnson in George W. Bush's administration. Burman noted that contracting out, or competitive sourcing, was a dominant theme during the Reagan, Clinton, and George W. Bush administrations. Interview with Mr. Burman in Washington, DC, January 6 and February 24, 2009.

17. See John D. Donahue, *The Privatization Decision: Public Ends, Private Means* (New York: Basic Books, 1989); Paul C. Light, *The True Size of Government* (Washington, DC: Brookings Institution Press, 1999); and Paul C. Light, *A Government Ill Executed: The Decline of the Federal Service and How to Reverse It* (Cambridge, MA: Harvard University Press, 2008).

18. Kosar, "Contracting for Services (Outsourcing)" in "Privatization and the Federal Government," 15.

19. John R. Luckey, "OMB Circular A-76: Explanation and Discussion of the Recently Revised Federal Outsourcing Policy," CRS Report for Congress (Washington, DC, updated September 10, 2003). For an update, see also L. Elaine Halchin, "Circular A-76 Revision 2003: Selected Issues," CRS Report for Congress (Washington, DC, updated January 7, 2005).

20. P. W. Singer, *Corporate Warriors: The Rise of the Privatized Military Industry* (Ithaca, NY: Cornell University Press, 2003), ix–x. On p. 79, Singer discusses the difficulty of even knowing about the universe of private military contractors. This methodology challenge is also raised by Christopher Kinsey, *Corporate Soldiers and International Security: The Rise of Private Military Companies* (London and New York: Routledge, 2006), 1–2.

21. In his position paper for a new administration, Dan Guttman argues strongly for transparency and the availability of information. "Because reliance on contractors to perform the basic work of government remains invisible in substantial respects, independent analyses of how and how well the system works are few and far between." Guttman, "Government by Contract: The White House Needs Capacity to Review and

Revise the Legacy of 20th Century Reform" (Washington, DC: National Academy of Public Administration, August 2008), 22. In my interview with members of the permanent staff of the Committee on Oversight and Government Reform of the U.S. House of Representatives in Washington on January 7, 2009, they emphasized how difficult it is to obtain information from the private security contractors (PSCs), even though the committee, unlike most, has subpoena power and can conduct depositions. The lack of transparency is an important issue in the excellent analysis by Deborah Avant and Lee Siegelman, on the impact of PSCs on American democracy. See Avant and Sigelman, "Private Security and Democracy: Lessons from the U.S. in Iraq," *Security Studies* 19, 2 (April–June 2010), 230–265, especially 262.

22. For example, two of the largest contracting firms, MPRI and DynCorp, were acquired by other, even larger firms. In June 2000, MPRI was acquired by L-3 Communications; DynCorp was acquired by Computer Sciences Corporation in 2003 and "now has nearly 14,000 employees in 30 countries." Jennifer K. Elsea, Moshe Schwartz, and Kennon H. Nakamura, "Private Security Contractors in Iraq: Background, Legal Status, and Other Issues," CRS Report for Congress (Washington, DC, updated September 29, 2008), 8. For a sense of the buying, and selling, of private contracting companies see, for example, Jody Ray Bennett, "Good Year for Private Security," *Security Watch* (Zurich: International Relations and Security Network, January 19, 2010); available at www.isn.ethz.ch/isn/Current-Affairs/Security-Watch/.

23. These reports to Congress are embargoed for a week or so, then become available at www.sigir.mil. For the legal bases, see SIGIR, "Enabling Legislation as Amended," (Washington, DC: Author, 2009), and see as well their book-length summary of some of their main findings: SIGIR, *Hard Lessons: The Iraq Reconstruction Experience* (Washington, DC: SIGIR, 2009), available at www.sigir.mil/Default.aspx. A similar organization, the Special Inspector General for Afghanistan Reconstruction (SIGAR), was founded by Congress in 2008.

24. I interviewed auditors and other experts at SIGIR February 26, 2009, who told me that until six months previously there had been very little credible data available.

25. It appears that other academic authors have not systematically focused on the contract as the nexus of the relationship between the firm and the USG. In Chapter 10, "Contractual Dilemmas," P. W. Singer raises only some operational and conceptual issues. Singer, *Corporate Warriors*, 151–168. Also, Benedict Sheehy, Jackson Maogoto, and Virginia Newell ostensibly deal with the contract, but the discussion is very abstract, and the data is dated. See Chapter 2, "The Corporate Form and the Private Military Corporation," in Sheehy et al., *Legal Control of The Private Military Corporation* (Basingstoke, UK: Palgrave-Macmillan, 2009), 33–65.

26. "Report of the Commission on Army Acquisition and Program Management in Expeditionary Operations (Gansler Commission)," October 31, 2007, 3; available at www.army.mil/docs/gansler_commission_report_final_071031.pdf.

27. Robert Mendel, *The Privatization of Security* (Boulder, CO: Lynne Rienner Publishers, 2002), 11.

28. Congressional Budget Office (CBO), "Contractors' Support of U.S. Operations in Iraq" (Washington, DC: CBO, August 2008).

29. Ibid., 1, "Introduction and Summary." All of the preceding quotes are from this page. This report refers to a total of $446 billion for contracting in Iraq, but this total is an underestimate, as it does not include contract costs in countries outside the Iraq theater.

30. Ibid., 7. SIGIR, "Agencies Need Improved Financial Data Reporting: Summary," (SIGIR-09-005) (Washington, DC: Author, October 30, 2008).

31. Ibid., 12.

32. Ibid., 2.

33. Emphasis added. SIGIR, "Comprehensive Plan for Audits of Private Security Contractors to Meet the Requirements of Section 842 of Public Law 110-181," Issued October 17, 2008, updated May 8, 2009, 1. Available at www.sigir.mil website.

34. Author interviews at SIGIR with the deputy director, the assistant inspector general for audits, and several auditors, Arlington, Virginia, February 26 and June 16, 2009. In the latter interview I met with the three senior auditors working on the PSCs, including David R. Warren, assistant inspector general for audits. This point is supported by William M. Solis, director of defense capabilities and management for the Government Accountability Office (GAO), in "Operation Iraqi Freedom: Preliminary Observations on DOD Planning for the drawdown of U.S. Forces from Iraq," statement before the Commission on Wartime Contracting in Iraq and Afghanistan (GAO-10-179) November 2, 2009. He states, "Experience has shown that requirements for contracted services will likely increase during the drawdown . . ." Solis, Operation Iraqi Freedom, 9.

35. SIGIR reports that, as of September 30, 2009, there were 25,500 private security contractors in Iraq. There were, at the same time, 120,000 U.S. military personnel. SIGIR, "Quarterly Report to the United States Congress," October 30, 2009, 47. In a more recent report, the figures are 20,738 PSCs to 75,000 U.S. troops. See "Quarterly Report to the United States Congress," SIGIR, July 30, 2010, 58.

36. For this list I drew specifically on Elsea et al., "Private Security Contractors in Iraq," 3.

37. Nicholas Dew and Bryan Hudgens, "The Evolving Private Military Sector: A Survey," February 20, 2008, 21–22. Available at www.acquisitionresearch.org.

38. "Contractor Performing Functions in Areas of Combat Operations," SEC. 862 of the National Defense Authorization Act (NDAA) for Fiscal Year 2008, Public Law 110-181, December 5, 2007. Section 862 is included in the Appendix.

39. "Comprehensive Plan for Audits of Private Security Contractors to Meet the Requirements of Section 842 of Public Law 110-181," SIGIR, updated May 8, 2009. This

document is signed by Stuart W. Bowen Jr., inspector general, and David R. Warren, assistant inspector general-audit, whom I interviewed on this topic on June 16, 2009.

40. Nicholas Dew and Bryan Hudgens, "The Evolving Private Military Sector," 21–22; and Nicholas Dew and Ira Lewis, "The Evolving Private Military Sector: Toward a Framework for Effective DoD Contracting," Acquisition Research Sponsored Report Series, February 10, 2009 (NPS-CM-09-003); available at www.acquisitionsresearch .org. See also Kenneth H. Curtis, Paul. J. Marko, and John J. Parma, "Understanding Market Segments and Competition in the Private Military Industry," MBA Professional Report, Naval Postgraduate School, December 2009.

41. Deborah D. Avant, *The Market for Force: The Consequences of Privatizing Security* (New York: Cambridge University Press, 2005). Avant defines PSCs according to the nature of their contract, while Singer, in *Corporate Warriors*, looks at the structure of the firms themselves.

42. Dew and Hudgens, "The Evolving Private Military Sector," 20, and table 2, on p. 21. The references are to Singer, *Corporate Warriors*, 93; and Avant, *The Market for Force*, 17.

43. Dew and Hudgens diagram what they refer to as a "revised 'Tip of the Spear'" to illustrate the data on capabilities from Avant, *The Market for Force*. Dew and Hudgens, "The Evolving Private Military Sector," 19.

44. Dew and Hudgens, "The Evolving Private Military Sector," 6.

45. Ibid., 8 and 9.

46. Ibid., 44–50. Singer dedicates Chapter 4 to the topic, "Why Security Has Been Privatized," in *Corporate Warriors*, 49–70.

47. David M. Walker, comptroller general of the United States, "DoD Needs to Reexamine Its Extensive Reliance on Contractors and Continue to Improve Management and Oversight," Testimony before the Subcommittee on Readiness, Committee on Armed Services, U.S. House of Representatives, 110th Congress, second session, March 11, 2008, GAO-08-572T: 4–5.

48. Author interview with Arch Barrett, Austin, Texas, December 8–10, 2008.

49. The data for 1990 are from "Selected Manpower Statistics Fiscal Year 1990," AD-A235 849, Washington Headquarters Services, Directorate for Information Operations and Reports, Department of Defense. Data for 1997 and 2009 are available at http://siadapp.dmdc.osd.mil/personnel/MILITARY/history/tab9.

50. CBO, "Contractors' Support of U.S. Operations in Iraq," 13. It should also be noted that DoD was the lead agency for postwar Iraq in accord with President George W. Bush signing National Security Presidential Directive 24, on January 20, 2003. See Nora Bensahel, "Mission Not Accomplished: What Went Wrong with Iraqi Reconstruction," *The Journal of Strategic Studies* 29, 3 (June 2006), 458.

51. Author interview with former State Department official. This also was an ongoing theme in my interviews with Douglas Brooks, who is president of the International

Peace Operations Association. See the interviews for the dates of these meetings. For a useful analysis of the Bureau of Diplomatic Security, see the statement of Jess T. Ford, director of international affairs and trade, GAO, Testimony before the Subcommittee on Oversight of Government Management, the Federal Workforce, and the District of Columbia, Committee on Homeland Security and Governmental Affairs, U.S. Senate, 111th Congress, 1st session, GAO-10-290 T, December 9, 2009.

52. See Richard N. Haass, *War of Necessity War of Choice: A Memoir of Two Iraq Wars* (New York: Simon & Schuster, 2009).

53. Richard Haass refers to "the effective silencing of the Joint Chiefs of Staff by Secretary of Defense Donald Rumsfeld." This relates to the administration's unrealistic assessment of what could be achieved in Iraq. Ibid., 18–19. This key point has been dealt with extensively in credible sources. For example, Richard Haass states:

> The second Iraq war was a war of choice twice over: that it was fought and how it was fought. More than anything else the relatively low number of troops brought to the theater (approximately 150,000, roughly one-third the number of American troops in the previous Iraq war) all but guaranteed the United States and its few coalition partners would not be in a position to assert and maintain order once the formal battles were concluded. The 150,000 number was about one-third the level of forces called for in war plans developed at Central Command in the late 1990s. (Ibid., 253–54)

See also Bensahel, "Mission Not Accomplished"; and Nora Bensahel et al., *After Saddam: Prewar Planning and the Occupation of Iraq* (Santa Monica, CA: RAND, Arroyo Center, 2008). Joseph Collins lists ten "Errors in Decisionmaking and Execution," of which eight concern lack of manpower. See Joseph J. Collins, "Choosing War: The Decision to Invade Iraq and Its Aftermath," Occasional Paper, Institute for National Strategic Studies, National Defense University, April 2008, 16.

54. Secretary of Defense Robert Gates, Hearing to Receive Testimony on the Challenges Facing the Department of Defense, U.S. Senate Committee on Armed Services, 111th Congress, 2nd session, January 27, 2009, 8.

55. In an interview with a member of the permanent staff of the House of Representatives, I was informed that originally, under Title 10, there was a prohibition on the use of PSCs. After 9/11, however, it was waived because of the need for activated reservists to guard facilities.

56. John R. Luckey, "OMB Circular A-76: Explanation and Discussion of the Recently Revised Federal Outsourcing Policy," CRS Report for Congress, September 10, 2003, 3. Emphasis in original.

57. Walker, "DoD Needs to Reexamine Its Extensive Reliance," 5–6, 7.

58. Ibid., 8–9.

59. The short definition: "The term 'inherently governmental function' means a function that is so intimately related to the public interest as to require performance

by Federal Government employees." John R. Luckey, Valerie Bailey Grasso, and Kate M. Manuel, "Inherently Governmental Functions and Department of Defense Operations: Background, Issues, and Options for Congress," CRS Report for Congress, R40641, Washington, DC, June 15, 2009, 9.

60. Steven Cohen and William Eimicke, *The Responsible Contract Manager: Protecting the Public Interest in an Outsources World* (Washington, DC: Georgetown University Press, 2008), 159–168.

61. The literature I am referring to includes Donahue, *The Privatization Decision*; and Light, *The True Size of Government* and *A Government Ill Executed*. The most relevant CRS Reports are those that deal with privatization and inherently governmental functions. For the former see Kevin R. Kosar, "Privatization and the Federal Government: An Introduction," CRS Report for Congress, December 28, 2006, and for the latter see Luckey, et al., "Inherently Governmental Functions," updated September 14, 2009. Note that this document is updated regularly, with the same title and document number and a different date.

Chapter 6

1. "Contractors Performing Private Security Functions in Area of Combat Operations," Section 862 of the National Defense Authorization Act (NDAA) for Fiscal Year 2008, Public Law 110-181 (December 5, 2007). This legislation directs the secretary of defense to deal specifically with the PSCs. Section 862 is in the appendix. The guidance to SIGIR is from section 842 of the same NDAA. They also call attention to "discussions with key congressional staff," prior to launching a "Comprehensive Plan for Audits of Private Security Contractors to Meet the Requirements of Section 842 of Public Law 110-181." Special Inspector General for Iraq Reconstruction (SIGIR), Washington, DC, updated May 8, 2009.

2. See Frederick M. Kaiser, Walter J. Oleszek, T. J. Halstead, Norton Rosenberg, and Todd B. Tatelman, "Congressional Oversight Manual," Congressional Research Service (CRS) Report for Congress (RL 30240), updated January 2, 2007.

3. The GAO details their instruction to study PSCs in "Military Operations. High-Level DOD Action Needed to Address Long-Standing Problems with Management and Oversight of Contractors Supporting Deployed Forces," Government Accountability Office (GAO) Report to Congressional Committees (GAO-07-145), December 2006, updated from 2003: 3. Appendix I reviews the methodology, including all of the governmental and contracting organizations in the United States, Iraq, Kuwait, and United Arab Emirates.

4. Representative Henry Waxman, who assumed the chairmanship of the committee after the 2006 elections gave the Democratic Party a majority in both houses of Congress, immediately ramped up the committee's activities on the conduct of post-combat operations, an area his Republican predecessor had neglected.

5. See the committee website at http://oversight.house.gov/story.asp?ID=1509; also, author interviews with committee professional staff members, Washington, DC, January 7, 2009.

6. On these incidents, see Jeremy Scahill, *Blackwater: The Rise of the World's Most Powerful Mercenary Army* (New York: Nation Books, 2007).

7. "Urgent Reform Required: Army Expeditionary Contracting," report of the Commission on Army Acquisition and Program Management in Expeditionary Operations (henceforward the Gansler Commission Report), October 31, 2007, 43. The commission interviewed or took testimony from approximately150 practitioners and experts.

8. David M. Walker, comptroller general of the United States, "DOD Needs to Reexamine Its Extensive Reliance on Contractors and Continue to Improve Management and Oversight," Testimony before the Subcommittee on Readiness, Committee on Armed Services, House of Representatives, 110th Congress, second session, GAO-08-7572T, March 11, 2008, Highlights section [no page number]. Emphasis added.

9. The commission also notes that "the 'Operational Army' is expeditionary and on a war footing, but does not yet fully recognize the impact of contractors in expeditionary operations and on mission success, as evidenced by poor requirements definition." Gansler Commission, "Urgent Reform Required," 1, note 2; available at www.army.mil/docs/gansler_Commission_Report_Final_071031.pdf.

10. Ibid., 20.

11. Ibid., 4. Interview with Dr. Jacques S. Gansler at University of Maryland, College Park, on February 23, 2009.

12. I have introduced the term *contract management process* here at the suggestion of Professor Rene G. Rendon, a faculty member in the NPS Graduate School of Business and Public Policy, in written response on August 14, 2009. The centrality of the contract emerged as the main theme in the interviews with both the would-be regulators and those they would regulate, the contactors. In my interview with members of the permanent staff of the Committee on Oversight and Government Reform in the House of Representatives on January 7, 2009, they agreed, "Effectiveness is in terms of the contracts." This also was a central theme in interviews with General Harry E. "Ed" Soyster, of MPRI in Arlington, Virginia, on January 8, 2009, and Dr. Gansler, regarding the reform of Army contracting.

13. See the list of interviews for the individuals and affiliations.

14. Suzanne Simons, *Master of War: Blackwater USA's Erik Prince and the Business of War* (New York: Harper Collins, 2009), 5.

15. Linda Robinson, *Tell Me How This Ends: General David Petraeus and the Search for a Way Out of Iraq* (New York: Public Affairs, 2008).

16. "Contractors' Support of U.S. Operations in Iraq," Congressional Budget Office (CBO) Paper, Washington, DC, August 2008, 13.

17. U.S. Government Accountability Office (GAO). "Department of Defense. Additional Actions and Data Are Needed to Effectively Manage and Oversee DOD's Acquisition Workforce," GAO Report to Congressional Requesters (GAO-09-342) (Washington, DC: Author, March 2009), 1–2.

18. GAO. "High-Risk Series: An Update," GAO Report to Congress (GAO-09-271) (Washington, DC: GAO, January 2009), Highlights, no page number.

19. Ibid., 43.

20. Ibid.

21. Ibid., 73.

22. Walker, "DoD Needs to Reexamine Its Extensive Reliance," 1–2.

23. Ibid., 4. This point was made also in my interview with Rene Rendon on January 16, 2009. Dr. Rendon reiterated this point in his written comments to me on August 14, 2009. This is a constant theme in contract management: that contracting for services is much more complicated than contracting for things.

24. Ibid., 1. According to Walker, "DOD is by far the largest federal purchaser of service contracts—ranging from housing to intelligence to security." Ibid., 4.

25. Ibid., 14.

26. Rendon, written comments.

27. The former point was made by permanent staff of the U.S. House of Representatives and staff of the Office of the Secretary of Defense (OSD), also on June 17, 2009. The latter point was made by members of the Waxman Committee permanent staff on January 17, 2009, the SIGIR auditor staff on June 16, 2009, in the House, and the GAO staff on June 16, 2009. The absence of a doctrine was stressed again and again in meetings at the Naval Postgraduate School with Professor Cory Yoder in 2009.

28. CBO, "Contractors' Support of U.S. Operations in Iraq," 20.

29. Walker, "DoD Needs to Reexamine Its Extensive Reliance," 14.

30. Ibid., 14–16.

31. Simons, *Master of War*, 73. See also, Lt. Gen. Ricardo S. Sanchez, with Donald T. Phillips, *Wiser in Battle; A Soldier's Story* (New York: HarperCollins, 2008), 340, in which Sanchez describes an incident with Blackwater regarding the relay of bogus information.

32. Gansler Commission Report, 39–46

33. Ibid., 45–46.

34. Ibid., 44–45. See glossary for meaning of these acronyms.

35. Kelley Poree, Capt., USAF, Katrina Curtis, Capt., USAF, Jeremy Morrill, Capt., USAF, and Steven Sherwood, LCDR, USN, "The Joint Effects-Based Contracting Execution System: A Proposed Enabling Concept for Future Joint Expeditionary Contracting Execution," Graduate School of Business and Public Policy, Naval Postgraduate School, Monterey, California, December 30, 2008: 26.

36. CBO, "Contractors' Support of U.S. Operations."

37. Ibid., 7. This means that they are unable to determine what is supposed to be done under the contract.

38. Ibid., 8.

39. These interviews were with permanent staff of the U.S. House of Representatives, Nicholas Dew on February 19, and GAO on June 16, 2009, and with Cory Yoder in several meetings through 2009. Many of those I interviewed are critical of the Defense Contract Audit Agency (DCAA). Senator Claire McCaskill (D-MO), one of the chief congressional critics of the recent problems at the DCAA, released a statement about the reassignment of agency director April Stephenson: "'This is just a first step in a long list of changes that need to happen at DCAA,' McCaskill said. 'There is a culture at DCAA and the Defense Department that has allowed the agency to go so far down this very wrong path. While I am encouraged by Comptroller Hale's recent decision, the Defense Department still has a long way to go before it restores DCAA's credibility as an auditing agency.'" Quoted in Ed O'Keefe, "Contracting cost cuts on target, OMB says," *Washington Post*, December 21, 2009; available at www.washingtonpost .com/wp-dyn/content/artile/2009/1.

40. Rendon, interview. January 16, 2009. Also, Rene G. Rendon, "Defense Acquisition Workforce," in Rene G. Rendon and Keith F. Snider, eds., *Management of Defense Acquisition Projects* (Palmdale, CA: Lockheed Martin Corporation, for the American Institute of Aeronautics and Astronautics, Inc., 2008), 267–280. As he states on page 270, they do not have an acquisition workforce in this service area.

41. This was a main theme in a number of interviews with extremely well-informed experts, including Burman, Brooks, SIGIR, Gansler, Green, and Yoder. See the list of interviews.

42. Gansler Commission Report, 30. See also Moshe Schwartz, "Training the Military to Manage Contractors during Expeditionary Operations: Overview and Options for Congress," CRS Report for Congress, December 17, 2008, 1, He writes,

> However, while a number of contracting officers and other acquisition officials are in Iraq, most of DOD's acquisition workforce is generally not deployed or embedded with the military during expeditionary operations. As the number of contactors in the area of operations has increased, the operational force—the service men and women in the field—increasingly rely on, interact with, and are responsible for managing contractors. Yet, a number of military commanders and service members have indicated they did not get adequate information regarding the extent of contractor support in Iraq and did not receive enough pre-deployment training to prepare them to manage or work with contractors. ("Schwartz, Training the Military," 3)

Schwartz draws heavily on Walker, "DOD Needs to Reexamine Its Extensive Reliance."

43. Gansler Commission Report, 35, table 9.

44. Ibid., 36–37.

45. The Honorable Jacques S. Gansler, "Acquisition Reform: Achieving 21st Century National Security," testimony before the Senate Armed Services Committee, 111st Congress, 1st session, March 3, 2009, table on p. 3. See also the Federal News Service for a transcript of his testimony, March 3, 2009.

46. Gansler interview, February 23, 2009. He also noted that the Defense Contract Management Agency did have four general officers and currently has none, while the U.S. Air Force number was cut in half.

47. Gansler Commission Report, 30.

48. Rendon, interview.

49. Walker, "DOD Needs to Reexamine Its Extensive Reliance," 16. Walker also makes reference to the Gansler Commission Report, which states "that the Army lacks the leadership and military and civilian personnel to provide sufficient support to either expeditionary or peacetime mission. . . . As we noted in our 2006 report, [34] without adequate contract oversight personnel in place to monitor its many contracts in deployed locations such as Iraq, DOD may not be able to obtain reasonable assurance that contractors are meeting their contact requirements efficiently and effectively." Ibid., 17.

50. Ibid., 20.

51. Gansler Commission Report, 43.

52. SIGIR, "Need to Enhance Oversight of Theater-Wide Internal Security Services Contracts," (SIGIR-09-017). Washington, DC: April 24, 2009, ii.

53. Ibid., 10.

54. Interview with Jason Venner, David Warren, and Bob Pelletier on June 16, 2009. The Merit System Protection Board (MSPB) researched and published a report dated May 2006 on the CORs. A number of findings stand out from the survey on which this report is based. First, DoD dwarfs the rest of the departments or agencies in sheer scale. Of the total dollars that go to contracting, among all the agencies they studied, DoD accounted for $132 billion of the total of $185 billion and was 59 percent of all actions in the survey. DoD, it becomes clear, is in a category all by itself in this cross-agency study of the CORs. The results seem, in general, to fairly reflect what the CORs are doing: "47% of the CORs experienced less than the intended outcome in at least one of the outcome categories." "Contracting Officer Representatives: Managing the Government's Technical Experts to Achieve Positive Contract Outcomes," Report to the President and Congress, MSPB, Washington, DC, May 1, 2006, 58.

55. John K. Needham, director of acquisition and sourcing management, "Acquisition Workforce: DOD Can Improve Its Management and Oversight by Tracking Data on Contractor Personnel and Taking Additional Actions," Testimony before the

Oversight and Investigations Subcommittee, Committee on Armed Services, House of Representatives, 111th Congress, 1st session (GAO-09-616T), April 28, 2009.

56. Ibid. Needham also refers to data found in GAO, "Additional Actions and Data Are Needed."

57. William M. Solis, director, defense capabilities and management, "Military Operations: High-Level DOD Action Needed to Address Long-Standing Problems with Management and Oversight of Contractors Supporting Deployed Forces." GAO report to Congress (GAO-07-145), December 2006.

58. Ibid., Highlights (no page number).

59. Ibid., opening summary (no page number). To appreciate the continuity in recognition, but not remedy, of the problems, it is worth reading the original report. See "Acquisition Workforce: Department of Defense's Plans to Address Workforce Size and Structure Challenges," GAO (GAO-02-630), April 2002. In my interview on June 17, 2009, with staff at the Office of the Secretary of Defense Assistant Deputy Undersecretary (Logistics & Material Readiness/Program Support), responsible for implementation of recommendations within DoD, they offered some relevant details regarding implementation. I will deal with these in the conclusion.

60. Solis, "High-Level DOD Action Needed:" Highlights (no page number).

61. Ibid.

62. Ibid., Highlights.

63. Ibid., 4.

64. Ibid., Highlights.

65. They continue to make the same points. See, for example, David M. Walker, comptroller general of the United States, "Defense Acquisitions: DOD'S Increased Reliance on Service Contactors Exacerbates Long-Standing Challenges," Testimony before the Subcommittee on Defense, Committee on Appropriations, House of Representatives, 110th Congress, 2nd session, (GAO-08-621T), January 23, 2008; Needham, "DOD Can Improve Its Management and Oversight"; and William M. Solis, "Warfighter Support: Cultural Change Needed to Improve How DOD Plans for and Manages Operational Contract Support," Testimony before the Subcommittee on National Security and Foreign Affairs, Committee on Oversight and Government Reform, House of Representatives, 111th Congress, 2nd session (GAO-10-829T), June 29, 2010.

66. Allan V. Burman, "The Role of Contractors in Government: Have We Gone Too Far?" *The Public Manager* (March 22, 2008); and Burman, "Inherently Governmental Functions: At a Tipping Point? Should the Government Rethink Its Long-Standing Policy on Contracting Out Work?" *The Public Manager* (March 22, 2008).

67. Walker, "DOD Needs to Reexamine Its Extensive Reliance," 8; see also pp. 8–12 on this issue.

68. Needham, "DOD Can Improve Its Management and Oversight," 3.

69. Valerie Bailey Grasso, "Defense Contracting in Iraq and Afghanistan: Issues and Options for Congress," CRS Report for Congress (RL 33834), February 19, 2009. For some insights into the political positions see, on the proindustry side, Roger D. Carstens, Michael A. Cohen, and Maria Figueroa Kupcu, "Changing the Culture of Pentagon Contracting," Privatization of Foreign Policy Initiative of the New America Foundation, October 2008; and the letter, found in the Appendix of this book (Letter to OFPP of OMB, by Contracting Industry Representatives, dated June 8, 2009).

70. Ibid., 5, and 5–8.

71. John R. Luckey, Valerie Bailey Grasso, and Kate M. Manuel, "Inherently Governmental Functions and Department of Defense Operations: Background, Issues, and Options for Congress," CRS (R 40641), June 15, 2009. It is notable that the CRS continues to publish updates to this report to assist the Congress on this extremely important issue. See Luckey et al., "Inherently Governmental Functions," (same document number), dated September 14, 2009. Newer CRS reports on this topic will be cited in the Conclusion.

72. Interviews with professional staff made clear that the definition of what is inherently governmental is crucial to reform. In addition to the sources cited in note 71 for insights from a legal "industry perspective," see Tara Lee, "Redefining Inherently Governmental: The Push to Redefine the Function and Its Consequences," *Journal of International Peace Operations* 4, 1 (July–August 2008), 9–10. Note that the website Open CRS-CRS Reports for the People has made the CRS reports on this topic readily available. See http://opencrs.com/document/R40641.

73. On January 21, 2010, a divided U.S Supreme Court, in a five to four decision, ruled that the government may not ban political spending by corporations in candidate elections. For details see Adam Liptak, "Justices, 5–4, Reject Corporate Spending Limit," *New York Times*, January 21, 2010; available at www.nytimes.com/2010/01/22/us/politics/22scotus.html.

74. See, for example, Andrew Alexandra, Deane-Peter Baker, and Marina Caparini, eds., *Private Military and Security Companies: Ethics, Policies and Civil–Military Relations* (London and New York: Routledge, 2008); and, more recently, Benedict Sheehy, Jackson Maogoto, and Virginia Newell, *Legal Control of the Private Military Corporation* (Basingstoke, UK: Palgrave Macmillan, 2009).

75. Simons, *Master of War*, 145.

76. Interview with Michael J. Heidingsfield, Washington, DC, February 26, 2009.

77. The sources I draw on include Mark Lindemann, "Civilian Contractors under Military Law," *Parameters* 37 (Autumn 2007), 83–94; Samuel P. Cheadle, "Private Military Contractor Liability under the Worldwide Personal Protective Services II Contract," *Public Contract Law Journal* 38, 3 (Spring 2009), 689–708; Steven L. Schooner, "Fear of Oversight: The Fundamental Failure of Businesslike Government," *American University Law Review* 50, 3 (2001); Matthew C. Weed, "U.S.–Iraq Agreements:

Congressional Oversight Activities and Legislative Response," CRS Report for Congress (RL 34568), May 15, 2009; R. Chuck Mason, "Status of Forces Agreement (SOFA): What Is It, and How Has It Been Utilized?" CRS Report for Congress (RL 34531), June 18, 2009; R. Chuck Mason, "U.S.–Iraq Withdrawal/Status of Forces Agreement: Issues for Congressional Oversight," CRS Report for Congress (R 40011), July 13, 2009; "Rebuilding Iraq: DOD and State Department Have Improved Oversight and Coordination of Private Security Contractors in Iraq, but Further Actions Are Needed to Sustain Improvements." Washington, DC: U.S. General Accounting Office (GAO-08-966), July 2008; and Kara M. Sacilotto, "Iraq SOFA: Issues Abound for Contractors," *Federal Contracts Report* 91, 2 (January 20, 2009), 44–45. My interviews with Doug Brooks, Jeff Green, Michael Love, and Tara Lee in 2009 are also relevant to these legal issues. See the list of interviews.

78. Jennifer K. Elsea, Moshe Schwartz, and Kennon H. Nakamura, "Private Security Contractors in Iraq: Background, Legal Status, and Other Issues," CRS Report for Congress (RL 32419), updated September 29, 2008: 14. A more comprehensive listing of possibly applicable laws is provided in "Rebuilding Iraq," 24–30.

79. For example, the Montreaux Document of September 17, 2008, resulted from a meeting of seventeen countries regarding rules and good practices relating to private military and security companies operating in armed conflicts. It relates to the Status of the Protocols Additional to the Geneva Conventions of 1949 and to the protection of victims of armed conflicts. The document "contains a set of over 70 good practices designed to assist States in complying with these obligations. Neither parts are legally binding, nor are they intended to legitimize the use of PMSCs in any particular circumstance." Summary of United Nations "General Assembly Security Council" (A/63/467-S/2008/636), October 6, 2008.

80. Elsea et al., "Private Security Contractors in Iraq," 19.

81. Martin Chulov, Ed Pilkington, and Enas Ibrahim, "Iraq Threatens Action after Blackwater Case Collapses," World News, *Guardian* Online, January 1, 2010; available at www.guardian.co.uk/world.

82. Elsea et al., "Private Security Contractors in Iraq," 20.

83. Ibid.

84. Lindemann, "Civilian Contractors under Military Law," 88.

85. Ibid.

86. Ibid.

87. Mason, "Status of Forces Agreement (SOFA)," 16.

88. Ibid., 90.

89. Mason, "U.S.–Iraq Withdrawal," 7–9.

90. Kara M. Sacilotto, "Iraq SOFA: Issues Abound for Contractors." *Federal Contracts Report* 91, 2 (20 January 20, 2009), 45. Tara Lee and Ryan Berry raise a series of issues in "Contracting under the SOFA," *Journal of International Peace Operations* 4, 4

(January–February 2009): 7–10. It is difficult for any industry outsider to comprehend how many of these problems are in fact real.

91. Cheadle, "Private Military Contractor Liability," 691.

92. Chulov et al., "Iraq Threatens Action."

93. I am encouraged to see that I am consistent with Renee De Nevers, a respected scholar who suggests self-regulation in lieu of the legal regulation I am examining here. De Nevers states,

> Regulations governing PSCS thus exist at the international and state level, but their scope is incomplete. The fact that the United States, whose regulations governing PSCS are the most comprehensive, has had trouble determining PSC accountability, points to the need for a more effective regulatory framework at both levels. This also suggests that alternative regulatory mechanisms such as self-regulation deserve further exploration.

See Renee De Nevers, "(Self) Regulating War? Voluntary Regulation and the Private Security Industry," *Security Studies* 18, 3 (2009), 491–492. Unfortunately, but not surprisingly, De Nevers finds that "it would be a mistake to trust to self-regulation alone. As it is currently configured, this industry does not lend itself to obligatory self-regulation." Ibid., 516.

Chapter 7

1. Project on National Security Reform (PNSR), "Turning Ideas into Action: A Progress Report" (Washington, DC: Author, September 30, 2009).

2. See SIGIR, "Quarterly Report to the United States Congress," July 30, 2010, 58.

3. Or, as stated by Peter A. Hall and Rosemary C. R. Taylor, "[Institutions are] the formal or informal procedures, routines, norms and conventions embedded in the organizational structure of the polity or political economy. They can range from the rules of a constitutional order or the standard operating procedures of a bureaucracy to the conventions governing trade union behaviour or bank-firm relations." Hall and Taylor, "Political Science and the Three New Institutionalisms," *Political Studies* 44 (1996), 938.

4. During the week of August 23, 2010, Ms. Admire conducted follow-up interviews with officials at four of the main venues for this analysis: the International Peace Operations Association, Special Inspector General for Iraq Reconstruction, the office of the secretary of defense, and the Commission on Wartime Contracting, as well as with a number of industry lawyers.

5. PNSR, "Turning Ideas into Action."

6. For updates on PNSR's work, visit www.pnsr.org/.

7. 2009 National Defense Authorization Act, Section 321, *Federal Register* (U.S. Congress) 74, 102 (May 29), 25775.

8. President Obama's memo is titled, "Memorandum for the Heads of Executive Departments and Agencies: Subject: Government Contracting," the White House, dated March 4, 2009. It is included in the appendix as President Barak Obama's Memorandum for Heads of Departments and Agencies, March 4, 2009. The quote and discussion are in James R. Luckey, Valerie Bailey Grasso, and Kate M. Manuel, "Inherently Governmental Functions and Department of Defense Operations: Background, Issues, and Options for Congress," CRS Report for Congress (Washington, DC: Congressional Research Service, September 14, 2009), 6.

9. Ibid.

10. The *Federal Register* 75, 61 (March 31, 2010).

11. For insights into the industry position, see the eight-page letter to Julia Wise, Office of Federal Procurement Policy, dated June 8, 2009, which is included in the Appendix to this book. See also Roger D. Carstens, Michael A. Cohen, and Maria Figueroa Kupcu, "Changing the Culture of Pentagon Contracting," Privatization of Foreign Policy Initiative of the New America Foundation, October 2008.

12. Robert Brodsky, "Inherently Governmental Rule Sparks Little Consensus," *Government Executive* (June 3, 2010); available at www.govexec.com/story_page_pf .cfm?articleid=45414&.

13. It is important to note that the Policy Guidance (2009-01) issued by the assistant secretary of the Army regarding the use of contractors, specifically states "that service contract requirements do not include inherently governmental functions." Yet the concept of what is inherently governmental had not been tightened up, so this guidance, which at first glance appears rigorous, in fact is only more vague wording. See "Memorandum for all USASMDC/ARSTRAT Employees," SMDC-RDC-AP, Policy Guidance 2009-01, Department of the Army, August 11, 2009.

14. L. Elaine Halchin, Kate M. Manuel, Shawn Reese, and Moshe Schwartz, "Inherently Governmental Functions and the Work Reserved for Performance by Federal Government Employess: The Obama Administration's Proposed Policy Letter," CRS Report for Congress, January 3, 2011.

15. Richard Fontaine and John Nagl, "Contractors in American Conflicts: Adapting to a New Reality," Working Paper, Center for a New American Security, December 2009, 15.

16. Jennifer K. Elsea, "Private Security Contractors in Iraq and Afghanistan: Legal Issues," CRS Report for Congress, December 22, 2009; and Jennifer K. Elsea, "Private Security Contractors in Iraq and Afghanistan: Legal Issues," CRS Report for Congress, January 7, 2010.

17. The two reports, issued only two weeks apart, are basically identical, although the latter report is one page longer than the former. Elsea, "Private Security Contractors in Iraq," January 7, 2010, 29–30.

18. Ricardo M. Urbina, U.S. District Judge, "Memorandum Opinion," U.S. District Court for the District of Columbia, doc. 217, 31 December 31, 2009. The ninety-page decision can be found at http://letterofapology.com/wp-content/uploads/2009/12/blackwateropinion.pdf.

19. The most up-to-date article I can find on the topic states, in the abstract, "This article suggests ways in which such accountability [legal accountability of private companies] *can be put in place*, such that PMSCs can actually serve the cause of securing local and regional stability as a first step toward establishing a much safer environment for people and for business." Don Mayer, "Peaceful Warriors: Private Military Security Companies and the Quest for Stable Societies," *Journal of Business Ethics* 89 (2010), 387–401, esp. 387. Emphasis added.

20. This important document can be found in the Appendix.

21. Author interview at the Office of the Secretary of Defense Assistant Deputy Undersecretary (Logistics & Material Readiness/Program Support), Washington, DC, June 17, 2009; follow-on interview by Kristyn Admire with staff of this office, August 24, 2010.

22. The position, and the responsibilities that go with it, are found in Department of Defense Directive Number 3020.49, March 24, 2009.

23. "Private Security Contractors (PSCs) Operating in Contingency Operations," Department of Defense Instruction No. 3020.50, July 22, 2009.

24. "The Interim Final Rule on Private Security Contractors (PSCs) Operating in Contingency Operations," *Federal Register* 74, 136 (July 17, 2009). The rule was open for comment and it will ultimately be included in the FAR (probably around 52.225-19) after it receives final approval from OMB.

25. Emphasis added. "Field Commanders See Improvements in Controlling and Coordinating Private Security Contractor Missions in Iraq," Special Inspector General for Iraq Reconstruction (SIGIR), (SIGIR 09-022), July 28, 2009. Also, while the title of the SIGIR report is positive, another by GAO that deals with implementation of Section 861 of the NDAA for FY 2008 is less so. See the statement of John P. Hutton, director of acquisition and sourcing management, in GAO, "Contingency Contracting. Further Improvements Needed in Agency Tracking of Contractor Personnel and Contracts in Iraq and Afghanistan" (GAO-10-187), November 2, 2009. A more recent SIGIR document's summary states that "over $2.5 billion in U.S. funds are vulnerable to waste and fraud." See SIGIR, "Long-Standing Weaknesses in Department of State's Oversight of DynCorp Contract for Support of the Iraqi Police Training Program," (SIGIR 10-008), January 25, 2010.

26. See "Operational Contract Support," Joint Publication 4-10, Office of the Joint Chiefs of Staff, October 17, 2008. It should be noted that a more positive view of JP 4-10 is put forth in Al Borzoo, Constance S. Short, Ken Brockway, and Col. Stan L.

VanderWerf, USAF, "Joint Acquisition Command Doctrine: A Success Story," *Defense Acquisition Review Journal* 16, 3, October 2009: 268–283.

27. Information on this document, DoDI 3020-41, was provided by the Office of the Secretary of Defense Assistant Deputy Undersecretary (Logistics & Material Readiness/Program Support), Washington, DC, on June 17, 2009, from a PowerPoint presentation dated May 2009, for the U.S. Army War College.

28. CJCS Dependence on Contractors Task Force.

29. In a personal communication to the author on September 20, 2010, Barbara J. Bishop, Director Operational Contract Support (OCS) Education and Material Readiness, Office of the Deputy Assistant Secretary of Defense (Program Support), stated, "At this time, there is no mandate in place for officer to take these classes prior to deployment nor are there metrics to track who has taken the classes. These are issues that we will be working on within the next few months."

30. In several of my interviews I was informed that the CORs would be trained online. This training can be accessed at https://acc.dau.mil/cor. As a U.S. government employee, professor, and researcher who often is required to travel, I have had to fulfill at least a dozen on-line trainings, several of them annually. My doing so, however, does not make me an expert at any of them. They are simply one more requirement that has to be met.

31. See the Quadrennial Defense Review Report, Department of Defense, February 2010, 55–56. Even more important is the congressionally mandated Quadrennial Defense Review Independent Panel, which states, among other points similar to mine, the following:

> Contractors can and should have an important role in supporting the Comprehensive Approach, but better management and improved oversight is essential. In addition to the ongoing Department of Defense review of what constitutes inherently governmental tasks, better oversight should include designating an Assistant Secretary of Defense-level official to oversee and standardize management of contractors in contingencies; increasing the number and improving the training of contracting officers; integrating contractors and contractor-provided tasks into contingency plans; and integrating contractor roles into pre- deployment training and exercises.

Stephen J. Hadley and William J. Perry, *The QDR in Perspective: Meeting America's National Security Needs In the 21st Century* (Washington, DC: United States Institute of Peace, 2010).

32. For the budget submission, see "DOD Releases Defense Reviews, 2011 Budget Proposal, and 2010 War Funding Supplement Request—Update," Office of the Assistance Secretary of Defense (Public Affairs), no. 084-10, February 1, 2010, available at www.defense.gov/releases/release.aspx?releaseid=13281.

33. Patrick Purcell, "Federal Employees: Pay and Pension Increases since 1969," CRS Report for Congress, January 20, 2010. It seems telling as well that even military salaries are better than are those of civilians. In a study for Congressman Steny H. Hoyer, U.S. House of Representatives, the Congressional Budget Office on January 20, 2011, stated the following:

> According to CBO's analysis, median cash compensation for military personnel—including the tax-free cash allowances for food and housing—exceeds the salaries of most federal civilians of comparable education and work experience. In addition, according to prior studies, noncash and deferred benefits are also higher for military personnel than for federal civilian workers. (1–2)

Retrieved on January 24, 2011, from www.cbo.gov/ftpdocs/120xx/doc12042/01-20 -Compensation.pdf.

34. Paul C. Light, *A Government Ill Executed: The Decline of the Federal Service and How to Reverse It* (Cambridge, MA: Harvard University Press, 2008), 206.

35. Currently there are several of these initiatives. See, for example, "DOD News Briefing with Secretary Gates from the Pentagon," August 9, 2010, concerning "how the Pentagon does business," available at www.defense.gov/transcripts/transcript.aspx ?transcriptid=4669. For an assessment, see Stephen Daggett, "Preliminary Assessment of Efficiency Initiatives Announced by Secretary of Defense Gates on August 9, 2010," Congressional Research Service Memorandum (7-5700), August 12, 2010.

36. On February 24, 2011, the Commission published "At what risk: Correcting over-reliance on contractors in contingency operations" as their Second Interim Report to Congress. Available at www.wartimecontracting.gov/.

Appendix 2

1. 10 USC §2383 is the only statute that seeks to define the term "closely associated with inherently governmental functions." Other statutes simply cross-reference to 10 USC §2383. It is inappropriate to enshrine in a statute, e.g. 10 USC §2383, a definition that can be significantly modified unilaterally through regulations, although we recognize that there are numerous examples, even the federal procurement context, where this approach has been used.

2. We use government rather than agency employee here because, in some instances, one agency may choose to use federal employees of another agency to perform these inherently governmental functions. One example is when a contracting officer employed by the General Services Administration awards a contract or a task order funded by another agency for supplies or services needed by the requesting agency.

3. Government Contractors: Are Service Contractors Performing Inherently Governmental Functions, GAO/GGD-92-11 (November 1991) page 2.

4. A-76 uses "substantial" while the FAR uses "significant" when it mentions discretion. The FAIR Act does not use any phrase to modify the term "discretion."

5. If federal employees can occupy positions that do not perform inherently governmental functions or are not critical, those employees, aka commercial employees, can be overseen by a private employee, commercial employee because they are performing commercial work. This assumes the directing and control is not so detailed as to become personal services.

6. OMB Circular A-76 uses the term "activity", without definition, to mean a function that a person performs, e.g. an inherently governmental activity, and a collection of positions that are a logical grouping for purposes of competing for performance by a contractor or government employees.

INTERVIEWS

I conducted personal interviews with individuals I identified as the research project progressed who would be able to provide me with information and insights on the topics in this book. The warm reception I received from this array of professionals was truly gratifying. Everyone I spoke with made clear that the issue of reform, not only of contractors but to some degree also of national security policy making, could benefit from objective analysis by a bureaucracy and industry outsider. It must be noted that the professional staff of the U.S. Congress can speak only on background and must not be named in any publication. I regret that I am not able to single them out by name for their generosity in sharing both their time and invaluable expertise.

Gordon Adams: Stimson Center, Washington, DC, on January 6, 2009. Professor Gordon Adams is an academic with expertise in defense economics and has held positions in the U.S. executive and legislative branches. He has been directly involved in several defense reform initiatives.

Arch Barrett: Lago Azul, outside Austin, Texas, December 8–10, 2008. Mr. Barrett was a USAF colonel during the Vietnam War and later served as a staffer in the House of Representatives, where he was the single most important author of the Goldwater-Nichols Defense Reorganization Act of 1986. He oversaw the implementation of Joint Professional Military Education via the Skelton Panel on Professional Military Education and later served as principal deputy assistant secretary of the Army.

Kathy Brinkley: Meeting in Washington, DC, on February 24, 2009. Kathy Brinkley is a long-time contracting officer at the Military Sealift Command. She is an expert on contacting, including on contracting officer representatives.

Doug Brooks: Washington, DC, February 24, June 15, September 16, and October 7, 2009. Doug Brooks is president of the International Peace Operations Association and is in constant contact with the contractors, executive and legislative branch officials, NGOs, think tanks, and university programs. After 2010, IPOA has been renamed the International Stability Operations Association.

Kara Bue: Arlington, Virginia, several meetings; and Monterey, California, March 26, 2009. Kara Bue is a partner with Armitage International of Arlington, Virginia. From 2003–2005, Ms. Bue served as deputy assistant secretary of state for regional stability within the Bureau of Political-Military Affairs, where she worked on military policy in Iraq and Afghanistan.

Allan Burman: Jefferson Solutions in Washington, DC, on January 6 and on February 24, 2009. Mr. Burman is president of Jefferson Solutions. He previously held very high positions in both OMB, where he was director of the Office of Federal Procurement Policy, and DoD and remains active in teaching, researching, writing, and testifying on issues regarding defense planning and economics. Mr. Burman introduced me to the concept of "inherently governmental functions," which turned out to be a key element in this research.

Theodore Chuang and Russell Anello: Washington, DC, January 7, 2009. Theodore Chuang was deputy chief investigative counsel, and Russell Anello was counsel on the permanent staff of the House Committee on Oversight and Government Reform. They helped me understand the issues involved in the hearings on PSCs being chaired by Representative Henry Waxman.

Carole Coffey: Meeting at Government Accountability Office, Washington, DC, June 16, 2009, along with James A. Reynolds. Mrs. Coffey and Mr. Reynolds are the primary expert staff at GAO working on contracting, specifically contractors in contingency operations.

Pete Cornell: Defense Security Cooperation Agency, Crystal City, Virginia, on January 16 and February 23, 2009. Mr. Cornell was division chief for management at the programs directorate of DSCA. He is very familiar with contract oversight as well as the different authorities for spending U.S. government funds here and abroad.

Ginger Cruz: SIGIR, Crystal City, Virginia, on February 26, 2009. Ms. Cruz is deputy inspector general at SIGIR, where she has served since shortly after it was created in 2003.

Nicholas Dew: Mountain View, California, February19, 2009, and NPS, several times beginning in June 2009 until mid-2010. Nicholas Dew, an Associate Professor at the Graduate School of Business and Public Policy at the Naval Postgraduate School, has researched and published extensively on PSCs. He also supervises masters theses on all aspects of contracting out. Professor Dew not only made his research available to me but also helped me define the research topic and how I might pursue it.

Robert Dickson: Arlington, Virginia on June 18 and September 16, 2009. Mr. Dickson has long experience in the Departments of Defense and State and extensive background in the Defense Contract Administration Service Management Area. He is now executive director of the Commission on Wartime Contracting in Iraq and Afghanistan.

Sam Farr: Monterey and San Francisco, January 5, 2009, and Washington, DC, June 17, 2009. Congressman Sam Farr has depth and experience in both U.S. civil–military relations and contracting out and a great interest in the research of the Naval Postgraduate School.

Jacques Gansler: University of Maryland, College Park, on February 23, 2009. In addition to his extensive service in high-level positions in DoD, Dr. Gansler was the main force in the Commission on Army Acquisition and Program Management in Expeditionary Operations and its report "Urgent Reform Required: Army Expeditionary Contracting."

Cathy Garman: House of Representatives, June 17 and 7 October 7, 2009. Cathy Garman is a member of the permanent staff of the House Armed Services Committee. Among other issues, she is an expert on "inherently governmental functions."

John Gastright: Arlington, Virginia, on January 9, 2009. John Gastright had previously served in the Department of State. He is currently vice president for Government Affairs, Communications, and Marketing for DynCorps.

Jeffrey Green: Washington, DC, February 25, June 17, and September 15, 2009. Jeffrey Green is president of J. A. Green & Company, which represents organizations, including the International Peace Operations Association, and contractors. He is a former counsel to the House Armed Services Committee.

Michael Heidingsfield: Washington, DC, February 26, 2009. Michael. Heidingsfield is senior assistant sergeant at arms in the U.S. Senate. A professional law enforcement officer and USAF officer, he was recruited by DynCorps in 2004–2005, where he was in charge of the police training program in Iraq.

Andrew Hunter: Washington, DC, February 24, 2009. Andrew Hunter is a member of the permanent staff of the Armed Services Committee of the House of Representatives. He deals extensively with contracting and with Iraq.

Danny Kopp: SIGIR, Crystal City, Virginia, February 25 and June 16, 2009. Danny Kopp was senior writer at SIGIR, in charge of outreach. He not only informed me about SIGIR but also set up further meetings that are listed separately.

Christopher Lamb: Washington, DC, January 8, 2009. Dr. Christopher Lamb was the research director of the Project on National Security Reform. He has served in both the Departments of State and Defense, and at the time of writing he was a researcher and author on several themes of national security and defense.

Tara Lee: Washington, DC, October 7, 2009. Tara Lee is an attorney with DLA Piper, LLP (US). Previously a judge advocate general in the military, Ms. Lee specializes in contracting out and has written extensively on the legal framework with regard to private security contractors.

Peter Levine: Washington, DC, February 26, and September 15, 2009. Peter Levine is general counsel on the Senate Armed Services Committee. He works closely with Senator Carl Levin on the topic of "inherently governmental functions," among other issues.

James R. Locher III: Arlington, Virginia, February 23, June 15, and September 16, 2009. James Locher was the main author of the Goldwater-Nichols Defense Reorganization Act on the Senate side; served as assistant secretary of defense for the new Special Operations and Low Intensity Conflict section, which he had helped create; and is executive director of the Project on National Security Reform.

Michael Love: CSC on 6 October 6, 2009. Michael Love, assistant General Counsel at CSC, works extensively on issues of contracting. He participates actively in "industry" meetings and in meetings with congressional staffers, regulators, and auditors. He is also involved in the American Bar Association section on national security law.

Debbie Merrill: Washington, DC, January 6, June 17, and September 15, 2009, and others. Debbie Merrill is legislative director for Congressman Sam Farr and a long-time national security and defense expert in the U.S. House of Representatives.

Scott Marcy: Monterey, California, January 29, 2009. Colonel Marcy, USA (ret.) dealt with training and management for the U.S. Army and worked for MPRI between 2006 and 2009.

Christopher Mayer and Victor Alexander David Rostow: Arlington, Virginia, February 26, 2009. They are both with the Office of the Assistant Secretary of Defense for Global Security Affairs, working on contracting management reform in DoD.

Gary Motsek: Washington, DC, June 17, 2009. Mr. Motsek is the assistant deputy undersecretary (Logistics & Material Readiness/Program Support) at the Office of the Secretary of Defense, where he implements reforms regarding contracting for the department.

Kelley Poree: Monterey, California, January 26, 2000. Capt. Kelley Poree, USAF, is a Contracting Officer who was in Iraq during the transition from the Coalition Provisional Authority to the provisional Iraqi government in 2004. He was there again in 2006, when he worked at the Joint Contracting Command.

Rene Rendon: Monterey, California, January 16, 2009, and many times thereafter until mid-2010. Rene Rendon is Associate Professor of Acquisition Management at the Graduate School of Business and Public Policy at the Naval Postgraduate School and is coeditor of *Management of Defense Contracting Projects*.

Robin H. "Sak" Sakoda: Several meetings in Monterey, California, 2009–2010. "Sak" Sakoda is a partner with Armitage International, L.C. He served as senior policy advisor and executive assistant to the deputy secretary of state from December 2002 through January 2005. Mr. Sakoda served as the senior Japan director in the Office of the Secretary of Defense in 1995, as the U.S. and Japan reviewed and revised the guidelines for U.S.–Japan defense cooperation.

James Schweiter: Washington, DC, January 7, and June 16, 2009. James Schweiter is a lawyer with McKenna Long & Aldridge, LLP, and has previously held positions in the executive and legislative branches. He is an expert on contracting and has represented several of the most important PSCs.

Steven Schooner: Washington, DC, September 15, 2009. Dr. Steven Schooner is Professor of Government Procurement Law at the George Washington University Law School and has written extensively on contracting. Immediately before joining the Law School, he was associate administrator for procurement law and legislation at the Office of Federal Procurement Policy in the Office of Management and Budget.

SIGIR Auditors: Crystal City, Virginia, June 16, 2009. This meeting, set up by Mr. Danny Kopp, was with three senior auditors: Jason Venner, David Warren, and Bob Pelletier, all of whom have done extensive audits, investigations, and studies on PSCs.

Harry "Ed" Soyster: Alexandria, Virginia, January 8, 2009. Ed Soyster is a retired Army lieutenant general who began working with one of the biggest contracting firms, MPRI, in 1992, and continued there until he retired in 2003.

Tim Wilkins: Washington, DC, June 17 and September 15, 2009. Captain Wilkins is the military deputy/advisor in logistics & material readiness/program support, Office of the Secretary of Defense Assistant Deputy Undersecretary (Logistics & Material Readiness/Program Support).

Elliott "Cory" Yoder: Monterey, California, several meetings in early and mid-2009 until mid-2010. CDR Yoder, USN (ret) was a contracting officer and since 2006 has been a Senior Lecturer at the Graduate School of Business and Public Policy at the Naval Postgraduate School. His publications propose remedies for weaknesses in the contracting process and are cited in the Gansler Commission Report.

Dov Zakheim: Washington, DC, February 27, 2009. Dr. Dov Zakheim was comptroller of the Department of Defense and held other very high-level government positions. He is currently with Booz Allen Hamilton consultants. He is a member of the Commission on Wartime Contracting.

SELECTED BIBLIOGRAPHY

Abrahamsson, Bengt. *Military Professionalization and Political Power*. Beverly Hills and London: Sage Publications, 1972.

Aguero, Felipe. *Soldiers, Civilians and Democracy: Post-Franco Spain in Comparative Perspective*. Baltimore: The Johns Hopkins University Press, 1995.

———. The New "Double Challenge": Simultaneously Crafting Democratic Control and Efficacy Concerning Military, Police and Intelligence. in Alfred Stepan, ed., *Democracies in Danger*. Baltimore: The Johns Hopkins University Press, 2009.

Alexandra, Andrew, Deane-Peter Baker, and Marina Caparini, eds. *Private Military and Security Companies: Ethics, Policies and Civil–Military Relations*. London: Routledge, 2008.

Armitage, Richard L., and Joseph S. Nye Jr., cochairs. "CSIS Commission on Smart Power: A Smarter, More Secure America." Final report, Washington, DC: Center for Strategic and International Studies (CSIS), November 6, 2007.

Avant, Deborah D. *Political Institutions and Military Change: Lessons from Peripheral Wars*. Ithaca, NY: Cornell University Press, 1994.

Avant, Deborah D., and Lee Sigelman. "Private Security and Democracy: Lessons from the US in Iraq." *Security Studies* 19, 2 (April–June 2010).

Baker, James A. III, and Warren Christopher, co-chairs. "The National War Powers Commission Report." Miller Center for Public Affairs, University of Virginia, July 2008.

Barnard, Chester. *The Functions of the Executive*. Cambridge, MA: Harvard University Press, 1962. (Originally published in 1938.)

Barrett, Archie D. *Reappraising Defense Organization: An Analysis Based on the Defense Organization Study of 1977–1980*. Washington, DC: National Defense University Press, 1983.

Barton, Frederick, and Noam Unger. "Civil–Military Relations, Fostering Development, and Expanding Civilian Capacity." Workshop Report. Brookings Institution and CSIS, April 2009.

Bendix, Reinhard. *Max Weber: An Intellectual Portrait*. New York: Anchor Books, 1962.

Bensahel, Nora. "Mission Not Accomplished: What Went Wrong with Iraqi Reconstruction." *The Journal of Strategic Studies* 29, 3 (June 2006).

Bensahel, Nora, and Olga Oliker, Keith Crane, Richard R. Brennan Jr., Heather S. Gregg, Thomas Sullivan, and Andrew Rathmel. *After Saddam: Prewar Planning and the Occupation of Iraq*. Santa Monica, California: RAND, Arroyo Center, 2008.

Best, Richard A. Jr. "Proposals for Intelligence Reorganization, 1949–2004." Report for Congress. Congressional Research Service (CRS), July 29, 2004.

Betts, Richard K. *Enemies of Intelligence: Knowledge & Power in American National Security*. New York: Columbia University Press, 2007.

Biddle, Stephen, and Stephen Long. "Democracy and Military Effectiveness." *Journal of Conflict Resolution* 48, 4 (August 2004).

Borzoo, Al, Constance S. Short, Ken Brockway, and Col. Stan L. VanderWerf, USAF. "Joint Acquisition Command Doctrine—A Success Story." *Defense Acquisition Review Journal* 16, 3 (October 2009).

Brooks, Risa A. *Shaping Strategy: The Civil–Military Politics of Strategic Assessment*. Princeton, NJ: Princeton University Press, 2008.

Brooks, Risa A., and Elizabeth A. Stanley, eds. *Creating Military Power: The Sources of Military Effectiveness*. Stanford, CA: Stanford University Press, 2007.

Brown, Cody M. "The National Security Council: A Legal History of the President's Most Powerful Advisers." Report for the Project on National Security Reform (PNSR), Washington, DC, December 2008.

Bruneau, Thomas C. "Democracy and Effectiveness: Adapting Intelligence for the Fight against Terrorism." *International Journal of Intelligence and Counterintelligence.* 21, 3 (Fall 2008).

Bruneau, Thomas C., and Steven C. Boraz, eds. *Reforming Intelligence: Obstacles to Democratic Control and Effectiveness*. Austin: University of Texas Press, 2007.

Bruneau, Thomas C., and Alex MacLeod. *Politics in Contemporary Portugal: Parties and the Consolidation of Democracy*. Boulder, CO: Lynne Rienner Publishers, 1986.

Bruneau, Thomas C., and Florina Cristiana (Cris) Matei. "Towards a New Conceptualization of Democratization and Civil-Military Relations." *Democratization* 15, 5 (December 2008).

Bruneau, Thomas C., Florina Cristiana (Cris) Matei, and Sak Sakoda. "National Security Councils: Their Potential Functions in Democratic Civil–Military Relations." *Defense & Security Analysis* 25, 3 (September 2009).

Bruneau, Thomas C., and Scott D. Tollefson, eds. *Who Guards the Guardians and How: Democratic Civil-Military Relations*. Austin: University of Texas Press, 2006.

Bryden, Alan, and Marina Caparini, eds. *Private Actors and Security Governance*. Berlin: Lit Verlag, 2006.

Bryden, Alan, and Heiner Hänggi, eds. "Reform and Reconstruction of the Security Sector." Geneva: DCAF, 2004.

Builder, Carl H. *The Masks of War: American Military Styles in Strategy and Analysis*. Baltimore: Johns Hopkins University Press, 1989.

Caforio, Giuseppe, ed. *Social Sciences and the Military: An interdisciplinary Overview*. London and New York: Routledge, 2007.

Camacho, Paul. "A Forum on Privatization with Comments on the Relevant Literature Found in Armed Forces & Society." *Armed Forces & Society*. 36, 4 (2010).

Carafano, James Jay. *Private Sector, Public Wars: Contractors in Combat—Afghanistan, Iraq, and Future Conflicts*. Westport, CT: Praeger Security International, 2008.

Catallo, Jennifer. "Who Is a Mercenary? Changing Concepts, Waning Taboos." Political Concepts Working Paper Series No. 36. Committee on Concepts and Methods, November 2009; available at www.concepts-methods.org/index.php.

Caudle, Sharon. "Homeland Security: Approaches to Results Management." *Public Performance & Management Review* 28, 3 (March 2005).

Cheadle, Samuel P. "Private Military Contractor Liability Under the Worldwide Personal Protective Services II Contract." *Public Contract Law Journal* 38, 3 (Spring 2009).

Chesterman, Simon, and Angelina Fisher, eds. *Private Security, Public Order: The Outsourcing of Public Services and Its Limits*. New York: Oxford University Press, 2009.

Chesterman, Simon, and Chia Lehnardt, eds. *From Mercenaries to Market: The Rise and Regulation of Private Military Companies*. New York: Oxford University Press, 2007.

Cockayne, James, Emily Speers Mears, Iveta Cherneva, Alison Gurin, Sheila Oviedo, and Dylan Yaeger. "Beyond Market Forces: A Feasibility Study for a Standards Implementation and Enforcement Framework for the Global Security Industry." London: International Peace Institute, September 8, 2008; available at www.ipinst.org/GSI.

Cohen, Eliot. *Supreme Command: Soldiers, Statesmen, and Leadership in Wartime*. New York: The Free Press, 2002.

Cohen, Eliot, and John Gooch. *Military Misfortunes: The Anatomy of Failure in War*. New York: Vintage Books, 1990.

Collins, Joseph J. "Choosing War: The Decision to Invade Iraq and Its Aftermath." Occasional Paper 5, Institute for National Strategic Studies. Washington, DC: National Defense University Press, April 2008.

Commission on Army Acquisition and Program Management in Expeditionary Operations (the Gansler Commission). "Urgent Reform Required: Army Expeditionary Contracting." Report of the Commission. Washington, DC: Author, October 31, 2007.

Commission on Wartime Contracting in Iraq and Afghanistan. "At What Cost? Contingency Contracting in Iraq and Afghanistan Interim Report." Washington, DC: Author, June 10, 2009.

Congressional Budget Office (CBO). "Contractors' Support of U.S. Operations in Iraq." Washington, DC: Author. August 2008.

Cottey, Andrew, Timothy Edmunds, and Anthony Forster, eds. *Democratic Control of the Military in Postcommunist Europe: Guarding the Guards.* New York: Palgrave, 2002.

Cullen, Patrick, and Peter Ezra Weinberger. POI Report: Reframing the Defense Outsourcing Debate: Merging Government Oversight *with Industry Partnership.* Washington, DC: Peace Operations Institute, 2007.

Dale, Catherine. "National Security Strategy: Legislative Mandates, Execution to Date, and Considerations for Congress." CRS Report for Congress, updated September 23, 2008.

Dale, Catherine, Nina Serafino, and Pat Towell. "Organizing the U.S. Government for National Security: Overview of the Interagency Reform Debates." CRS Report for Congress (RL 34455), April 18, 2008.

Defence Reform Commission. "The Path to Partnership for Peace: Report of the Defence Reform Commission." Sarajevo, Bosnia and Herzegovina: Defence Reform Commission, September 25, 2003.

Demarest, Geoffrey B. "The Overlap of Military and Police Responsibilities in Latin America." *Low Intensity Conflict & Law Enforcement* 4, 2 (Autumn, 1995).

De Nevers, Renee. "(Self) Regulating War? Voluntary Regulation and the Private Security Industry." *Security Studies* 18 (2009).

Desch, Michael C. *Civilian Control of the Military: The Changing Threat Environment.* Baltimore: The Johns Hopkins University Press, 2001.

———. *Power and Military Effectiveness: The Fallacy of Democratic Triumphalism.* Baltimore: The Johns Hopkins University Press, 2008.

Dew, Nicholas, and Bryan Hudgens. "The Evolving Private Military Sector: A Survey." Acquisition Research Program, Graduate School of Business and Public Policy. Monterey, CA: Naval Postgraduate School, February 20, 2008; available at www.acquisitionsresearch.org.

Donahue, John D. *The Privatization Decision: Public Ends, Private Means.* New York: Basic Books, 1989.

Dunigan, Molly. *Victory for Hire: Private Security Contractors' Impact on Military Effectiveness.* Stanford: Stanford University Press, 2011.

Durch, William J. *UN Peace Operations and the "Brahimi" Report."* Washington, DC: The Henry L. Stimson Center, revised October 2001.

Edmunds, Timothy. "Defining Security Sector Reform," in "Civil–Military Relations and Security Sector Reform in the 21st Century." *CMR Network* 3 (October 2001).

———. "Security Sector Reform: Concepts and Implementation." DCAF, November 2001; available at www.dcaf.ch/cfs.

———. "What Are Armed Forces For? The Changing Nature of Military Roles in Europe." *International Affairs* 82, 6 (November 2006).

———. *Security Sector Reform in Transforming Societies: Croatia, Serbia and Montenegro.* Manchester, UK: Manchester University Press, 2007.

Ehrart, Hans-Georg, and Albrecht Schnabel. *Security Sector Reform and Post-Conflict Peacebuilding*, Tokyo: United Nations University Press, 2005.

Elsea, Jennifer K. "Private Security Contractors in Iraq and Afghanistan: Legal Issues." CRS Report for Congress, January 7, 2010.

Elsea, Jennifer K., Moshe Schwartz, and Kennon H. Nakamura. "Private Security Contractors in Iraq: Background, Legal Status, and Other Issues." CRS Report for Congress (RL 32419), Washington, DC, updated 29 September 29, 2008.

Facultad Latinoamericana de Ciencias Sociales [FLACSO]. *Report on the Security Sector in Latin America and the Caribbean.* Santiago, Chile: FLACSO, 2007 (English edition, 2008); available at: www.flacso.cl.

Fainaru, Steve. *Big Boy Rules: America's Mercenaries Fighting in Iraq.* Cambridge, MA: Da Capo Press, 2008.

Farson, Stuart, Peter Gill, Mark Phythian, and Shlomo Shpiro, eds. *PSI Handbook of Global Security and Intelligence; National Approaches.* Volumes 1 and 2. Westport, CT: Praeger Security International, 2008.

Feaver, Peter D. *Armed Servants: Agency, Oversight, and Civil–Military Relations.* Cambridge, MA: Harvard University Press, 2003.

———. "Civil–Military Relations." *Annual Review of Political Science* 2 (1999): 211–241.

Finer, Samuel E. *The Man on Horseback: The Role of the Military in Politics.* New Brunswick, NJ: Transaction Publishers, 2002. (Originally published in 1962.)

Fischer, Martina, Hans J. Gießmann, and Beatrix Schmelzle, eds. *Berghof Handbook for Conflict Transformation.* Berlin: Berghof Research Center for Constructive Conflict Management, updated 2009. Available only on the web at www.berghof -handbook.net/uploads/download/dialogue2_wulf.pdf.

Flournoy, Michéle A., and Shawn W. Brimley. "Strategic Planning for National Security: A New Project Solarium." *Joint Forces Quarterly* 41 (2nd quarter 2006).

Fluri, Philipp, and Miroslav Hadzic, eds. *Sourcebook on Security Sector Reform: Collection of Papers.* Geneva and Belgrade: DCAF, March 2004. Available at www.dcaf.ch/ publications/.

Fontaine, Richard, and John Nagl. "Contractors in American Conflicts: Adapting to a New Reality." Working Paper, Center for a New American Security, December 2009.

Franke, Volker, and Marc Von Boemcken. "Final Report: Attitudes, Values and Professional Self-Conceptions of Private Security Contractors in Iraq: An Exploratory Study." Bonn: International Center for Conversion, August 2009.

Grasso, Valerie Bailey. "Defense Contracting in Iraq and Afghanistan: Issues and Options for Congress." CRS Report for Congress (RL 33834), February 19, 2009.

Grimmett, Richard F., Coordinator. "9/11 Commission Recommendations: Implementation Status," CRS Report to Congress (RL 33742), December 4, 2006.

———. "Instances of Use of United States Armed Forces Abroad, 1798–2008," CRS Report to Congress (RL 32170), February 2, 2009.

———. "War Powers Resolution: Presidential Compliance," CRS Report to Congress (RL 33532), September 23, 2009.

Gunther, Richard, Nikiforos Diamandouros, and H. Pulhe, eds. *The Politics of Democratic Consolidations in Southern Europe*. Baltimore: The Johns Hopkins Press, 1995.

Guttman, Dan. "Government by Contract: The White House Needs Capacity to Review and Revise the Legacy of 20th Century Reform." Washington, DC: National Academy of Public Administration, August 2008.

Haass, Richard N. *War of Necessity, War of Choice: A Memoir of Two Iraq Wars*. New York: Simon & Schuster, 2009.

Halchin, L. Elaine. "Circular A-76 Revision 2003: Selected Issues." CRS Report for Congress (RL 32017), Washington, DC, updated January 7, 2005.

Hall, Peter A., and Rosemary C. R. Taylor. "Political Science and the Three New Institutionalisms." *Political Studies* 44 (1996).

Herspring, Dale R. *The Pentagon and the Presidency: Civil–Military Relations from FDR to George W. Bush*. Lawrence: University Press of Kansas, 2005.

Hicks, Kathleen H. *Invigorating Defense Governance: A Beyond Goldwater-Nichols Phase 4 Report*. Washington, DC: Center for Strategic & International Studies, March 2008.

Hitch, Charles J., and Roland N. McKean. *The Economics of Defense in the Nuclear Age*. New York: Atheneum, 1978. (Originally published in 1960.)

Holt, Victoria K., and Tobias C. Herkman. *The Impossible Mandate? Military Preparedness, the Responsibility to Protect and Modern Peace Operations*. Washington, DC: Henry L. Stimson Center, 2006.

Human Rights First. "Private Security Contractors at War: Ending the Culture of Impunity." New York, 2008; available at www.humanrightsfirst.org/.

Huntington, Samuel P. *The Soldier and the State: The Theory and Politics of Civil–Military Relations*. Cambridge, MA: Belknap Press, 1981. (Originally published in 1957.)

———. *The Third Wave: Democratization in the Late Twentieth Century*. Norman: University of Oklahoma Press, 1991.

Janowitz, Morris. "Armed Forces and Society: An Interdisciplinary Journal." *Armed Forces & Society* 1, 1 (Fall 1974).

Journal of International Peace Operations; published bimonthly by peaceops.com; available at http://ipoajournal.org/mag/web/.

Kaiser, Frederick M. " GAO: Government Accountability office and General Accounting Office." Washington, DC: CRS Report for Congress (RL 30349), updated June 22, 2007.

———. "Statutory Offices of Inspector General: Past and Present." CRS Report for Congress (Order Code 98-379), updated September 25, 2008.

Kaiser, Frederick M., Walter Oleszek, T. J Halstead, Morton Rosenberg, and Todd Tatelman. "Congressional Oversight Manual." CRS Report for Congress (RL 30240), updated January 2, 2007.

Kean, Thomas H., commission chair. "Final Report on 9/11 Commission Recommendations, December 5, 2005." 9/11 Public Discourse Project, December 5, 2005; available at www.9-11pdp.org.

———. The 9/11 Commission Report: Final Report of the National Commission on Terrorist Attacks upon the United States. Washington, DC: U.S. Government Printing Office, July 22, 2004.

Kidwell, Deborah C. "Public War, Private Fight? The United States and Private Military Companies." Global War on Terrorism Occasional Paper 12. Fort Leavenworth, KS: Combat Studies Institute Press, 2009.

Kinsey, Christopher. *Corporate Soldiers and International Security: The Rise of Private Military Companies.* London and New York: Routledge, 2006.

Kitts, Kenneth. *Presidential Commissions and National Security: The Politics of Damage Control.* Boulder, CO: Lynne Rienner, 2006.

Kohn, Richard H. *The United States Military under the Constitution of the United States, 1789–1989.* New York: New York University Press, 1991.

———. "The Erosion of Civilian Control of the Military in the United States Today." *Naval War College Review* 55, 3 (Summer 2002).

Kosar, Kevin R. "Privatization and the Federal Government: An Introduction." CRS Report for Congress (RL 33777) Washington, DC, December 26, 2008.

Leander, Anna. *Eroding State Authority? Private Military Companies and the Legitimate Use of Force.* Rome: Rubbettino Editore, 2006.

Lee, Tara. "Redefining Inherently Governmental: The Push to Redefine the Function and Its Consequences." *Journal of International Peace Operations* 4, 1 (July–August 2008).

Lee, Tara, and Ryan Berry. "Contracting Under the SOFA." *Journal of International Peace Operations* 4, 4 (January–February 2009).

Light, Paul C. *The True Size of Government.* Washington, DC: Brookings Institution Press, 1999.

———. *A Government Ill Executed: The Decline of the Federal Service and How to Reverse It.* Cambridge, MA: Harvard University Press, 2008.

Linn, Brian McAllister. *The Echo of Battle: The Army's Way of War.* Cambridge, MA: Harvard University Press, 2007.

Linz, Juan J. *The Breakdown of Democratic Regimes: Crisis, Breakdown, and Reequilibration.* Baltimore: The Johns Hopkins University Press, 1978.

Linz, Juan J., and Alfred Stepan. *Problems of Democratic Transition and Consolidation: Southern Europe, South America, and Post-Communist Europe.* Baltimore: The Johns Hopkins University Press, 1996.

Locher, James R. III. *Victory on the Potomac: The Goldwater Nichols Act Unifies the Pentagon.* College Station: Texas A&M University Press, 2004.

Luckey, John R. "OMB Circular A-76: Explanation and Discussion of the Recently Revised Federal Outsourcing Policy." CRS Report for Congress (RS 21489), Washington, DC, updated September 10, 2003.

Luckey, John R., Valerie Bailey Grasso, and Kate M. Manuel. "Inherently Governmental Functions and Department of Defense Operations: Background, Issues, and Options for Congress." CRS Report for Congress (R40641). Washington, DC: Congressional Research Service, September 14, 2009.

Machiavelli, Niccolo. *The Prince*, translated and edited by Robert M. Adams. New York: W. W. Norton & Company, 1977. {Originally written in 1513.}

Mason, R. Chuck. "Status of Forces Agreement (SOFA): What Is It, and How Has It Been Utilized?" CRS Report for Congress (RL 34531), June 18, 2009.

———. "U.S.–Iraq Withdrawal/Status of Forces Agreement: Issues for Congressional Oversight." CRS Report for Congress (R 40011), July 13, 2009.

May, Ernest R. "When Government Writes History: A Memoir of the 9/11 Commission." *The New Republic* (May 23, 2005).

McCoy, Katherine E. "Beyond Civil–Military Relations: Reflections on Civilian Control of a Private, Multinational Workforce." *Armed Forces & Society* 36, 4 (2010).

Mendel, Robert. *The Privatization of Security.* Boulder, CO: Lynne Rienner Publishers, 2002.

Morelli, Vincent, and Paul Belkin. "NATO In Afghanistan: A Test of the Transatlantic Alliance." CRS Report for Congress (R33627), updated December 3, 2009.

Moskos, Charles C., John Allen Williams, and David R. Segal, eds. *The Postmodern Military: Armed Forces After the Cold War.* New York: Oxford University Press, 2000.

Munck, Gerardo L., and Richard Snyder. "Debating the Direction of Comparative Politics: An Analysis of Leading Journals." *Comparative Political Studies* 40, 1 (January 2007).

Murdock, Clark A., lead investigator. "Beyond Goldwater-Nichols: Defense Reform for a New Strategic Era." Phase 1 Report. Washington, DC: Center for Strategic and International Studies (CSIS), March 2004.

Murdock, Clark A., and Michèle A. Flournoy, lead investigators. "Beyond Goldwater-Nichols: Defense Reform for a New Strategic Era." Phase 2 Report. CSIS, July 2005.

Nathan, James A. "Revising the War Powers Act." *Armed Forces & Society* 17, 4 (Summer 1991).

National Commission on Terrorist Attacks (the 9/11 Commission). *The 9/11 Commission Report: Final Report of the National Commission on Terrorist Attacks upon the United States*. New York: W. W. Norton & Company, 2004.

Needham, John K., director of acquisition and sourcing management. "GAO Acquisition Workforce: DOD Can Improve Its Management and Oversight by Tracking Data on Contractor Personnel and Taking Additional Actions." Testimony before the Oversight and Investigations Subcommittee, Committee on Armed Services, House of Representatives, 111th Congress, 1st session (GAO-09-616T). April 28, 2009.

Nielsen, Suzanne C., and Don M. Snider, eds. *American Civil–Military Relations: The Soldier and the State in a New Era*. Baltimore: The Johns Hopkins University Press, 2009.

Office of the Director of National Intelligence. "Intelligence Community Directive Number 601. Human Capital: Joint Intelligence Community Duty Assignments." Washington, DC: Author, May 2006, amended in September 2009.

Okun, Arthur M. *Equality and Efficiency: The Big Tradeoff*. Washington, DC: The Brookings Institution, 1975.

Olldashi, Arjana. "Civil–Military Relations in Emerging Democracies as Found in the Articles of *Armed Forces & Society*." Political Science Department, Texas State University-San Marcos, 2002. Available at http://ecommons.txstate.edu/arp/54/.

Olmeda, José. *Democracias frágiles: las relaciones civiles-militares en el mundo ibero-americano*. Valencia, Spain: Tirant lo Blanch, 2005.

Owen, Mackubin Thomas. *US Civil–Military Relations after 9/11: Renegotiating the Civil–Military Bargain*. New York: Continuum, 2011.

Packer, George. *The Assassins' Gate: America in Iraq*. New York: Farrar, Straus and Giroux, 2005.

Pelton, Robert Young. *Licensed to Kill: Hired Guns in the War on Terror*. New York: Three Rivers Press, 2006.

Petersen, R. Eric. "Congressional Nominations to U.S. Service Academies: An Overview and Resources for Outreach and Management." CRS Report for Congress (R33213), December 29, 2005.

Pion-Berlin, David. *Through Corridors of Power: Institutions and Civil-Military Relations in Argentina*. University Park: Pennsylvania State University Press, 1997.

———, ed. *Civil–Military Relations in Latin America: New Analytical Perspectives*. Chapel Hill: University of North Carolina Press, 2001.

Pion-Berlin, David, and Harold Trinkunas. "Democratization, Social Crisis and the Impact of Military Domestic Roles in Latin America." *Journal of Political and Military Sociology* 33, 1 (Summer 2005).

Pridham, G., ed. *Transitions to Democracy*. Aldershot, UK: Dartmouth, 1995.

Project on National Security Reform (PNSR). "Forging a New Shield: Executive Summary." Washington, DC: Author PNSR, November 2008.

———. "Turning Ideas into Action: A Progress Report." Washington, DC: Author, September 30, 2009.

Przeworski, Adam. *Democracy and the Market: Political and Economic Reforms in Eastern Europe and Latin America*. New York: Cambridge University Press, 1991.

Quinn, Dennis J., ed. *The Goldwater-Nichols DOD Reorganization Act: A Ten-Year Retrospective*. Washington, DC: National Defense University Press, 1999.

RAND Corporation (Sarah K. Cotton, Ulrich Petersohn, Molly Dunigan, Q Burkhart, Megan Zander-Cotugno, Edward O'Connell, Michael Webber). *Hired Guns. Views about Armed Contractors in Operation Iraqi Freedom*. Santa Monica: RAND, 2010.

"Rebuilding Iraq: DOD and State Department Have Improved Oversight and Coordination of Private Security Contractors in Iraq, but Further Actions Are Needed to Sustain Improvements." Washington, DC: U.S. General Accounting Office (GAO-08-966), July 2008.

Red de Seguridad y Defensa de América Latina (RESDAL). *A Comparative Atlas of Defence in Latin America*. Buenos Aires, Author: 2008.

Rendon, Rene G., and Keith F. Snider, eds. *Management of Defense Acquisition Projects*. Palmdale, CA: Lockheed Martin Corporation, for the American Institute of Aeronautics and Astronautics, 2008.

Ricks, Thomas. *Fiasco: The American Military Adventure in Iraq*. New York: Penguin Press, 2006.

———. *The Gamble: General David Petraeus and the American Military Adventure in Iraq, 2006–2008*. New York: Penguin Press, 2009.

Robinson, Linda. *Tell Me How This Ends: General David Petraeus and the Search for a Way Out of Iraq*. New York: Public Affairs, 2008.

Roman, Peter J., and David W. Tarr. "The Joint Chiefs of Staff: From Service Parochialism to Jointness." *Political Science Quarterly* 113, 1 (1998).

Russell, James A. "Innovation in War: Counterinsurgency Operations in Ambar and Ninewa Provinces, Iraq, 2005–2007." *The Journal of Strategic Studies* 33, 4 (August 2010).

Russell, James A. *Innovation, Transformation, and War: Counterinsurgency Operations in Anbar and Ninewa Provinces, Iraq, 2005–2007*. Stanford, CA: Stanford University Press, 2011.

Sacilotto, Kara M. "Iraq SOFA: Issues Abound for Contractors." *Federal Contracts Report* 91, 2 (January 20, 2009).

Sanders, Ronald P., Associate Director of National Intelligence for Human Capital. "National Security Reform: Implementing a National Security Service Workforce." Testimony before the Senate Subcommittee on Oversight of Government Management, the Federal Workforce, and the District of Colombia, 111th Congress, 1st session, April 30, 2009.

Sarkesian, Sam C., John Allen Williams, and Stephen J. Cimbala. *U.S. National Security: Policymakers, Processes, & Politics*, 4th edition. Boulder, CO: Lynne Rienner Publishers, 2008.

Schooner, Steven L. "Fear of Oversight: The Fundamental Failure of Businesslike Government." *American University Law Review* 50, 3 (2001).

——. "Why Contractor Fatalities Matter." *Parameters* 38, 3 (Autumn 2008).

Schwartz, Moshe. "Training the Military to Manage Contractors during Expeditionary Operations: Overview and Options for Congress." CRS Report for Congress (R40057), December 17, 2008.

Search for Common Ground. "Resource Guide on Security Sector Reform." Washington, DC,: Author, December 21, 2005; available at www.sfcg.org/programmes/ilr/security1.pdf.

Sedra, Mark. "European Approaches to Security Sector Reform: Examining Trends through the Lens of Afghanistan." *European Security* 15, 3 (September 2006).

Serafino, Nina M. "The Global Peace Operations Initiative: Background and Issues for Congress." Washington, DC: CRS Report for Congress, updated October 3, 2006.

——, coordinator. "The Department of Defense Role in Foreign Assistance: Background, Major Issues, and Options for Congress." CRS Report for Congress (RL 34639), December 9, 2008.

Scahill, Jeremy. *Blackwater: The Rise of the World's Most Powerful Mercenary Army.* New York: Nation Books, 2007.

Serra, Narcis. *La transicion military: Reflexiones en torno a la reforma democratica de las fuerzas armadas.* Barcelona: Debate, 2008. Published in English as *The Military Transition: Democratic Reform of the Armed Forces*, Peter Bush, trans. Cambridge, UK: Cambridge University Press, 2010.

Serra, Narcis. "Beyond Threats to Democracy from the Armed Forces, Police, and Intelligence: The Spanish Case," in Alfred Stepan, ed., *Democracies in Danger*. Baltimore: The Johns Hopkins University Press, 2009.

Shapiro, Ian, Stephen Skowronek, and Daniel Gavin, eds. *Rethinking Political Institutions: The Art of the State.* New York: New York University Press, 2006.

Shearer, David. "Private Armies and Military Intervention." Adelphi Paper no. 316. International Institute for Strategic Studies. New York: Oxford University Press, 1998.

Sheehy, Benedict, Jackson Maogoto, and Virginia Newell. *Legal Control of the Private Military Corporation.* Basingstoke, UK: Palgrave Macmillan, 2009.

Shenon, Philip. *The Commission: The Uncensored History of the 9/11 Investigation.* New York: Twelve Publishers, 2008.

Shuman, Howard E., and Walter R. Thomas, eds. *The Constitution and National Security: A Bicentennial View.* Washington, DC: National Defense University Press, 1990.

Simon, Herbert A. *Administrative Behavior.* New York: Macmillan and Company, 1961.

Simons, Suzanne. *Master of War: Blackwater USA's Erik Prince and the Business of War.* New York: Harper Collins, 2009.

Singer, P. W. "Can't Win with 'em, Can't Go to War without 'em: Private Military Contractors and Counterinsurgency." Policy Paper Number 4. Washington, DC: Brookings Institution, September 2007.

Skelton, Ike. *Whispers of Warriors: Essays on the New Joint Era.* Washington, DC: National Defense University Press, 2004.

Snider, Don M., and Miranda A. Carlton-Carew, eds. *U.S. Civil–Military Relations: In Crisis or Transition?* Washington, DC: Center for Strategic & International Studies, 1995.

Solis, William M., director, defense capabilities and management. "Military Operations: High-Level DOD Action Needed to Address Long-Standing Problems with Management and Oversight of Contractors Supporting Deployed Forces." GAO Report to Congress (GAO-07-145). December 2006.

Special Inspector General for Iraq Reconstruction (SIGIR). "Agencies Need Improved Financial Data Reporting for Private Security Contractors." (SIGIR-09-005). Washington, DC: SIGIR, October 30, 2008.

———. "Enabling Legislation as Amended." Washington, DC: SIGIR, 2009.

———. *Hard Lessons: The Iraq Reconstruction Experience.* Washington, DC: SIGIR, 2009.

———. "Need to Enhance Oversight of Theater-Wide Internal Security Services Contracts." (SIGIR-09-017). Washington, DC: SIGIR, April 24, 2009.

———. "Comprehensive Plan for Audits of Private Security Contractors to Meet the Requirements of Section 842 of Public Law 110-181." Updated May 8, 2009.

———. "Quarterly Report and Semiannual Report to the United States Congress." July 30, 2009.

———. "Long-Standing Weaknesses in Department of State's Oversight of DynCorp Contract for Support of the Iraqi Police Training Program." SIGIR 10-008, January 25, 2010; available at www.sigir.mil.

Stepan, Alfred. *The Military in Politics: Changing Patterns in Brazil.* Princeton, NJ: Princeton University Press, 1971.

———, ed. *Authoritarian Brazil: Origins, Policies, and Future.* New Haven, CT: Yale University Press, 1973.

———. *Rethinking Military Politics: Brazil and the Southern Cone.* Princeton: Princeton University Press, 1988.

Stepan, Alfred, ed. *Democracies in Danger.* Baltimore: The Johns Hopkins University Press, 2009.

Stephenson, James. *Losing the Golden Hour: An Insider's View of Iraq's Reconstruction.* Dulles, VA: Potomac Books, 2007.

Stinchcombe, Arthur L. *Constructing Social Theories*. New York: Harcourt, Brace & World, 1968.

Strachan, Hew. "The Lost Meaning of Strategy." *Survival* 47, 3 (Autumn 2005).

———. "Making Strategy: Civil–Military Relations after Iraq." *Survival* 48, 3 (Autumn 2006).

Stanger, Allison. *One Nation under Contract: The Outsourcing of American Power and the Future of Foreign Policy*. New Haven, CT: Yale University Press, 2009.

Szayna, Thomas S., Kevin F. McCarthy, Jerry M. Sollinger, Linda J. Demaine, Jefferson P. Marquis, and Brett Steele. "The Civil-Military Gap in the United States: Does It Exist, Why, and Does It Matter?" No. MG-379-A. Santa Monica, CA: RAND Corporation, 2007.

Trinkunas, Harold A. *Crafting Civilian Control of the Armed Forces in Venezuela: A Comparative Perspective*. Chapel Hill: University of North Carolina Press, 2006.

Tulchin, Joseph S., Raul Benitez Manaut, and Rut Diamint, eds. *El Rompecabezas: Conformando la seguridad hemisferica en el siglo XXI*. Buenos Aires: Prometeo Libros, 2006.

U.S. Agency for International Development, U.S. Department of Defense, and U.S. Department of State. "Security Sector Reform." Washington, DC, February 2009.

U.S. Congress. Report of the Panel on Military Education of the 100th Congress of the Committee on Armed Services, House of Representatives. 101st Congress, 1st session, April 21, 1989.

———. "National Security Reform: Implementing a National Security Service Workforce." Testimony before the Senate Subcommittee on Oversight of Government Management, the Federal Workforce, and the District of Colombia. Dr. Ronald P. Sanders, Associate Director of National Intelligence for Human Capital. 111th Congress, 1st session, 30 April 2009.

U.S. Government Accountability Office (GAO). "Acquisition Workforce: Department of Defense's Plans to Address Workforce Size and Structure Challenges." (GAO-02-630). Washington, DC: GAO, April 2002.

———. "Defense Contracting: Army Case Study Delineates Concerns with Use of Contractors as Contract Specialists." (GAO-08-360). March 2008.

———. "High-Risk Series: An Update. Strategic Human Capital Management." GAO Report to Congress (GAO-09-271). Washington, DC: GAO, January 2009.

———. "Department of Defense. Additional Actions and Data Are Needed to Effectively Manage and Oversee DOD's Acquisition Workforce." GAO Report to Congressional Requesters (GAO-09-342). Washington, DC: GAO, March 2009.

———. "Contingency Contracting: DOD, State, and USAID Continue to Face Challenges in Tracking Contractor Personnel and Contracts in Iraq and Afghanistan" (GAO-10-1), October 2009; available at www.gao.gov.

Walker, David M., comptroller general of the United States. "Defense Acquisitions: DOD'S Increased Reliance on Service Contactors Exacerbates Long-Standing Challenges." Statement of David M. Walker, Comptroller General of the United States. (GAO-08-621T). January 3, 2008.

———. "DOD Needs to Reexamine Its Extensive Reliance on Contractors and Continue to Improve Management and Oversight." Testimony before the Subcommittee on Readiness, Committee on Armed Services, U. S. House of Representatives. 110th Congress, 2nd session, March 11, 2008.

Warner, Michael, and J. Kenneth McDonald. "U.S. Intelligence Community Reform Studies since 1947." Washington, DC: Center for the Study of Intelligence, April 2005.

Weber, Max. *Economy and Society: An Outline of Interpretive Sociology.* Edited by Gunther Roth and Claus Wittich. Berkeley: University of California Press, 1978.

Wedel, Janine R. *Shadow Elite: How the World's New Power Brokers Undermine Democracy, Government, and the Free Market.* New York: Basic Books, 2009.

Weed, Matthew C. "U.S.–Iraq Agreements: Congressional Oversight Activities and Legislative Response." CRS Report for Congress (RL 34568), May 15, 2009.

Wheeler, Winslow T. *The Wastrels of Defense: How Congress Sabotages U.S. Security.* Annapolis: Naval Institute Press, 2004.

Wheeler, Winslow T., and Lawrence J. Korb. *Military Reform: A Reference Handbook.* Westport, CT: Praeger Security International, 2007.

Williams, Cindy, and Gordon Adams. "Strengthening Statecraft and Security: Reforming U.S. Planning and Resource Allocation." MIT Security Studies Program Occasional Paper. Massachusetts Institute of Technology, Cambridge, MA, June 2008.

Williams, Kiernan, and Dennis Deletant. *Security Intelligence Services in New Democracies: The Czech Republic, Slovakia and Romania.* Basingstoke, UK: Palgrave, 2001.

Wills, Garry. *Bomb Power: The Modern Presidency and the National Security State.* New York: Penguin Press, 2010.

Woodward, Bob. *Plan of Attack.* New York: Simon & Schuster, 2004.

———. *The War Within: A Secret White House History.* New York: Simon & Schuster, 2008.

Yoder, Elliott Cory. "The Yoder Three-Tier Model for Optimal Planning and Execution of Contingency Contracting." Acquisition Research Working Paper Series (NPS-AM-05-002); available at www.nps.navy.mil/gsbpp/acqn/publications.

Yoo, John. *Crisis and Command: The History of Executive Power From George Washington to George W. Bush.* New York: Kaplan Publishing, 2010.

Zegart, Amy. *Flawed by Design: The Evolution of the CIA, JCS, and NSC.* Stanford, CA: Stanford University Press, 1999.

———. *Spying Blind: The CIA, the FBI, and the Origins of 9/11.* Princeton, NJ: Princeton University Press, 2007.

Master's Theses, Naval Postgraduate School, Monterey, California

Dunar, Charles J., Jared L. Mitchell, and Donald L. Robbins. *Private Military Industry Analysis: Private and Public Companies.* 2007.

Harris, Neil J. *Contractors and the Cost of War: Research into Economic and Cost-Effectiveness Arguments.* 2006.

Heskett, Jonathan D. *The Potential Scope for use of Private Military Companies in Military Operations: An Historical and Economical Analysis.* 2005.

Jorgensen, Brent M. *Outsourcing Small Wars: Expanding the Role of Private Military Companies in U.S. Military Operations.* 2005.

Kornburger, Michael D., and Jeremy R. Dobos. *Private Military Companies: Analyzing the Use of Armed Contractors.* 2007.

O'Brien, James M. *Private Military Companies: An Assessment.* 2008.

Poree, Kelley, Capt. USAF, Katrina Curtis, Capt. USAF, Jeremy Morrill, Capt. USAF, and Steven Sherwood, Lt. Cdr. USN. "The Joint Effects-Based Contracting Execution System: A Proposed Enabling Concept for Future Joint Expeditionary Contracting Execution." 2008.

INDEX

The term *PSCs* refers to private security contractors.

Abrahamsson, Bengt, 16
Abu Ghraib prison, 109, 163
Accountability of PSCs, 158–159, 229n19
ACLU. *See* American Civil Liberties Union (ACLU)
Adams, Gordon, 233
Admire, Kristyn, 156, 159, 227n4, 229n21
Afghanistan: combat operations (2001) in, 37, 76, 86, 87; and expeditionary or contingency contracting, 128-129; and Global War on Terror, 77; and interagency process, 72-73; literature on war in, 14–15; peacekeeping forces in, 194n22; postconflict stabilization or "nation building" in, 37, 211n73; protection for State Department personnel in, 122; PSCs in, 2, 112, 113, 126, 129, 131, 159, 160, 213n12; Romanian armed forces in, 194n22; and SIGAR, 2, 127, 163
Africa, 30, 55, 121. *See also specific countries*
African Union, 36
AF&S. See *Armed Forces & Society* (*AF&S*)
Air Force, U.S.: and Goldwater-Nichols Defense Reorganization Act (1986), 58; military education for officers in, 199n18; and National Security Act (1947), 82; opposition to Goldwater-Nichols Defense Reorganization Act

(1986) by, 84; and private contractors, 4; size of, 122, 197n1
Air Force Academy, 55–56
Air Force Institute of Technology, 56
Alice in Wonderland (Carroll), 64
American Civil Liberties Union (ACLU), 54
American Civil-Military Relations, 20
Amnesty International, 55
Anello, Russell, 234
Argentina, 17, 44, 46, 55, 56
Armed forces. *See* Air Force, U.S.; Army, U.S.; Marines, U.S.; Navy, U.S.; *and headings beginning with* Military
Armed Forces & Society (*AF&S*), 15, 21–27, 151, 189n29, 191n47
Armitage, Richard L., 96
Army, U.S.: contracting officers (COs) and contracting officer representatives (CORs) in, 138–139, 154, 223n54, 230n30; contract managers as civilian versus military in, 137–138; and contractors excluded from inherently governmental functions, 228n13; dollar value of contracts by, 137; expeditionary contracting by, 220n9; and Goldwater-Nichols Defense Reorganization Act (1986), 58; military education for officers in, 199n18; number of contracts by, 137; opposition to Goldwater-Nichols Defense Reorganization Act (1986) by, 84; and private contractors, 4; and PSCs in Iraq and Afghanistan, 4, 129, 135;

The authorized representative in the EU for product safety and compliance is:
Mare Nostrum Group
B.V Doelen 72
4831 GR Breda
The Netherlands

www.ingramcontent.com/pod-product-compliance
Lightning Source LLC
Chambersburg PA
CBHW020340270326
41926CB00007B/255